# Masquerade Balls in Regency Britain

# Masquerade Balls in Regency Britain

Anne Glover

First published in Great Britain in 2025 by
Pen & Sword History
An imprint of Pen & Sword Books Limited
Yorkshire – Philadelphia



ISBN 978 1 03610 294 4



A CIP catalogue record for this book is available from the British Library.



Typeset by Mac Style
Printed in the UK by CPI Group (UK) Ltd, Croydon, CR0 4YY.

The Publisher's authorised representative in the EU for product safety is Authorised Rep Compliance Ltd., Ground Floor, 71 Lower Baggot Street, Dublin D02 P593, Ireland.
www.arccompliance.com

For a complete list of Pen & Sword titles please contact

PEN & SWORD BOOKS LIMITED
47 Church Street, Barnsley, South Yorkshire, S70 2AS, England
E-mail: enquiries@pen-and-sword.co.uk
Website: www.pen-and-sword.co.uk
or
PEN AND SWORD BOOKS
1950 Lawrence Road, Havertown, PA 19083, USA
E-mail: uspen-and-sword@casematepublishers.com
Website: www.penandswordbooks.com

# Contents

# Acknowledgements

I would like to thank the many resources I have relied upon for researching this book, including the British National Newspaper Archives, who bring history to life. It is a gift to be able to easily access primary sources from an ocean away. Included in my thanks is the Yale Center for British Art, The Met, The Rijksmuseum, Wellcome Collection, the New York Public Library, and Wikimedia Commons for access to public domain artwork from the era.

My deep gratitude goes to my editor, Sarah-Beth Watkins, who took a chance on an amateur historian, my copyeditor Sarah Hodder for her keen eye, and all those at Pen & Sword Books for their dedication to history.

Thank you to all the Regency Readers who have supported my research and writing for several decades, spurring me on with their curiosity and thirst for learning about the British Regency.

Finally, this work would not be possible without the incredible support of my husband, James, who has been with me for the entire journey, holding my hand and letting me hibernate to produce this labour of love. I love you with everything that I am.

# Introduction

On a Thursday night in June 1777, Mrs Cornelys hosted a masquerade styled rural. Carlisle House was lush with picturesque décor consisting of fauna and flora, brightly illuminated rooms, and with a band of music to provide the soundtrack to merriment and dancing. The reigning masquerade promoter of the day had returned to the scene a few years prior after a stint in debtor's prison. She was given the management of Carlisle House, which had been auctioned off in 1772, from 1775 until bankruptcy in 1779. The June event was one of two very popular rural themed masquerades she would host during her last days of freedom. The newspaper was surprised at how sumptuous the feast of cold meats and various wines were, given the low entrance fee.[1] It was by most accounts a successful masquerade.

The details of this event hinted at the masquerades that had come before and those that would follow for decades after; the bright lights, abundant greenery, and plush supper spread were just three key elements that would come to define a successful masked ball. A lively band, choice wines, and fair entrance fee were familiar elements. Masquerades, by 1777, had already become more than a novel diversion. There was a pattern and rhythm to their success that could be replicated, almost as if factory made, well into the early days of industrialisation. And although critics would declare the death of the masquerade by the end of the 1700s, in reality there was consistent production of masked events and fancy balls throughout the long Regency. And they were a production.

This production owed itself to the successes and failures of the previous century; the history of masquerades in Great Britain had a beginning in the eighteenth century. Inspired and imported from Italy's Carnival, it was established as a new form of gathering and entertainment, primarily for the upper classes. Like the theatre or balls, the masquerade would present an opportunity for the fashionable and powerful to engage in fantasy and escapism in disguise, but it would also serve as a place for likeminded people to congregate. A few significant impresarios would fan the flames of this trend so that it would carry through the whole century, and beyond, with only minor waxing and waning in public interest. Both private and public masquerades, small and large, would develop and refine a specific formula for the event, with traditions that would last into the next century. Many of these details were reflected in Mrs Cornelys' 1777 fete. It was a significant cultural phenomenon providing a unique lens into British culture of the time.

Count John James Heidegger is commonly credited with the importation of the masquerade to England in the early eighteenth century. Or, at least, bringing it to the public en masse as a site of consumption. There were a few aristocrats who, it has been suggested, introduced masquerades on a private, home-based scale yet when most think about the public, for profit masquerade, Heidegger is an acknowledged founder. A Swiss Count, Heidegger had spent some time in Venice and after a failed year in London as a Swiss negotiator, he tried his hand at opera management. Remembering the experiences of Carnival in Italy, he had an idea to introduce masquerades to the British Isles. It was finally a stroke of luck, as the idea would be his most successful. He became a promoter for masquerade balls at the Haymarket Theatre by 1713.

Heidegger was an imperfect hero in the history of masquerades. Known for his violent temper, he was frequently labelled as extremely ugly for a harshness of features. This notoriety gave way to a bet between Heidegger and the Earl of Chesterfield that the Earl could not find an uglier person in all of London. One woman was brought forth, but Heidegger was universally declared the winner. Heidegger was also known to be a drunk.[2] Regardless of his personal flaws, he was nonetheless successful once he turned his focus to bringing the masquerade to London and perfecting it as a form of entertainment through his entrepreneurial hunger and skills at organisation and event planning. Masquerades and the opera, while derided by some like Hogarth, brought success for Heidegger who was reportedly making £5000 a year at the height of his career. By the time of his death in 1749, the masquerade was a staple in many popular London locales, including the Ranelagh and Vauxhall Pleasure Gardens, inspired by Heidegger's success. A Heidegger masquerade was public, but subscription based, and known to attract several hundred participants per event. His masquerades were held primarily at the Haymarket Theatre and emphasised music and fashion. Contemporaries would refer to them as a promiscuous assembly.[3] Fancy dress and masquerades were often interchangeable, setting a standard for not only a mask but a costume and persona to be part of the fun. The setting in a theatre lent the events that air of performance that helped support the idea of play. Masquerades often enjoyed royal patronage, with King George I being a particular fan. While the clergy eventually forced a temporary halt to masquerades, Heidegger would reinvent them as a ridotto and would be awarded with the king's approval.[4]

Heidegger would pass away at his home in Richmond in 1749. He was succeeded as the reigning masquerade promoter by Mrs Cornelys. A German-born singer by profession, she settled in London around 1756 and shortly gained possession of the former Earl of Carlisle's mansion in Soho Square, Carlisle House. The fashionable address was near many of the aristocratic town homes of the time period, serving as the centre for much of the activity for those of rank or note. Sometimes referred to as an adventuress by her peers, Cornelys was well known for throwing lavish masquerades with over the top decorations and top tier food and drink. According to many, Mrs Cornelys' masquerade balls were unparalleled in their magnificence and brilliance. Beginning at nine and ending at six the following morning, the masquerade brought royals, gentry, ambassadors, and other respectable characters to a Carlisle House that had been so extensively renovated as to resemble a fairy palace.

Mrs Cornelys, whose Carlisle House was the most frequented masquerading haunt for the latter half of the Georgian decade, was known to not only flaunt convention and general sensibilities, but also to violate the law. A grand jury heard, during a trial for conducting theatrical entertainment without a license, her events described as disorderly, with assorted loose and idle persons rioting the whole night, generally misbehaving, and creating a broader public disturbance.[5] Cornelys' masquerades utilised the subscription model to assure top quality patronage at her events. Her success with throwing lavish events saw her purchase a country home. However, she frequently advertised that her events were charity functions to mask that she was making money without proper approval. This would bring the law down around her ears and force her to stop her money-making venture. Throughout her reign of fashionable events, she would continually be running on River Tick, serving time in a debtor's prison until Carlisle House was seized and its contents auctioned off around 1772. She would resurface for a few years, before suffering insolvency once again. By the end of the Georgian era, she would die in the Fleet Prison, after languishing in relative obscurity for several decades.

Heidegger and Cornelys' events would not be the only masquerades during the Georgian era. By the 1770s, other venues had caught on to the lucrative event as a nice diversification from plays, balls, and concerts. The Pantheon had at least one masked ball per year, and the Ranelagh Pleasure Gardens would also host the occasional masquerade. In 1773, the first iteration of Almack's Assembly Rooms held a masquerade ball. Contemporaries complimented the excellent music, entertainment, and elegant attendees. Masquerades were no longer novel, but by and large they were a lucrative diversion.

In part, the diversion was from convention. Masquerades hinted at opportunities to flaunt convention, show skin, and engage in amorous liaisons. A Hammersmith masquerade sometime in the 1770s was reported to host masqueraders with bare knees, a truly shocking display. While masquerades would continue to operate on a fine line of respectability, as they became more of a common entertainment at public venues, like the Pantheon, much of the lewd and lascivious behaviour would be tamed into something more respectable. This included having well respected women and men offer their name in support of the events. A Pantheon event in 1782 had the Prince of Wales, the Duchess of Devonshire, Major St Leger, and several other lords and ladies partnering for an organised cotillion showcase. Decked out in Spanish-inspired costume, the dance they introduced was new and coordinated.[6] A King's Theatre masquerade followed quickly, the same year, with many of the same people and a profusion of wine, supper, and good wit and humour.[7] It was a harbinger of the style of events that would emerge during the long Regency.

Castle (1986) suggested that at the close of the eighteenth century, the golden age of masquerades in Britain was also reaching its end. However, this is not borne out by the evidence. In 1830, the *Weekly Times (London)* declared that masquerades had become as common as to require little advanced notice.[8] In fact, at any given decade during the long Regency there were at least three, and up to five or six venues, regularly providing masquerade events. On top of the three to five reported private masquerades held annually, it perhaps is more accurate to say that the public taste for masquerades did not wane in the nineteenth century, but instead the dynamics of the masquerade changed.

Terry Castle's seminal work emphasised the masquerade in the eighteenth century as a site of play among classes. Castle (1986) suggested that the masquerade was a vehicle for subverting class and gender boundaries, exploring sexual freedom, and undermining etiquette and decorum. Some current scholars take issue with that depiction, questioning whether there was truly a freedom or wildness about the events. Undoubtedly, some were known to devolve into debauchery, vice, and criminal activity but new research posits that was the exception rather than the rule.

A review of primary sources suggests that there is likely some truth in both depictions. Some people used the anonymity of a masquerade to behave in a manner at odds with their ordinary identity. In other cases, a guest's identity was known but the masquerade setting was still a useful excuse to try on another identity, albeit likely a stereotypical one. The intent is hard to truly understand without interview of the participants, but generally the costumes of the British masquerade that emerged from character and fancy dress suggest categories that imply intent: comedic, sexy or risqué, heroic or powerful. However, it is arguable whether this subversive play had the impact of true social change or, instead, served to reproduce cultural norms. Even while some may have engaged in bacchanalian excesses, the access to these events that were largely in London and in the best parts of town, support the argument that the players were select and their performances specifically aimed at their counterparts. The rich and fashionable, rather than rubbing elbows with the middle and lower classes, were insulated from any real risk by the barriers of access and etiquette.

Newer research focuses on the intersection between cultural appropriation and costume, imperialism and rising racism. In cataloguing the various costumes from the Georgian and Regency era, it's apparent all cultures, foreign and domestic, were ripe for mascot-ism. The gentry at masquerades could play at being poor or richer, from another country, a profession, or a figure from a bygone era. The language to describe indigenous-based costumes is the most inflammatory and ripe for criticism, but contextualised, the portrayal of people from working or middle class is also problematic. People, mostly wealthy or influential, would dress in the garbs of different religions, races, or walks of life but in such a way as to amuse, entertain, delight, or excite their friends and acquaintances.

What is notable is that as the nineteenth century dawned, masquerades had been successful events in Great Britain for a century. Both private and public events allowed for masked fancy dress or costumes, where people could pretend to be someone else, temporarily relieving the strain of the social mask. Yet, as the socio-political climate transitioned from eighteenth to nineteenth century, and all the shifting cultural tides, masquerades were at once a constant and an agent of change in the Regency. Evident in much of the contemporary reporting, masquerades were seen as a mechanism for relieving the mantle of British restraint but more importantly were a source for satire for many elements of culture. These events had some of the notable spectacles and interactions from the Regency era. Masquerades, particularly public events, allowed the option for the burgeoning middle class to gain entrance to the glittering fancy dress balls of the gentry and allowed women the rare freedom to flirt with public outings where the risqué was a design feature. Regardless of the scholarly debates about the levels of free expression and liberation masquerade exhibited, these small transgressions were microcosms of a changing world hastened by invention, restructuring economies, and the push for more equality.

The official Regency era was the window of time, 1811 to 1820, when Prince George IV ruled as regent. For the purposes of this book, I will be using the broader time frame of 1795 to 1837 to cover the third and final timespan of the Georgian era until Queen Victoria's accession to the throne. This larger time span is frequently acknowledged as the long Regency, owing to King George's battle with mental health and the prince's role in governance during the time period. There are also socio-political, economic, and broader cultural similarities that make sense to group the Regency under this time span. The roughly forty-three-year period is a time of change but also stagnation. There are minor shifts over this time period, but generally it is unified by fashion, cultural influences, trends, and the ever expanding Empire.

The Regency is frequently portrayed as the era of decadence before the impending backlash and swing towards repressive morality in the Victorian era. On the precipice of rapid industrialisation, with British colonialism reaching an impasse and a dialogue opened to discuss slavery and exploitation, it however represents a unique window of time by which to truly understand the cultural exchange taking place at the masquerade. For some, it was a harkening back to the eighteenth century tradition. For others, it represented a reboot and opportunity to alternatively place themselves in a narrative about gender or class. Still for others, there was a cultural interplay of national identity and the Empire woven into the very fabric of these events that makes them particularly interesting for scrutiny.

Historical romance novels portray the masquerade as a place for intrigue and assignations, with the climax of unmasking exposing desires to the censor or delight of society. Yet, costumes can also be experienced as a form of tourism and consumption, by which the masqueraders sought to depart their realities and find themselves in a land of absurdity that would provide a vehicle to eschew oppressive norms and etiquette. In some sense, the mask was the original avatar, fulfilling the same subconscious and conscious desires of individuals. The mechanisms at play are fascinating and offer unique insight into the socio-cultural and political underpinnings of the era.

The shift in the masquerade, including the increasing standardisation of these events, are what make the Regency masquerade a platform for understanding broader aspects of Regency culture. Using primary sources, the first ten chapters focus on examining the record and providing the details of the Regency masquerade. The where, what, when, why, and how's of private and public events are explored to begin painting a picture of masquerades in the early nineteenth century. These details will help to tease out underlying trends, themes, and the overall pattern of masquerades during the long Regency. On the whole, there is startling sameness about these events despite differences in venue, spectacle, and decade. Using examples gleaned from primary sources, these chapters will highlight these similarities and also differences so that a clear, established pattern can be identified. This section of the book has been organised to first set the scene, by examining the most common venues for the Regency masquerade. There were changes from the beginning of the Regency to the end, yet every decade had at least two venues that regularly held masquerade balls.

Capping the review with a look at private masquerades, a study of décor will follow. By breaking down the common elements that many of the venues and private homes featured at masquerades for décor, whether lights, chalked floors, or outdoor spaces, décor will be understood as a space for symbolism and identity reproduction. Entertainment at masquerades follows the discussion of décor, highlighting the music, dancing, performances, and refreshments that formed the standard run of show. As we examine newspaper and memoirs that report on masquerades, several themes emerge. In particular, an escalating emphasis on spectacle becomes apparent as the large venues attempt to establish their events as premier destinations for the rich and fashionable. Finally, analysis of the categories of costumes that appear over and over at these events intends to showcase the inherent interests and beliefs of the Regency masquerader.

The remaining chapters shift to extracting meaning from these details, exploring the emergent themes and discussing them within the context of scholarly research on the Regency, masquerades, and British identity. The intent is to provide a thorough picture of masquerade between the late 1790s into the late 1830s, and to highlight what the masquerade can tell us not only about the age but also about people more generally. Of particular interest are national identity, cultural appropriation, gender, and the subsequent impact the framing of these identities had on future generations. It's not an exhaustive study, but instead intended to be a first step into understanding the historical record of the long Regency and the role masquerade events played during this time.

A review of primary sources, including memoirs, newspaper articles, and guidebooks on Regency masquerades reveal a sort of formula for success. Critical and positive reviews continuously, over the long Regency, highlight a shortlist of needs for the masquerade event to make it profitable and well-received. The features that made up this formula included the venue (and therefore the guest list), the décor, the entertainment, and the costumes. The entertainment, particularly for the Regency, includes not only the music and dancing, but also food and beverage and assorted spectacle. Some of these features were established in the Georgian era, with the introduction of masquerades as a commercial event, but much of it was refined over some forty odd years of the long Regency period. While perhaps not surprising that many of the costumes and characters at these events were relevant over the forty year span, and that the standards for run of show were perfected over that time period, it is surprising at how little variation there was in the type of refreshments, the music selection, the décor, and the overall experience.

In the Regency era, the location for a masquerade was nearly as significant as the costume one donned. The level of exclusivity of a venue would often have a direct correlation to its reputation. In a review of newspaper and memoir coverage of masquerades, it's clear there was a hierarchy of venues for masquerades during the early nineteenth century. Private masquerades were exclusive events by nature, with the exception of a Cyprian ball, and were particularly popular for more intimate gatherings where attendees knew all or most of the other guests. These could be held in the host or hostesses home or a venue would be rented out for the occasion. They were held in London and, on occasion, at an individual's country estate. Generally, the size of the gatherings would not exceed three or four hundred people, and most required a clear invitation that would be vetted at the door for admittance.

The next tier of venues, in terms of exclusivity, were subscription masquerades held regularly at the Argyll Rooms. Entrance required approval of a patroness or patron to gain an invitation and subscription and therefore was the premier location for exclusive masquerading for the Regency party goer of the fashionable and upper class. In the latter years of the long Regency, newspapers would grouse that even the Argyll Rooms were devoid of respectable women so that there was some whiff that, for a young lady, attendance at an Argyll Rooms masquerade would be risqué. However, judging by lists of those in attendance, it was commonplace for the crowd to be filled with various gentry and fashionable people.

Public balls were attractive for some of the *haute ton* because of the titillating idea that they might frequently find themselves intermingled with low company. Truthfully, except for pickpockets, sex workers, and others who might professionally benefit from attendance, the price of admission necessarily meant that public balls were still exclusive to those who could afford it. In most cases, this meant the gentry would be mingling at most with the middle class, which for some was still a dangerous prospect. In addition, paid performers would often be in attendance, in character, to enliven the atmosphere. There was some variation even within the public venues on the level of understood exclusivity, likely due to admission fees and access. Yet the idea of being part of the motley crowd was still appealing to those seeking a thrill and adventure.

By the late Georgian era, there were more locations regularly hosting masquerade events than in the early and middle Georgian era. This offered a selection to participants depending on the type of experience they were in search of. Argyll Rooms, the Pantheon, Vauxhall and Ranelagh Pleasure Gardens, and Haymarket represented the most frequent masquerade locations within London, at least for the early Regency period. Farther flung cities would also boast masquerades, including popular summer destinations like Bath and Margate. And private homes would still represent another opportunity for various circles to explore costume and fancy dress performances with a hundred or more of their closest friends and neighbours. The newspapers would report on these events sometimes in a list of 'Fashionable Arrangements' or 'Fashionable World' for the week, and at other times detailed accounts highlighting attendees, decoration, food and beverage, and commentary on costumes.

The venues devoted to entertainments like the masquerade varied in size and design, but shared the common theme of spectacle as an enhancement for events. There is little doubt the public or subscription events were driven by money as much as the desire to entertain. But the prevalence of private events suggests that, beyond entertainment and income, the masquerade held an attraction for Regency society. A clear picture of the popular and common venues for masquerades during the Regency era will help lay a foundation for understanding the socio-economic and broad cultural impacts and praxis of masquerades.

## Chapter One

# Fashionable Institution (Argyll Rooms)

The house in little Argyll Street was dressed for a Ladies' Grand Subscription Masquerade in June 1806. The grand hall and staircase dripped with tasteful displays of artificial roses and other flowers interwoven with variegated lamps, and the occasional shrub peppered the lush garden atmosphere. A large transparency awaited guests at the top of the staircase, decorated with the prince's feathers and an inscription that read: 'If the precaution taken to preserve this spot sacred from introducing have proved fruitless, let the masque that covered the deception at least continue to screen the intruder'. The first few hours were spent delighting in the display of character costumes and fancy dress. Supper was set at two o'clock in the morning to a dizzying array of society's most fashionable peers and people, the event continuing with dancing and song until nearly half past nine in the morning.[1] And thus one of the premier masquerade venues of the long Regency was thrust into the London spotlight.

Its ambitions were bolstered by a past history of masquerade and entertainment, despite being beleaguered by a piecemeal design. The remnants of the Duke of Argyll's London mansion, a sprawling, dull and stolid place with little architectural pretence,[2] had been demolished in 1736 to make way for the construction of Little Argyll Street. Argyll House was not a memorable or stately landmark so there was no great concern with the partial demolition. In reality, Argyll House was more of a hodgepodge of buildings, so that it was easy enough for the duke to take the forecourt of one of the buildings in exchange for some land, leaving the north and south wings. After the demolition, Lord Ilay, the duke's brother who had lived in the home since the early 1700s, began to build a new house on the plot the duke had leased him. Lord Ilay would live there until his death in 1761, having succeeded to the title of the Duke of Argyll upon the death of his brother in 1743.

What was left of the original mansion were the north and south wings along Little Argyll Street and Regent Street. The north wing, after the duke's passing, was occupied by Sir Raymond and then Lady Monoux in 1757. William Joliffe purchased it around 1771 for a low price. Joliffe was a politician who served in parliament until 1802, when he passed away. Joliffe was described in letters from the 1770s as a consummate entertainer, often giving balls, masquerades, and other entertainments for the ton.[3] It was these early events that would likely help to inspire the Argyll Rooms' future. Joliffe's son, Hylton, would sell the house on Little Argyll Street to Colonel Henry Greville after his father's death for, reportedly, £70. Greville would quickly make his way to establishing the home as a London hot spot.

Greville was the second of three sons, all who had military careers. Their sister also was a notable Whig hostess. The Colonel was deployed during the American Revolutionary War, becoming a prisoner of war during the British surrender at Yorktown. It was in Yorktown Greville was involved in the Asgill Affair. The diplomatic incident would be well known in London, as ministers were involved in trying to intervene. Just eight years later, in 1790, Greville would be appointed to serve in Ireland with the 4th Regiment of Dragoon Guards until he decided to leave the army to pursue the career of a theatrical impresario. Although his military career had brought him some public attention, it was his ventures in the world of entertainment that would ultimately earn him lasting fame, if not lasting wealth. Yet his military career helped to establish him and build the network that would support his career as an impresario.

The Argyll Rooms were the second venture of Greville, following the dissolution of the Pic-Nic Society after much public derision and a failure to make money. The Pic-Nic Society, or the Dilettanti, held meetings in Tottenham Street. These meetings primarily consisted of a theatrical or musical performance by persons of fashion, a lavish supper, and alcohol.[4] The Society and their events lasted only for a year with an account of the last event in the *Morning Post* calling Greville a dupe for trying to establish a French theatre in London.[5] Greville did try to revive it again the following year, but was unsuccessful. He briefly started a weekly newspaper called the *Pic-Nic* for theatrical reporting, which was just as quickly dispensed with. During the Pic-Nic Society's short lifespan, Gillray produced a variety of prints showcasing the group and their events.

Greville was an interesting character. His mother, Frances Greville, had been a celebrity poet during the Georgian era, and his father, Fulke Greville, was a member of parliament. He was notably handsome, a remarkable sportsman, and terrible with money, but driven to entertain. Therefore, it was unsurprising that he immediately made moves to find his next entertainment scheme after the failure of the Pic-Nic ventures. He purchased the north wing of the former Argyll Rooms and proceeded to have it renovated. The cost of renovations was reported to be upwards of £10,000, funds likely obtained from investors. In 1806, Greville held two balls to test the new Fashionable Institution later styled the Argyll Rooms.

Prior to Greville's launch of the Fashionable Institution in 1806, the house in Little Argyle street was hired by Lady Lambert to carry on the tradition of masquerades from the previous owner, William Joliffe. Joliffe was said to have built one of the rooms expressly for the purpose.[6] Lady Lambert found her own home in Manchester Square insufficient for a large ball and the north wing of the former Argyll House worked well for her purpose. Lady Lambert's June 1805 masquerade was reported on in *The British Press*. The coverage provided sufficient detail to understand the event was grand. The entire house was used, with decorations including a large lamp illuminating the staircase and the 35 by 25 foot ballroom decorated by a profusion of fragrant shrubs and flowers, with a floor chalked with delicate ornamentation. The card rooms were framed by sizeable pillars encased in floral wreaths. Overall, the theme was Elysium, with many guests dressing in the spirit of the Greek afterlife. More commonplace costumes included Punch, a tailor, a lawyer, nuns, an old tabby, and the Weird Sisters. The guest list was full of the rank and file from the fashionable and titled of London.[7]

Lady Lambert's event was as good as a soft launch for the Fashionable Institution, but Greville did not rest until the establishment was perfect. The sizeable expenditures would help to transform the once mismatched mansion into a premier venue. *The Picture of London* (1809) would describe the Fashionable Institution following Greville's renovations; the entrance and lobbies were framed with Corinthian pillars and lit by gilt lamps welcoming visitors into the rooms. The ground floor held three large supper rooms, the first decorated in grey with scarlet drapery, the second with stone colour and green trellis wallpaper with salmon drapery, and the third dressed in a similar, yet less elegant style as the second room. All three featured glass and gilt lamps and chandeliers that were frequently recounted in newspaper descriptions, impressing visitors with elegance and the air of wealth.

A staircase would often be staged for events with impressive scenery in the form of a transparency, lights, or flora and fauna, encouraging masqueraders to make their way to the grand saloon that would serve as ballroom or theatre, with an oblong shape and twenty-four boxes in three richly gold moulded tiers. The middle tier was decorated with antique brass bass reliefs, and the upper tier featured scrolls in a stone colour and ethereal blue. Bronze circular chandeliers with cut glass pendants were hung over each box, with draperies in scarlet. An orchestra and stage were featured at one end of the room, with the motto 'The Pleasant Oblivion of a Busy Life' in Latin above. Corinthian pillars, bass relief panels, and blue and gold accents adorned the middle room, which was lined with benches upholstered in scarlet and lit by eight glass chandeliers. The floor would be chalked in a theme set for the evening. Adjacent were the refectory, painted with landscapes and flower wreaths, and a billiard room. On the other side of the room was a spacious card room done up with scarlet window coverings and featuring a painted ceiling. The blue room was a small apartment next to that, with light blue drapery and sofas, and a ceiling painted to mimic an open sky with an eagle canopy holding the bronze and gold chandelier.

The room was decorated with elegance and taste, designed to imply that no expense had been spared to entertain the fashionable set. It was deliberate, with tickets to events varying from one guinea a lady and two guineas per gentlemen to ten shillings each. The 1809 *Picture of London* gave the subscription terms as ten guineas for a lady, twelve for a gentleman and sixteen for a lady with an unmarried daughter. The subscription would have included anywhere from eight to twelve events during the Season, mostly musical or dancing events commensurate with Greville's license. With upwards of five to six hundred attendees per event at its height, the Argyll Rooms were opulent but productive. Masquerades were a significant part of its success.

The first subscription masquerade would happen on June 2, 1806, unveiling a new room hung with paper in the design of treillage and vines. Five supper rooms were set with the grandest holding a pyramid of glass circles with the names of the lady patronesses of the event. Transparencies decorated the staircase, one a figure of Minerva and the other likenesses of the twelve lady patronesses. Supporting these creations were wreaths of laurel and evergreens woven through the balustrade, while a military band positioned at the foot of the staircase greeted masqueraders with continuous music. White muslin hung on the walls and was decorated with artificial flowers, and a stage was erected to elevate Mr Gow's celebrated orchestra. The floor was chalked with Egyptian imagery and doves at the corners, and the ballroom was hung with crimson curtains. Another room was done up in the Turkish style and the fitting rooms were decorated to resemble vineyards. One newspaper advertisement promised one of the most elegant events to ever be presented to the fashionable world.

The event itself did not kick off until one in the morning, with the Prince of Wales and the Duke of Cambridge arriving a half an hour later to greet the crowd of some 500 people. While two thirds of the party was dressed simply in a domino, the *Morning Post* recounted the costumes of attendees who had stretched their creativity. All the costumes were eclipsed by the arrival of a group at two in the morning dressed as the characters from Tom Thumb. They entertained the crowd with dancing that they called *Lady Godiva of Coventry's Minuet* to the tune of *Like a Cat I'll Squall*, and then sang several songs to the amusement of the party until supper. More singing and dancing continued until the late morning. It was noted a masked lady rumoured to be the Duchess of York accompanied the prince and the Duke of Cambridge, causing speculation when she did not remove her mask for the entire evening.[8] It had been a memorable affair.

Buoyed by the success, Greville acted quickly. Another subscription masquerade was soon advertised for July 1, 1806. The July masquerade repeated the successes of the first event, although staged costumes in house for convenience. The advertisement also provided directions for servants to better manage traffic.[9] After two successful events, Greville obtained a license in 1807 from Lord Chamberlain to host music, dancing, burlettas, and dramatic performances. Masquerades would begin in earnest in 1807 in April, and also be repeated in June and July. By all accounts the masquerades continued to be crowded. Greville's confirmed victory as a promoter was clear not only in the popularity of his fetes, but in his ability to acquire a license.

Obtaining a license could often be a hard won prospect, and would represent one source of instability for the various masquerade venues over the nineteenth century. As a result of the Licensing Act of 1737, the Lord Chamberlain had the power to act as theatrical censor and grant licenses to theatricals, balls, musicals, and any manner of other commercial entertainment. The Lord Chamberlain system of censorship and licensing had the unique impact of subjecting commercial enterprise to the whims of the elite and powerful just as forces like industrialisation were changing the landscape.[10] Greville would have a complicated history with the Lord Chamberlain and licensing, including introducing and maintaining masquerades at several venues.

Masquerades were a special dance covered under Greville's license. Unique to the Argyll Rooms, these events were supported by subscriptions and the supervision of patronesses. Much like Almack's, a voucher was required for access to the Argyll Rooms and it would maintain a relatively strict admittance practice throughout its life making it one of the more elite venues. In 1806, at the outset, two Dukes, Lady Jersey, and numerous other ladies controlled who was admitted to the events. The patronesses would change over the years, but the names read like a virtual who's who of the ton, many times the same patronesses from Almack's Assembly Rooms. In 1811, the *Globe* listed the patronesses for a masquerade in May as the Duchess of Gordon (Jane Gordon), the Duchess of Bedford (Georgiana Russell), Countess Cholmondeley, and Countess Jersey. The Duchess of Gordon was named by Horace Walpole as the 'Empress of Fashion' and known for her lavish parties and political influence for the Tory Party. Sarah Villiers, Countess of Jersey was also a notable Tory and leader of the ton. She was a long reigning patroness of Almack's Assembly Rooms, and was given the ironic nickname of 'Silence' because she was said to never stop talking. Some contemporaries found her theatrical, ill-bred, rude, and a tragedy queen but she was unmistakably a Society trendsetter. Its undoubtable the sponsorship of these illustrious leaders of Society helped to establish the Argyll Rooms as a fashionable location.

Between 1806 and 1811, the Argyll Rooms would host at least two masquerades a year. Characteristically happening in April through July, the event dates were apparently chosen to reduce any conflict with other fashionable parties occurring during the early summer months.[11] The masquerades would routinely start at midnight, opening the doors to the elegant, tasteful establishment in anticipation of the various titled and fashionable people who would attend in dominos, character costume, and fancy dress, and close when the party waned by five or six in the morning. With the support of so many Society leaders and a select, refined experience on offer, the Argyll Rooms masquerades were London's most exclusive public, albeit subscription-based, event. The newspapers fairly tripped over themselves to deliver compliments to the elite establishment and guests. The great taste of the June 1808 Argyll Rooms masquerade greeted only around 300 of the elite, but the *Morning Post* was still effusive in their praise of the events at the Argyll Institution.[12] A May 1809 event was praised for its select and fashionable attendance.[13] The June 1809 masquerade was attended by 400 people.[14]

Despite the high attendance numbers, the Argyll Rooms did not make Greville's fortune. By 1811, Greville was ill, deeply in debt, and unable to sell the Argyll Rooms. Likely due to family pressure, Greville went abroad in 1812 and would eventually die in Port Louis, Mauritius. He gave the Argyll Rooms, at the time of his departure, over to his debtor, Stephen Slade, who paid off the remaining mortgages and took over ownership. Slade had already begun to get his name out there, hosting benefit masquerade balls at the Argyll Rooms in 1809 and 1810.[15] Greville's family was said to discharge the rest of Greville's debt, likely in exchange for his exile. Slade continued to nurture the business Greville had started, including hosting masquerades. The 1810 Argyll Rooms masquerade was said to belie the opinion that masquerades were not well suited to the British character. So well attended by respectable and fashionable people set on mirth and gaiety, dancing was said to go from open until close at five the next morning, spurred on by great character costumes and good supper and wine.[16]

Slade was a glass and china dealer by trade who had been called 'Conductor of the Household'. Slade was successful for the first few years of his ownership, aided by the upstart Philharmonic Society that was founded in 1813 and would make the Argyll Rooms its first home, as well as several notable theatrical productions. Masquerades were a part of his various schedule of entertainments, including hosting both the infamous Dandies Ball and Cyprian Ball. Yet it would not be complete smooth sailing for Slade. In late 1814 Slade was notified that demolition of the building was required for the creation of Regent Street. Famous architect John Nash had a vision for Regent Street, and Slade was a thorn in his side as he refused to give up the Rooms. Slade effectively delayed action until 1819, when he was forced to sell but later awarded £22,750 by a jury. Following the demolition of the original rooms, new rooms designed by Nash were erected on the east side of Regent Street for the Regent's Harmonic Institution. Some suggest that the Philharmonic Society had originally chosen the location because of Nash's interest, speculating his creation would be an ideal performing space, attracting the interest of the elite.

Cost overruns resulted in additional investor turmoil and the new Argyll Rooms landed in the hands of Thomas Welsh. It would continue to flourish as the fashionable institution it had been named to be, in large part because of the influence of the Philharmonic Society. This group would hold concerts at the Argyll Rooms until 1830, when a fire would force them to move to Hanover Square Rooms, and then St James's Hall.[17] Despite the change of ownership over the years, proprietors adhered to the successful model initiated by Greville for balls. Masquerades were limited in number every year and supported by patronesses who made up the upper ranks of the Regency ton. In 1813, one event listed the patronesses as Countess Cholmondeley, Countess Besborough, Countess Cowper, Viscountess Castlereagh, Lady Charles Bentinck, Lady Asgill, and Mrs Dorothy Boehm. In 1829, the patronesses were listed as the Duchess of Northumberland, Lady Lucy Clive, Lady Harriet W. Wynn, Lady Synebov, Lady Rodney, Mrs Rice Trevor, Mrs Williams Wynn, and Mrs Hughes. From year to year, and even event to event, the patronesses changed for the Argyll Rooms.

Many of the names will be familiar as patronesses of Almack's Assembly Rooms, including Lady Cowper and Lady Castlereagh. The Countess Cholmondeley, later Marchioness, was married to a scoundrel and womaniser and was known to run a faro bank that ruined many a person. Countess Besborough was also married to a gambling addict who was known to be abusive. The Countess narrowly avoided divorce when caught cheating. She was also a gambler. Lady Asgill was known as part of the Duchess of Devonshire's set, and enjoyed the theatre and entertainments. She also was the wife of Sir Charles Asgill, who was the namesake of the Asgill Affair incident with prisoners of war during the American Revolutionary War, in which Greville was also involved. Asgill had been selected among the British officers for execution which was only commuted due to pressures on America by the French monarchy.

Mr Boehm was a successful merchant who had made his fortune in the East India Company. The Boehms were called social climbers by some accounts, having many dinner parties and an active social life. Mrs Boehm was known for her fashionable balls and masquerades, but the most lasting legacy was that it was at her fete that news of the victory at Waterloo reached the Prince Regent and many of the ton's ears, bringing a sharp end to her party.[18] The Viscountess Lucy Clive, nee Graham, was the third daughter of the Duke of Montrose. Her husband, in 1839, would inherit an earldom and she would afterward be known as Lucy Herbert, Countess Powis. Her name is frequently listed in the late Regency as she presented various young ladies to court.

Over the years, and at the masquerades, there would be some repetition in patronesses as well as new names to sponsor the masked events. Until the 1820s, there would be considerable overlap in patronesses between Almack's and the Argyll Rooms. These powerful taste makers would lend their credit to these events, in much the way of modern celebrity endorsements. There is no doubt that for the Argyll Rooms part of the success was in the exclusivity, or at least the suggestion of it. Unique from some of the rigid strictures of Almack's, however, the Argyll Rooms offered a venue less for the marriage mart and more for the haute ton to indulge.

The masquerades and balls were not exclusively sponsored by the patronesses. In July 1813, the Dandies Ball was held at the Argyll Rooms by four leading Beaus of the day, Brummell, Alvanley, Pierrepoint and Mildmay,[19] to celebrate considerable gambling winnings at hazard. It was not a masked event, The ball was highly anticipated, in part because the Prince Regent was rumoured to have expressed interest in attendance and this was following the infamous cut from Brummel; the cut was a favoured way to renounce acquaintance by pretending not to acknowledge the person either directly, indirectly, or through distraction. The prince, still stinging from his cut from Brummel on St James, delivered Brummel the cut direct at the Rooms, solidifying its moment in history.[20] The prince was said to have remarked that had Brummel taken his cut in his stride, he would have renewed his favour. Years later a children's book called *The Dandies Ball* would quickly become a favourite for its amusing plates and rhymes. There are various sources that also cite the location for this event at the Hanover Square Rooms, but the record from that year reflects the fete was held at the Argyll Rooms to a crowd of over 300 people.[21]

Four more notorious patronesses assembled a masked Venetian Carnival Ball on Tuesday, May 26 , 1818 at the Argyll Rooms. The Cyprian Ball, as it was also known, was promoted by Augusta Corri, known as Lady Hawke, with four other well-known courtesans said to include the infamous Harriet Wilson and her sisters Amy, Fanny, and Sophia. No wives or girlfriends of the haute ton were welcome, but the gentlemen appeared in droves. The newspapers reported there were 300 in attendance with dinner served at 2:30 am and the party lasted until 5:00 am. The event was reported to cost £2000, although the bill was likely paid by a protector. For the event, the Argyll

Rooms had been decorated with wreathed columns, including natural and artificial flowers from France. Chalked floors and flowing wine and delicacies on the banquet tables set off the venue and welcomed masqueraders. It was reported the company wore the standard costumes including dustmen, harlequin, shoe-blacks, and royals. Notable were Martha Gunn, the bathing woman of Brighton, Liston, Mathews, and Shakespeare. Every manner of dance, including quadrilles, waltzes, boleros, and fandangos was said to be engaged in until the sun rose.[22] The event was memorialised in a plate by Cruikshank and appeared in a satirical publication.

The coverage in the newspapers would not be the end of the story for Lady Hawke. A reader wrote to the editor of the *St James's Chronicle* and *London Evening Post* in June 1818 and questioned their advertisement of Lady Hawke's Ball. The 'Constant Reader' hinted the marriage of Lord Hawke and Lady Hawke was suspect, knowing Lord Hawke to be a widower and no marriage to have been announced.[23] It is likely the wide publication of Lady Hawke's masquerade brought attention to the union and created some embarrassment for Lord Hawke, who may have wished to keep his relationship more discreet. Lord Hawke would file suit against Augusta Corri in 1819, with Lord Hawke protesting her claims of marriage and claiming malicious libel. Lady Hawke's account of the lengths to which Lord Hawke went to court her, propose marriage, and then create a ruse of a special license were so compelling that his suit for libel was dismissed. The case would be discussed for decades after in legal reviews. The case was also intertwined with the resignation of Philharmonic Society musician and director Antony Corri in 1816, who would by 1817 flee London and reappear in Baltimore under the name Arthur Clifton. Augusta Corri had been Antony Corri's first wife, and it was this marriage that Lord Hawke used in his case to claim Augusta was a bigamist. There is some speculation that the reason for his sudden resignation and departure from Great Britain was due to the discovery of his true sexual orientation, but this has not been substantiated.[24] That the whole affair was essentially one real-life masquerade piled upon another is surely either great irony or a sign of the times, part of what made the play at masquerade so visceral and compelling for certain circles within the Regency.

The Cyprian Ball was an anomaly for the Argyll Rooms in so freely promoting sex workers and the upper class together. The Argyll Rooms were noted for displaying taste without ostentation and liberality without profusion, and most importantly keeping out vulgarity and vice by restricting admittance to the upper classes.[25] This would help support it through the early nineteenth century, as the Pantheon lost its exclusivity and began to attract an unsavoury element of thieves. Strengthened by its relationship with titled patrons and patronesses, and the Philharmonic Society, the Argyll Rooms relied on a careful curation of its image and the patronesses serving as gatekeepers for admittance. Although the newspapers, from time to time, would grouse that only notorious females deigned to attend the masquerades.[26] Judging from the frequently published lists of attendees and their costumes, this was no doubt an exaggeration.

From the beginning, a key component of the Argyll Room's success was its overt displays of wealth and exclusivity combined with themes of nature, light, and abundance. A June 1806 masquerade was described as magnificent, with the grand hall and staircase decorated tastefully in shrubs, large artificial roses, other flowers, and sparkling variegated lamps. The ballroom was decorated with white draperies, and more artificial roses and lamps, with the floor chalked with dancing figures, rounded by feathers, flowers, and finally a coloured Etruscan border. The attached room was decorated in the Egyptian style, and featured an array of fruits, ices, tea, coffee, orgeat, and lemonade. The ceilings were hung with costly cut diamond lustres, flowers woven through the light body to give a natural, romantic feel to the space. Beyond the refreshments was the prince's supper room that was dressed to resemble a vineyard, being covered in grapes and more flowers, and luxurious enough to serve the future king. Beyond the appointed princely room were five additional supper rooms with covers laid for more than 600 attendees. Revellers arrived at eleven thirty with supper at two, and the party did not break until nine thirty the next morning. It was one of the longer events of recollection.

The Argyll Rooms were also occasionally hired for private events. The Countess of Cork held another masquerade at the end of June 1806 which began at her home in New Burlington Street. The Countess had prepared her conservatory with an array of variegated lamps, in arches and festoons, and a floor covered in hay. After an evening of cards and refreshments, at two in the morning a procession went from the house on New Burlington Street to the Argyll Rooms, where a supper was set for the 300 attendees. *The British Press* reported that the lights and masks enlivened the streets of London with the Carnival spirit of Rome or Venice.[27] As carriage traffic was always a consideration for any London event, the short walk was welcome and likely caused a spectacle for those who happened by.

A May masquerade in 1809 was the first at the Argyll Rooms for the Season, opening at midnight and becoming a crush at one in the morning. Decorated in variegated lamps, laurel, and leaves, the Rooms featured two bands that evening. The ballroom was illuminated by Chinese lanterns and Grecian lamps, keeping the partiers dancing until six in the morning.[28] The event was heralded as one of the best in years, with a fashionable and select crowd in attendance.[29] Although the ladies in attendance were said to have enough beauty to compensate for deficiencies in blood, implying that most of the women in attendance were likely not of the same class as the gentlemen in attendance.[30] That June, Mrs Chichester followed the Countess of Cork's lead, having a masquerade that began at her house before ending at the Argyll Rooms.[31]

Beyond the Cyprian's Ball and the Dandies Ball, the 1810s were plentiful for masquerades at the Argyll Rooms and frequently described as popular and one of the highlights of the Season. The June 1814 event was described as fashionable and well-attended, with foreign dignitaries making up the numbers and lively dancing for the entertainment of the masqueraders.[32] A masquerade in March 1818 was reported to have a scarcity of ladies, with only 400 people at the event and although members of the haute ton were in attendance, the newspaper complained of the lack of novelty in costume. Redeemed by the enthusiasm of the masqueraders, the *Morning Herald* reported the party did not break until dawn.[33] Not every year or event was entirely successful, yet there appeared to still be an appetite from the gentry for masked entertainments.

By the 1820s, the Grand Masquerades reached a peak of attendance. The 'New Argyll Rooms' as they were sometimes styled in the newspaper advertisements, emphasised the ability to view the festivities from boxes without mixing with the motley group on the dance floor.[34] While some journalists proclaimed that masquerades had begun to take on the pallor of sameness, the Argyll Rooms was still noted for its superiority in these events.[35] An 1825 event was lauded for the number of distinguished guests and remarkably creative costumes including a postman that astonished the guests by correctly delivering letters to several distinguished persons in attendance and a group of parliamentary orators that gave a mock debate.

Different bands staged in the many rooms coupled with excellent food and drink helped to establish the event as a happy success.[36]

The novelty was worn thin, but the masked fetes still held an allure to the upper classes. An 1826 report shared vociferous clowns and impudent fruit girls annoyed attendees until everyone at the event became noisy and clamorous. The *Morning Post* complained that they had never before seen a more riotous and stupid assembly of characters.[37] By contrast an event in March of 1827 was said to be an unusually orderly and respectable affair, apparently in large part owing to a notable amount of restraint around the champagne.[38] The following May event was also noted for being smooth and nicely produced affair. The fact that so much emphasis was placed on a well-behaved crowd signalled an increase in ennui with masquerades, particularly with wild and raucous behaviour.

Indeed, much of the reporting of the 1820s Argyll Rooms masquerades vacillated between complaints of sameness and noisy, disreputable behaviour, and the occasional novelty coupled with orderliness and respectability. Charles Wright, wine purveyor, was accredited as the principal manager for much of the 1820s, until 1829. The November 1829 event was advertised with the promise that recent éclat, including new embellishments and décor, now dedicated to the Grand Masquerade at the Rooms was worth a revival of interest from the fashionable crowds.[39] However the revival would be short-lived. Like many of the great venues of the Georgian and Regency era, the Argyll Rooms succumbed to fire in 1830. Although it was rebuilt, it would never retain its previous popularity and signalled the end of the Regency subscription masquerade at the Argyll Rooms.

The Argyll Rooms in many ways continued Mrs Cornelys' Carlisle House tradition, creating a more intimate yet public masked event. With attendance numbers frequently only one to two hundred people more than the larger private masquerades of the long Regency, its chief attraction was some level of predictability but also the potential for a more risqué experience than the well-curated crowds of a private masquerade. Greville had managed, with his second venture, to create a space that was, for several decades, a mainstay in London entertainment spaces for the power elite.

It's not clear how much influence The Pantheon masquerades had on Greville's vision. The large venue would have masquerades until 1814, after having established masquerade events as one of their offerings in the Georgian era. A much larger venue with a less exclusive admittance scheme, the annual *Picture of London* would reference this site and the Opera House as locations for masquerades.[40] Compared with the Argyll Rooms, the Pantheon needed much more sizeable audiences to turn a profit and so was more prone to spectacle and over the top celebrations to entice attendance.

## Chapter Two

# The Pantheon

Two thousand people of fashion or rank gathered in The Pantheon's fourteen rooms in 1772. The names of those in attendance included those from the upper reaches of society. Characters including female conjurors, man in the moon, a dancing Stockwell Clock, and a sultana dripping with a sizeable fortune in diamonds graced the crowds.[1] Multiple reports would call it an unrivalled spectacle, a feast for the senses with good company, amusements, and quality libations. The Pantheon was not empty until nine in the morning the next day. According to any measure, it was a whirlwind success, kicking off The Pantheon's foray into masquerades.

The rooms would later be enlarged to accommodate the size of the crowds,[2] the first event a remarkable size for a masquerade. The popularity of the event and the venue was obvious to the promoters and so a masquerade of a similar size would be repeated in December of the same year.[3] By the next year, the crowds had dwindled to a mere 600, many in dominos or in familiar costume,[4] but it would in no way damper the enthusiasm for masquerades over the next forty years. The large size of the venue, with its spacious boxes, domed theatre, and many rooms that could accommodate a few thousand people, would give way to bigger and better spectacles, so that by the time the Pantheon's doors closed it was well remembered for its fantastic masquerades.

In the beginning, however, everything was speculative. The opening in February of 1772 saw crowds somewhere between 1500 to 2000 people, revelling in the magnificence of the establishment; its bold paintings and bright lights, the rotunda with its dome and statued tributes to gods and goddesses was designed to awe and impress.[5] The detailed architecture, which was a fusion of styles, coupled with its size, made it a popular venue for various entertainments. First opened as a theatre for musical events, the Pantheon's managers had quickly realised that they needed a diversified schedule of amusements to keep Londoners engaged. Masquerades became a keystone offering. Their first masked event, in 1772, was so well received that it was rumoured Mrs Cornelys had to postpone one of her masquerades for fear the Pantheon's event capitalised on the public thirst for novelty.[6] It happened the same year that Carlisle House was auctioned and Mrs Cornelys ended up in debtor's prison. After Mrs Cornelys swift departure from the production of masquerades, The Pantheon quickly became the late Georgian mainstay, alongside the Pleasure Gardens, for public masquerades.

The Pantheon was popular in part for splashing out on lavish décor, food, and assorted pleasures,[7] so that by the Regency era it was a well-established venue for masquerades. The Pantheon's location on Oxford Street and proximity to other fashionable establishments would help the venue maintain its success. Unlike the patroness model of the Argyll Rooms, the Pantheon did not require a subscription and therefore was accessible to those who could afford a ticket, including sex workers. One memoir suggested that had improper people not been part of the crowd, the company would have been thin of company.[8] Part of the attraction of the public venue was the promise of risqué interclass mingling, although how much that occurred or was artificially arranged through hired performers, it is not clear. What is evident is exclusivity was less of a focus than the Argyll Rooms, Willis Rooms, or private masquerades.

Not unlike the Argyll Rooms, the Pantheon would also have a roughly forty year run of success before ceasing to be a site for masked balls. Its larger size often lent the Pantheon to emphasise spectacle in events; fireworks, balloon ascensions, and rope walkers were translated from Vauxhall Gardens into the interior spaces or adjacent exterior to amuse guests. The spectacle was enhanced by the incredible architecture famous beyond Great Britain for its celebration of ancient cultures and modern building practices. Built in 1770 on Oxford Street from the designs of James Wyatt, Esquire, it was inspired by the ancient Pantheon in Rome. Erected through subscription, it was built primarily for theatrical and musical entertainments and also served as a temporary home for the Opera House after it burned down.

Around 1780, the price of assemblies at the Pantheon had been reduced along with an increased emphasis on showmanship and spectacle to combat waning public interest. A masquerade in 1783 was sponsored by Delphini, the famous clown, with tickets sold at three guineas a piece, a princely sum in honour of the prince achieving his majority.[9] Delphini, later recalled as the pet and protégé of the Prince Regent,[10] had hoped to further cement his favour with the lavish affair. While it was a spectacular event, the high cost of admissions reduced the numbers in attendance. Accounts had Delphini losing significant amounts at this speculative venture, but other masquerades that year and beyond were more successful suggesting cost of the tickets may have come into play.

Delphini's event, albeit unsuccessful financially, had helped promote the combination of spectacle and masquerades. In 1785, the February 8 Pantheon masquerade featured Lunardi's grand Union Jack hot air balloon suspended from the cupola with a basket draped in scarlet fabric. Lunardi, known as the Daredevil Aeronaut, had debuted in London to a crowd of some 200,000 people as he flew, with a dog, cat, and caged pigeon from the Artillery Ground to first touchdown in North Mymms to let off the cat who was unwell, and then resume his balloon flight to Standon Green End. The exhibition of his balloon at the Pantheon some months later, then, was a marvel. 1200 people were in attendance, with many of the typical costumes including a hairdresser, buffling cook, Punch, Merlin, and merry gingerbread woman. The party broke some time between six and seven in the morning, and was said to feature excellent food and wines.[11]

In 1786, another balloonist, Mr Uncles, exhibited his balloon which was fish-shaped and was accompanied by a display of four live eagles trained by Mr Uncles to guide the Persian silk balloon to its place. Mr Uncles would attempt flight with his balloon in July of the same year at Ranelagh for a crowd of 10,000 people only to have the balloon, with eagles attached, ascend roughly eight feet before dropping to the earth.[12] The crowd was amused and annoyed by the spectacle, and it is said Mr Uncles was never heard from again.[13] But despite the particular failures of Mr Uncles, balloon exhibitions would remain entwined with masquerades throughout the long Regency; ballooning would become a regular attraction for Vauxhall in its later years as the crowds increasingly demanded novelty and spectacle.

Sometime around 1786 or 1788, the Pantheon shareholders decided a more discriminating bar was needed for attendees and elected to restore the half guinea subscription fee to expressly discourage the bourgeois. An account of the early 1786 masquerade suggested that the guinea subscription often meant there was a diversity of classes represented at the masquerade,[14] although at roughly today's equivalent of £100, we can assume that most attendees were from the middle and upper classes. The air of exclusivity seemed to drive interest as much as over the top spectacle, with accounts that the late 1780s had masquerades comprising up to 1400 attendees. In many cases the prince and other royals attended these events.

The Pantheon was most popularly entered on Oxford Street, where visitors would enter from the portico (a stone front supported by pillars) to a vestibule. Then, a masquerader might enter through the central first and then second card rooms, or take one of the corridors dressed as galleries flanked on either side towards the rotunda or grand staircase. The rotunda was under a large dome with a cupola, sported by colonnades, and functioned as the main assembly room. Statutes representing Roman gods and goddesses, friezes, and ornate decoration traced the curves and recessed spaces of the rotunda. It is hard to overstate its opulence in design and execution, which was so fascinating that in its early years it was often open, for a fee, to visitors simply wanting to marvel at the space. Its fantastic interior helped enhance the masquerade experience, amplifying the spectacle of costume with its own feats of architecture and design.

However, the glories of the Roman inspired dome would be short lived. On January 14, 1792, the Pantheon burned to the ground when a fire originated in the painter's room and quickly took with it the rest of the space, creating a terrible vision of fire and smoke in the western quarter of London.[15] Naturally, this resulted in a temporary halt to events at the venue. By 1795, it was rebuilt, yet with less style and bombast; the rotunda resembled more of a theatre space surrounded by double tiers of spacious boxes with a painted ceiling and large glittering chandelier in the centre in a mostly rectangular space. The rebuilt Pantheon met with an indifferent reception compared with the original. The first event was a masquerade in April of 1795. There would be only a few masquerades in the remainder of the 1790s, mostly on account of the failure and subsequent disappearance of the would-be manager, Crispus Claggett. Claggett was the proprietor of Apollo Gardens, and had overseen the rebuilding of the Pantheon but met with such bad press and likely significant debt that he disappeared, never to be seen again, sometime in 1796 or 1797.[16] The loss of one of its primary architectural features and woes in management had the Pantheon flagging in popularity as Great Britain entered the Regency era. Shareholders stepped in in 1798 to re-establish their management.

Part of the transition to shareholder management was to continue the formula for success prior to the fire. Masquerades at the Pantheon were a regular event. One contemporary account stated the Pantheon held two masquerades a year, one immediately before Easter and the other after, or roughly sometime at the end of February and the beginning of May respectively.[17] This was more common prior to the nineteenth century. Into the Regency, masquerades at the Pantheon would increase in number per annum, with events in January, February, April and May. The day of the week the masquerades were held varied, but during the Regency Mondays seemed to be the most common, followed by Wednesdays. The events were well advertised and promised familiar amusements along with new enticements, including spectacles most commonly seen at the Pleasure Gardens.

Several annual masquerades after the revival were in honour of people or had other offerings, like prizes. Sometimes these two things were combined; the April 1801 Pantheon masquerade held a drawing (a lottery) and gave away medals made from silver. The medals had an image of Lord Nelson with his age and date of birth on the side. On the other side was a depiction of HMS *Neptune* in battle blowing up *L'Orient*, with the number of ships taken at the battle.[18] The HMS *Neptune* would later be refitted and be part of Lord Nelson's fleet for the Battle of Trafalgar. Many masquerades throughout the Regency involved similar tributes to the Napoleonic Wars and other conflicts the British Empire was engaged in, or in the resulting peace from resolution from revolutions or wars. Later generations would dress as Lord Nelson for masquerades,[19] but during the Regency he would occasionally be honoured along other military figures, like Wellington.

The February 1802 masquerade was dedicated to peace.[20] Transparency busts of Howe, Vincent, and Nelson as well as several unnamed other war heroes were hung over the orchestra, matching the elegance of the décor that included festoons of lamps.[21] While the crowd was evidently thick with the light-fingered gentry, as pickpockets were called, it did not discourage future events including another grand masquerade in April also in honour of peace.[22] Beyond military tributes, masquerades were also paired with fundraising for various causes. A November 1809 Pantheon masquerade was a benefit for prisoners in debt, proceeds from the fifteen shilling entrance fee going to the Society for Relieving Persons Confined for Small Debts.[23]

In January 1801, the Pantheon management dressed the grand saloon boxes up as different shops with giveaways for attendees, and the advertisement sought characters to staff the booths. The pop-up shops included: a whiskey shop with punch, cherry brandy and Irish whiskey; a confectioner's shop with jellies, ice cream, biscuits, and twelfth night cakes; a fruit shop offering oranges, apples, and grapes; and a haberdasher's shop giving away ribbons.[24] Styled as a Union Masquerade, in honour of the Union, the event featured two bands, with supper and wine as an added cost.[25] This idea would appear at other masquerades, playing in to the tendency for some masqueraders to play working class people. It was most popular at private events, but would be repeated more than once at a public venue. The novel use of the theatrical boxes was a welcome diversion, and the added enticement of prizes typically encouraged larger crowds.

In addition to spectacles and giveaways, the refreshments and supper were an added attraction for guests. While complimentary refreshments were part of the price of admission, often times the alcohol was limited to punch and wine. Complimentary refreshments were simple and included beverages like tea and orgeat. By contrast, the supper tables, which were usually opened at one, were veritable feasts of excess and luxury. At the Pantheon, supper was sometimes included in the admittance cost and other times an added cost. It was noted the added cost of five or seven shillings for supper, a fee that was added after the Pantheon had to be rebuilt from fire damage, reduced the popularity of supper and the events overall.[26] However, some of the events like the February 1805 grand masquerade would still include supper in the one guinea admission fee.[27] Reporting of a May 1805 Pantheon masquerade noted that not only did supper include every delicacy of the season, but the sherry and port was unlimited and of high calibre; unusual for the free wine that was usually served or for the alcohol available for an additional cost.[28] By many accounts, supper would often revive the crowds enough to dance into the morning.

To attract fashionable people looking for more exclusivity, The Pantheon frequently made private supper boxes available for an additional cost. The cost would not be disclosed in advertisements, and those interested would have to apply directly to the promoters to reserve a spot. After event reports would cite these private boxes as places for couples to rendezvous or to safeguard proprieties for ladies who wanted to watch the events but not mix with the motley crowd. This additional perk, like alcohol and dinner, widened the gap between the haves and the have nots. However, even the tiered access would not discourage those masqueraders intent on entertainment from attendance.

Beyond the food, décor, and spectacle, a key element of the masquerade were the costumes. Newspaper reports complained after most Pantheon masquerades of little creativity displayed by attendees in costumes so that the novelty of a masquerade was greatly lessened. In some instances, like reporting on the May 1804 event, writers were brutal calling the event a satire of masquerades.[29] However, the newspapers did often share the general air of entertainment and good humour so that these events still promised a good evening, if not one of monumental diversion. On the occasion when members of the gentry or fashionable crowds would be in attendance, it would make the news. Coverage of the February 1802 masquerade emphasised the event was well-attended by fashionable and genteel company.[30] The May 1803 masquerade was highlighted for the attendance of Lord Eardley and a large party of fashionables in attendance, with the only other commentary being recognition of the wines and supper provided by Waud.[31] One event in late January 1804 had a sizeable crowd, excellent music, good food and drink, and superior service made note as did the relative sobriety of the crowd and the lack of riot.[32] The year prior, The Pantheon had hosted 1200 people, deemed respectable by the press, who partied until seven in the morning, with name drops for the fashionable women and men in costume.[33]

The difference in reporting between the Argyll Rooms masquerades and the Pantheon masquerades was vastly different in tone, depth, and general assessment. The Argyll Rooms' commentary tended to be awestruck and positive while for the Pantheon there was a propensity for a more weary approach. The exception was when royalty was present attracting a significant crowd. The consistent themes in coverage with respect to the Pantheon during the Regency were vulgarity, vice, and the lack of original costumes or décor. Considering that the costumes mentioned were much in a similar vein as the Argyll Rooms, it is evident that it was the masquerader rather than the mask that lent a certain distaste; Thomas Rowlandson's 1809 *Pantheon Masquerade* tinted etching shows a lively crowd of masqueraders in a variety of costumes, including several harlequins, jesters, a judge, a washerwoman, and a man on stilts. From the lists of costumes from the Argyll Rooms masquerades, there is not a marked difference except that the number of people at the Argyll Rooms was obviously smaller. This fact enabled reporters to give a more thorough accounting of the titled and fashionable present, which would naturally discourage any direct criticism. The Pantheon's large size and lower bar for admittance often led to the venue being seen as a source of vulgar mixing of classes. A letter to the *Morning Chronicle* in 1770 went so far as to be explicit, stating that masquerades should only be an event for the rich and fashionable.[34]

As the first decade of the nineteenth century came to a close, the Pantheon saw a waning reputation. It had enjoyed relative success for several decades, and hosted some grand affairs, but it was not to be sustained. Reports of pickpockets at the events in the newspapers likely aided to the Pantheon's eventual demise, along with continued disparaging remarks about attendees lacking wit or creativity in their costumes. On occasion, an event would exceed expectations, particularly on those evenings like in March 1810 when costumes exceeded dominoes.[35] Promoters would go all out, mimicking other venues and offering a wide variety of refreshments like ice creams and jellies, and paid costume performers to entice attendance.[36] However, it was likely too little too late.

By 1810, the shareholders saw the writing on the wall and decided to lease the building again, rather than continuing with event promotion themselves as they had done since 1798. The Pantheon would be converted in 1811 to a theatre until public entertainment was brought to a halt in 1814 due to the Lord Chamberlain's crackdown. The Lord Chamberlain had done battle for three years with the license, mostly attributed to some unsafety with the building and roof, but also in restricting the investors to his original license. The Lord Chamberlain also wanted to exclusively deal with Greville, who had been intending to expand his events at the Argyll Rooms to the larger venue, yet negotiations with the lessee Nicholas Wilcox Cundy broke down. This was likely in part owing to Greville's precarious financial situation occurring at the same time. Cundy tried, in desperation, to open the Pantheon as an English Opera House in 1813 without a license but was quickly taken to court.[37]

Continued financial and legal troubles meant the building sat vacant for seven years. The Pantheon would be re-envisioned as a bazaar in 1833. The bazaar included sculptures and paintings, creating a reputation as a place for show and pretension. The bazaar featured a variety of products, including toys, hats, gloves, music, and other assortments.[38] Consumption was still the order of the day. The success of the bazaar faded over time and the space was then converted to an office and show rooms by wine merchants from 1867 until it was demolished in 1937. In its heyday, it was undoubtedly one of the premier masquerading venues for a broader class of people. It's growing influence in the last days of the Georgian era helped it to carry its presence as an entertainment venue through a portion of the Regency. Yet it could not overcome the prejudice and financial stress of such a large venue, and spectacle, in the end.

The Pantheon was not the only Georgian carry over masquerade venue. The Pleasure Gardens and the Haymarket Theatre would represent three additional options to satiate the public hunger for a masked event marked with spectacle and luxury. Although these venues would also meet similar fates including fires and closures, they represented continuity for the spectacular and the masquerade between the eighteenth and nineteenth century. In fact one venue, the King's Theatre near Haymarket, could arguably be stated to be the birthplace of the public British masquerade.

# Chapter Three

## Georgian Hold Overs – Haymarket and the Pleasure Gardens

Known by many names, during the Regency era the King's Theatre in Haymarket was a site for theatre, opera, and other forms of entertainment including masquerades. From around 1714 to 1837, it was primarily known as the King's Theatre, but alternatively would also be called the Opera House, Italian Opera House, or Haymarket Theatre. Haymarket Opera House was the original cornerstone of the Georgian masquerade. Originally constructed in 1705 by Sir John Vanbrugh, an architect and playwright with grand schemes that would be unrealised and force him to lease the theatre for the next several decades, the Opera House was originally intended to be the premier site for the opera. However, the grand design failed to deliver in function, and was found to have poor acoustics. This would swiftly put an end to becoming a famous Opera House, and it served better to be repurposed into an all-around entertainment venue.

In 1718, Heidegger picked up the lease. It is at the Haymarket where Heidegger established the masquerade in Great Britain, introducing the new commercial entertainment inspired by the Italian Carnival. During his reign in the first part of the century as premier masquerade impresario, Heidegger would see the rise in popularity as well as debate on masquerades. Scholars like Castle have argued that the eighteenth-century masquerade was focused in the hearts and minds of the public as the means for bacchanalian pursuits. This would be fertile grounds for moralists to rage about the decay of society, spurred on by the reduced restraint of the public masquerade. In the backdrop was the Haymarket, the site of these pleasure fests.

By the late eighteenth century, the Haymarket theatre would look very different both in tone and in architecture. After a fire destroyed the original theatre in 1789, it was rebuilt by 1791 with facades on Charles Street and Haymarket. Initially, the Lord Chamberlain denied the new manager, William Taylor, a performing license so that events were limited to private song and dance parties. After much negotiating, a General Opera Trust Deed was signed in 1792 and a committee of noblemen, appointed by the Prince of Wales, were to manage the facility. Taylor once again stepped in to manage as the committee never once meant, and the first public performance was launched in January 1793 with an opera. Masquerades were not common in the early days of Taylor's management. They would start, after a long hiatus, in earnest in 1801, building in popularity in keeping with the King's Theatre's reputation as a public place for people of fashion. Likely, there was also a sense of nostalgia for the birthplace of the masquerade that could draw crowds interested in taking part in the experience.

It was not enough that this was the original site of the London masquerade. Competing with, by 1801, established venues including the Pantheon meant that King's Theatre event had to distinguish themselves. The events were consistently enlivened by paid troops of professional actors dressed in costume mixed among the party goers to enliven the atmosphere.[1] This was a practice other venues would participate in, but King's Theatre was said to be the origins for a padded audience. Coupled with the typically larger crowds, masquerades at the King's Theatre represented more danger in intermingling with unknown quantities than the curated experience at the Argyll Rooms; for the party goer seeking more of the bacchanalian experience, the King's Theatre could better deliver the risqué. Or at least the appearance of such.

The building itself was an important factor in the masquerade experience. The first theatre was a much simpler building, with a three bay entrance and a brick façade. Some remodelling occurred in the 1770s, but the 1789 fire caused by arson destroyed the theatre so that it would have to be completely rebuilt. A new theatre was constructed on the site in 1791, the largest theatre in England at the time and considered to be one of the world's finest. It's newly enlarged size made it more conducive to large, more inclusive events. The new building was designed by Novosielski. Novosielski was a scene painter by trade, but was hired by Taylor prior to the fire to make structural modifications to the interior at a cost estimated between eight and ten thousand pounds with over two hundred workers.[2] Novosielski completely redesigned the interior so it was almost indistinguishable from its prior appearance, and would later be heavily critiqued for some follies in design. Given that he had little training in architecture or engineering, design flaws were inevitable.

The site consisted of two acres between Leicester Square and Gerrard Street. The façade had a rustic stone basement, three pillars, two windows, and assorted embellishments. In 1792, seven small houses along the theatre's east side were raised and a new concert room was erected to receive greats like Haydn. Thomas Leverton was hired between 1795 and 1796 to redesign the façade; however after lengthy negotiations it was never completed. A redesign to the façade was completed in 1820 from Nash and Repton's designs, with the iconic covered portico walkway, and several stories. Nash and Repton also directed the interior redecoration in 1818, to include new lighting with gas lustre and over 145 boxes.[3] Gas lighting was unique to the venue at the time, and attracted attention and interest. Later, seats with backs on them, called stalls, would replace the former benches in the pit in 1829. A print from 1821 shows a myriad of festive lights on the walls of the concert room in the shape of stars, initials, festoons, and other decorative patterns, and a collection of masked and unmasked revellers engaging in dancing, conversation, and play.

It was the installation of the concert room that would allow for the space to hold masquerades, as well as concerts and other assemblies. The gallery could hold 800 people, and was approximately 42 feet in depth, 62 feet wide. The concert room was 95 feet long by 46 feet, with a ceiling height of 35 feet, which gave it the grand countenance to lend itself to masquerades.[4] The concert room was typically where the King's Theatre would stage at least one band for the masquerade and often another band, like the military band, would be set at the entrance to welcome revellers.

An advertisement from 1805 showed dominos and masks were onsite for attendees to hire for the evening, and that the doors opened at 10 pm, supper was at 1 am, and the tickets cost ten shillings, sixpence.[5] Costumes and dominos on site was one arrangement, for convenience of patrons, that would help to ensure those in attendance appeared in some type of masked dress. The refreshments were most commonly advertised as tea, coffee, and the like with a supper typically provided. Entrance fees in 1803 were listed at one guinea.[6] An 1804 advertisement promised ice creams, lemonade, and orangeade in addition to tea and coffee, as well as wine to be paid for separately.[7] The same advertisement stressed all attendees were required to be in costume or a mask and domino, and shared several costumers and masquerade warehouses where a costume might be had. In the 1810s, the price for admission would remain the same as it had been in the early 1800s, fifteen shillings, or sometimes one guinea depending on the event.

Masquerades were typically held on Thursday nights at the King's Theatre, although an occasional masquerade might be held on a Monday or other day of the week. One Monday event in 1818 was reported to include around 3000 people there to celebrate the royal wedding. As with much of the newspaper reporting on masquerades in the Regency, humour was the highpoint of the event. The antics of a man dressed as a Scottish horse dealer were highlighted as his put on accent and humorous commentary created a trail of laughter throughout the crowded venue.[8] For the event, boxes were available at one guinea, whereas access to the gallery only cost five shillings.[9] The event included a Grand Allegorical Transparency with the portraits of Princess Elizabeth and the Prince of Hesse Hombourg, a variety of musicians and singers, and an appeal to foreign dignitaries and ambassadors.[10] A Mr Dogherty was given credit for the success of the masquerade, with promises of his continued management as incentive for fashionable world patronage.[11]

A series of changing ownership in the 1820s, followed by the need to entirely rebuild the north wall of the theatre and make repairs to the south wall caused waxing and waning of events. However, it was still an established venue for masquerading and revelry, as the Cruikshank image of supper at the Opera House from 1820 pictured. The fact that it was the chosen site for masquerades in Egan's *Tom & Jerry Life in London*, and the accompanying story that emphasised the masquerade as a place for showing talents as well as having fun indicated how much the King's Theatre's legacy as a location for masquerades was sewn in to the Regency culture. It also should be noted that Egan's commentary emphasised the crowd as a motley group which was language favoured by reporting to speak of the less than genteel crowds and the tendency towards ribaldry at the King's Theatre masquerades.[12]

Generally, the King's Theatre masquerades were not as broadly reported as those at the Argyll Rooms or Pantheon. When there was coverage, the commentary was usually brief and did not share many details about those in attendance, the décor, or refreshments. Although all the ads appealed to the nobility, ladies, and gentlemen, the size of the space and the relatively low cost of entry to the gallery would have been accessible to at least a skilled tradesperson. A report following an April 1826 masquerade remarked that a smaller amount of noisy, vulgar people ensured for a more successful event than had occurred on previous occasions, suggesting that the lack of exclusivity necessarily encouraged people behaving badly.[13] By 1828, the advertisements announced the boxes could be used to view the masquerade, rather than participate, taking a page out of the Pantheon's book. An 1829 ad went so far as to say a party of four could view the masquerade from the private box without mixing with the motley crowd, making it clear that the boxes were a way to separate the wealthy from the general admission.[14] The boxes were popular, in particular, with genteel ladies who wished to witness the events without taking the risk of entering the fray.

Limited coverage continued into the 1830s, despite the masquerades maintaining good size turnouts. Management had changed by the late 1820s, but there was continuity in the types of productions. A blurb about the February 1830 masquerade at the King's Theatre shared it was excessively crowded but, while there were some attendees in costume none stuck to character enough to amuse.[15] Press coverage for the upcoming April 7, 1834 event promised a brilliantly illuminated theatre, with the pit and stage made level to make a Grand Saloon perfect for dancing.[16] The last masquerades at the King's Theatre during the Regency period were in 1835.

In 1837, with Queen Victoria's ascension to the throne, the name of the theatre would be changed to Her Majesty's Italian Opera House. In the 1830s and beyond, the Italian Opera House would largely be an opera and theatre venue.

In addition to the King's Theatre, Ranelagh and Vauxhall Pleasure Gardens would also feature in both Georgian and Regency events including masquerades. Just as the King's Theatre needed to distinguish itself next to its Regency counterparts, the Pleasure Gardens would compete throughout the Georgian era into the Regency to capture the hearts and imaginations of the wealthy and fashionable of London. While masquerades were only one event in the myriad of balls and fetes on offer at these venues, masquerades were nonetheless a powerful enticement to visit these destinations and, if nothing else, bear witness to the spectacle.

In the village of Chelsea along the Thames, Ranelagh Gardens was a Georgian destination. Set up to be a direct competitor to Vauxhall Gardens, it was a place to see and be seen, after opening to the public in 1742. As an outdoor pleasure garden, it was a fashionable site for the gentry willing to pay the two shillings, six pence or one guinea entrance fee to enjoy masked parties, walks along dark tree lined pathways, and the various structures that defined the place. Originally the estate, including a home, of the Earl of Ranelagh, the house and gardens would be purchased in 1741 by a syndicate including Drury Lane Theatre Royal proprietor, James Lacy, and Sir Thomas Robinson. Lacy was said to be inspired by the various tea gardens springing up on the outskirts of London, and purchased Ranelagh with the goal of establishing an entertainment venue on a large scale.[17]

From the open season between April and July, when noble and fashionable families descended upon London, to its décor and entertainments, Ranelagh was designed to appeal to the upper classes. Ranelagh would be more exclusive, and therefore more fashionable, than Vauxhall Gardens. A higher admission fee helped elevate that exclusivity. The exclusivity, in turn, brought in aristocratic patrons who would also be a source of attraction for the broader nobility and fashionable. The Drury Lane syndicate was focused on creating a premier experience in an idyllic rural setting for the pleasure and entertainment of the wealthiest and most fashionable of London.

The heart of the gardens was the rotunda, which was modelled after the Roman Pantheon, albeit larger. William Jones, surveyor for the East India Company, built the rotunda which included a central fireplace, orchestra stand, a large organ, and fifty two candle boxes around the walls. In rococo style, it was a sizeable structure, with an external diameter of 185 feet, an internal diameter of 150 feet, with two rows of windows at the base and one along the middle that were often illuminated to excess.[18] It would be remembered as an extraordinarily large and elegant building, that astonished visitors and emphasised the bombast and grandiosity which Lacy had envisioned. Its rustic ground floor, with entrances supported by four Doric porticos invited visitors into its gallery. The rotunda would be remembered as an ingenious design meant to overwhelm the senses with its scale and feats of engineering.[19] The rotunda was the centrepiece, the place to see and be seen, with its magnificent lighting and Neoclassical promenades. Ranelagh also featured a Chinese pavilion and an ornamental lake to keep visitors entertained under the starry sky.

As Ranelagh increased in popularity, its entertainment schedule would widen and diversify. Throughout the late Georgian era, into the early Regency, masquerades would be introduced as an occasional event. Masquerades were held beginning in January throughout the rest of the year, on various weeknights. The pleasure gardens could hold thousands of people, but often events would number between five to six hundred people in attendance as Ranelagh charged a more expensive admission fee than Vauxhall. Such was the case for a May 1791 masquerade. On that evening, a troop of masked cavalry members entered the rotunda at a full gallop to be attacked by a group dressed as Amazons. This costume play was not uncommon and often a highlight of events. A portion of the rotunda had special floors placed that evening for dancing, and supper was in abundance.[20] Three years later in June, a masquerade at Ranelagh would attract 1500 visitors, although there was a lack of character costumes.[21]

The gardens were always well lit with lamps and transparencies, in much the same style as was popular at other venues, with the benefit of the natural manifold attractions of the outdoor space. The canal would, on occasion, be decorated by lamps.[22] Fireworks were one of the main attractions for night-time visitors. As with other venues, supper and wine would be served to sustain the crowd until the morning. The rotunda was often reserved for supper, and attendees could also find teas, coffees, and an assortment of refreshments throughout the evening. The masquerade events typically started around 10:00 pm and would go until four or five in the morning the next day. This schedule was adhered to regardless of the weather. Ranelagh's distance from town and the weather could not even dampen the January events, which were described as bustling and lively. The January 1801 event was pronounced as having been attended by numerous genteel persons, and very beautiful women, with standard list of character costumes. Grimaldi, the clown, gave a performance at the event and the entertainment, supper and wines were described with praise.[23] As with many other venues, one of the main critiques of a Ranelagh masquerade came down to the guest's costumes and performances. The newspapers would often grouse about the overabundance of dominos over masked characters. *Bell's Weekly Messenger* proclaimed the proverbial dullness of dominoes,[24] a theme that would be repeated across venues hosting masquerades during the Regency.

Despite the often less than creative attire of attendees, a Ranelagh masquerade often delivered an enjoyable experience. A masquerade in June 1802, held in honour of the King's birthday and in celebration of peace, was conducted in partnership with the Boodle's Club and featured supper, dancing, wine, and onsite character dresses and dominoes.[25] The event was said to attract more than 2000 people and was regarded as a splendid event.[26] The entrance was well decorated in lamps, with the ground beyond the gravel walk covered in green baize to appear like grass, and a temporary wooden floor was laid for the purposes of dancing. The event started with theatrical performances and singing, followed by dancing. A lottery was also drawn to award prizes to the guests, that included shawls, parasols, handkerchiefs, quizzing glasses, and other items inspired to bring laughter and excitement to the crowd. Festoons of flowers, three bands, and a lavish supper capped off the masquerade ball.[27] Remarkably, considering the attendance, it had been held the night after a Grand Masquerade at Cumberland House, which was also well attended; it was clear all of London wanted to see and be seen marking the royal occasion.

It was also not unusual for Ranelagh to feature back to back celebrations attracting the wealthy and fashionable of London. Being a popular site for lavish parties, management would often hold over décor from those events for masquerades the following evening so that if you missed the experience the first night, it was an added incentive to attend the masquerade. One such occurrence was in June 1803, after the Knights of Bath Ball, where arches constructed from bough and small lights welcomed visitors at the entrance and transparencies with the Insignia of the Order as well as the king and queen's initials were on display. Eight brilliant chandeliers, with 300 lights each, paired with a mixture of festoons of variegated lamps and lit up trees made the gardens bright and enchanting. A portion of the ground was boarded over for dancing, and accompanied with the illuminated grove and green baize ground cover. The *Morning Post* likened Ranelagh Gardens that evening to a fairy temple.[28] Despite the glorious reception of the event, it would be one of the last to invite the public into the rotunda.

The rotunda was closed in 1803 and the Gardens were closed and substantially reduced in 1805. Yet even with the demolition of the rotunda and the closure of Ranelagh Gardens in its former incarnation, masquerades would continue. A masquerade in August 1812 had approximately 1500 people in attendance, although largely unknown persons who were likely either from the middle class or from less fashionable sets. Masked characters would represent in abundance that evening, bringing with it fine weather and an overall merriness.[29] However, the slow trickle of events could not sustain its remnants and Ranelagh Gardens would be redesigned in 1860 in support of Chelsea Hospital.

Although masquerades at the Ranelagh were not frequent throughout the long Regency, the Pleasure Gardens nonetheless had an impact. The memory of masquerades at Ranelagh would have had an influence on the events throughout the Regency, tying spectacle, nature, and grandeur into the Carnival spirit. It would also provide a model for other venues seeking to offer an exclusive experience to the nobility and the fashionable. Yet Ranelagh cannot take all the credit for presenting an out of doors masquerade experience, as it was preceded and succeeded by Vauxhall Pleasure Gardens as a premier pleasure garden offering a spectacle filled masquerade event.

On the Thames, Vauxhall was a popular destination from the mid-seventeenth century through the Regency era. Situated in Lambeth, it was said to have been developed as early as the 1660s, styled as New Spring Garden. The lease would be awarded to the Tyers family in 1728, and the family ran Vauxhall for most of the Georgian era. It was opened to a broader, admission paying public under Tyers' management with a ridotto in June 1732. The Tyers family would continue to make improvements throughout the eighteenth century, increasing public entertainments and expanding the structures.[30] Tyers purchased the property in 1752, and was succeeded by his son in running Vauxhall upon his death in 1767. Their vision created a site of amusement that would be a popular destination through the nineteenth century. This would include not only the famous, if not infamous, walks but also the Prince's Pavilion, the rotunda, a saloon, supper room, two octagon temples, a theatre, and a high fireworks tower.[31] The best estimates of capacity ranged between 5000 to 15,000 people.[32]

The various pavilions served as supper boxes, with tables and accommodation for six to eight people around the grove. To the left of the entrance, a series of Corinthian pillars paralleled the Grand Walk just past the orchestra, and ending at the edge of the Cross Walk. A supper room was erected in 1794. The Prince of Wales had his own pavilion, directly next to the orchestra, and lavish with pillars, gilt ornaments, and crystal chandeliers. Nearby in the grove, for those not wanting the privacy of a supper box, were over a hundred tables by the orchestra.[33] The orchestra edifice was made of wood, painted white with floral coloured accents in a Plaster of Paris-like concoction referred to as plastic.[34] By 1818, an auction catalogue of Vauxhall would detail its many features including the Prince's Pavilion, 66 feet in length and ornamented with sienna pillars and balustrades; a noble supper room supported by cast iron pillars and mirrored doors, with a flight of stairs descending to a colonnade-covered walk and octagon temples; a temple used as the orchestra for instrumental and vocal performances; the picture room with two portraits of the king and queen and four large allegorical paintings by Haymen; the rotunda supported by pillars and featuring a painted ceiling, orchestra station, and an Indian-inspired portico; a supper room with a circular roof and supported by twenty-six ornamented pillars, embellished with landscape paintings and other allegorical devices; a covered walk with seven supper boxes and tables on the side; several treed walks; and outbuildings hidden from public view but including an ice house, paint room, three artists' workshops, a lamp house, bottle house and a room and stage for fireworks. There was also a brick house on site with ten bedrooms on the upper story and numerous rooms on the ground floor along with a newer, brick four stall stable, hay room, and coach field.[35]

With admission cheaper than Ranelagh, Vauxhall was accessible to more than the gentry, and the famous fireworks, cold suppers, fountains and walkways, music, and merriment attracted many to its pleasure gardens. Containing approximately twelve acres, the pleasure gardens formed a nearly perfect square. Until 1818 it was reached exclusively by boat and this tradition continued even after the construction of Vauxhall Bridge in 1816. The bridge had gone through several iterations, architects, and acts for funding by the time it was complete, and was initially named the Regent Bridge but then shortly renamed Vauxhall Bridge. The introduction of this bridge would allow carriages to deliver Vauxhall visitors on land to the pleasure gardens. Passage by boat would be complicated by introduction of large steam engine ships in the early Victorian era, but during the Regency the travel over the Thames in a small craft added to the romance, drama, and intrigue of a visit. Entering Vauxhall from the water gate was an illuminated covered walk, featuring a grand transparent portrait of the king. It would be one of many transparencies and light features that would add to the overall spectacle of the gardens.

The masquerade, or ridotto as it was sometimes called, was just one of many evening events held at Vauxhall. Masquerades, along with Grand Galas, became a feature around 1792 when the daily admission rate was increased from one to two shillings. Special events were typically three shillings. The higher admission fee did include tea and coffee.[36] The first successful masked ball, in 1792, was noted for the bright lights and usual character costumes.[37] Another masquerade in May 1794 featured the supper boxes dressed as fruit, music, millinery, jewellery, toy, perfume, and trinket shops with wares for sale, a precursor to the 1801 Pantheon event. There was even a have-for-a-penny shop. Exotic birds and animals were on display, as well as some theatricals. Ample refreshments, and 10,000 variegated lamps, as well as well-decorated buildings, made the evening a pronounced success.[38]

By the Regency era, a new crowd of pleasure seekers required novelty, thrills, and spectacle. Fireworks were introduced in 1798 and became a permanent fixture of the Vauxhall experience by 1813. Fireworks would often be combined by a concert or by performers including high rope dancers. The transparencies, brilliant lights, and performers would be matched by more common entertainments including supper and walks. For the purpose, a supper room had been added in 1786 to the left of the rotunda, and in 1810 through 1811, several of the grove trees were cut to make way for the erection of a vaulted colonnade and cast iron pillars. The colonnade would be draped with lamps and provided coverage during rains.[39] The standard season was from May to August.

These details make it hard to convey just how dazzling the sights and scenes at Vauxhall would be for the contemporary in attendance. Advertisements and articles often emphasised the rural charm of the pleasure gardens, but the sheer number of lights, transparencies, fireworks, and other features underscoring the experience was in large part due to the spectacle. Scholars have emphasised scopophilia, the pleasure of looking, as a key element to Vauxhall's allure.[40] Pavilions, gothic temples, and an orchestra stand were just some of the features of the venue, but most illustrious were the walks where a visitor might be enchanted by the lights. Music would play until supper was served in the pavilions. The ham, as thin as muslin, was famous and people could enjoy it and supper in supper alcoves, dressed with contemporary paintings like those of Hogarth. Fountains and walkways were illuminated with colourful lights, and the legendary cascade turned on at nine in the evening to the amusement of many. The cascade was hidden behind a curtain that would be raised to reveal a landscape including a miller's house and watermill. The whole was a large transparency, illuminated from behind, and the waterfall in motion with the waterwheel presented a moving picture to the astonished audience. The scene was enhanced by noises of cascading water. The spectacle would conclude after ten or fifteen minutes.[41]

These features were naturally present at the variety of events Vauxhall would be host to, but masquerades were often set apart with themes or a grander assembly of spectacle. Like the other venues, Vauxhall masquerades would often be held as a benefit or tribute to various people and causes. An August 1812 masquerade was given in honour of the military success on the Peninsula, with the names Ciudad Rodrigo, Almeida, Talavera, Badajoz, Vimeira, and Salamanca along the cover walk amid variegated lamps, Chinese lanterns, and balloons. The display was intended to excite feelings of pride while also aweing spectators with the fanciful design.[42] The event continued in much the same vein as other masquerades, with the crowd dispersing at dawn. The idyllic grounds and added spectacles of both performance and feature would typically be enough to attract sizeable crowds to Vauxhall throughout its lifetime.

Vauxhall was put up for auction in 1818, and finally purchased in 1821 by T. Bish, lottery office keeper, for £30,000.[43] A masquerade was held at Vauxhall that July in celebration of the coronation. A military band was set to in the orchestra, and dancing was in the rotunda, while the French ventriloquist, Alexandre, entertained on a small stage near the rotunda. The popular Ramo Samee, the famous Indian juggler and magician, appeared as part of the show. Mr Wilson and his tightrope dancing troupe were established in the painted saloon, walking on the perpendicular ladder, and the usually dark walks were alight with illuminated paintings. The supper included shellfish, boiled and roasted fowl, ham, salad, pigeon and meat pies, roasted lamb, jellies, pastries, ices and sweetmeats. However, despite the extravagance the newspaper pronounced there was no crowd and the new owner likely lost money.[44] A similar event was held in August 1821, with the *Morning Post* congratulating the proprietor for their arrangements, entrance fees that would prevent attendance by improper persons, and the interest the event garnered among the haute ton.[45] Despite early missteps under Bish's ownership, masquerades would remain part of the Vauxhall calendar.

This dedication to events would be bolstered by other investments in the venue. As a fascination with Chinese culture swept through London in the early nineteenth century, Vauxhall would enter the trend, renaming the cross walk as the Chinese walk and opening a Chinese entrance lined with more coloured lanterns. This re-envisioned feature would be an attraction to crowds, as well as continued tributes to the monarchy, military, and more generally luxury and spectacle. The grand events and spectacle would continue on and masquerades would appear somewhat irregularly throughout the last decade of the Regency into the Victorian era.

King's Theatre, Ranelagh Gardens, and Vauxhall Gardens represented the Georgian tradition of masquerades continuing on into the Regency era. Promoters sought not only to continue engagement with old audiences, but to also find new masqueraders. They would have frequent success by infusing luxury, spectacle, and a familiar pattern of events that promised entertainment to those who could afford the cost of admission. These three venues had a direct influence on the newer venues, like the Argyll Rooms, even as they all sought to distinguish themselves with unique features.

Beyond the King's Theatre, Vauxhall, the Argyll Rooms, and the Pantheon, other London venues would play host to masked and fancy dress balls during the Regency. While novelty was important to increase attendance, there is also an emergent pattern that becomes apparent throughout the record on the Regency masquerade that an examination of the more irregular masquerade venues help to tease out. It also represents the continued public interest with masquerades that would be sustained from the Georgian era and beyond.

## Chapter Four

# Occasional Masquerade Venues

There is intimation in much of the literature on the Georgian masquerade that masquerades would be almost extinct by the nineteenth century. But, in fact, it was still a popular pastime for many Londoners in search of amusement. Beyond the Argyll Rooms, the Pantheon, the King's Theatre and the Pleasure Gardens, masquerades could be found at other venues or private homes. Although not standard events, on occasion masquerades would be held at a variety of other locales in London including Almack's Assembly Rooms, Lowther Rooms, and the Theatre Royal. In many cases, these were special events for fundraising or to honour distinguished guests, and were hosted by groups including several gentlemen's clubs, like Boodles or Whites. These London venues would serve to maintain the popularity and public interest, at least those members of the public who could afford the luxury, in masquerades throughout the long Regency.

On occasion, Almack's Assembly Rooms would serve as host to a masquerade ball. It's small size, reputation, and generally selective entrance practices meant that it was one of the most exclusive venues for a masquerade. The Assembly Rooms, on King Street, were a much smaller venue than the Pantheon, more on par with the Argyll Rooms, with the average attendance around 500. The maximum capacity was said to be 700–800, although advertisements sought up to 1000 subscribers. The large ballroom was 100 feet by 40 feet, decorated with gilt columns and other Neoclassical elements like medallions, mirrors, and cut-glass lustres.[1] By 1820, the subscription fee was only seven shillings, but required a visitor name be listed in the lady patronesses' books, which intentionally made access exclusive.[2]

Beyond Almack's masquerades, that were a more rare occurrence, the venue itself would also lend itself to masquerades. The Assembly Rooms were also known as Willis's Rooms, typically as a way to distinguish it from the Almack's events. While Almack's was most known for its subscription balls on Wednesday evenings, the Rooms were also used for concerts, dinners, public meetings, dramatic readings, and other events, including fancy dress balls. Most of these events at the Willis's Rooms, as *Leigh's New Picture of London* (1834) was clear to point out, were unconnected to Almack's. Rather, Willis referred to the James Willis family who managed the assembly rooms from roughly 1792 until the late 1880s. The Willis management would see the assembly rooms have great success, in part because of its exclusivity. The rooms would experience an increase in masquerade events in the later part of the Regency, likely in part due to its declining reputation and the need for a diversified income.

The Duke of Wellington would be credited with the creation of the 24 June 1817 masquerade-style ball. Instead of the typical masked event, guests were asked to come in fancy dress, specifically in various costumes from all the nations of the world, but without a mask. Over 800 tickets were sold under the guise of it being the first ball of its type, with the newspaper blurb entitled Novelle Fete.[3] June 1817 was a busy time in London, with many celebrations in honour of the second anniversary of Waterloo, including a Waterloo ball at Almack's, the opening of Waterloo Bridge , a *Fete Champetre* at Windsor, and a Vauxhall event.[4] The masquerade fitted well in the staccato tempo of activity happening in and around London that early summer. It would also be a harbinger of the rise in maskless fancy dress balls that would overtake masquerades in the Victorian era.

Following Wellington's new fete, masquerades at Almack's or the Willis's Rooms would follow with more frequency. The Grand Fancy Dress Ball in June 1818 had 500 attendees from rank and fashionable, including the Duke and Duchess of Cambridge and the Duchess of York.[5] Almack's masque and fancy dress ball in July 1819 also entertained several dukes and other peers of the realm, with quadrille dancing starting at midnight and the event ending at four o'clock in the morning.[6] The advertisements expressly indicated that masks were admitted, suggesting that masks were optional at Almack's fancy dress balls,[7] at least after the 1817 Wellington occasion.

A masked and fancy dress ball had been held in June 1819 ahead of the July event. The crowd was packed with more than 500 guests. The evening dancing commenced at eleven, and royalty among the attendees included the Prince Regent, Prince Saxe Coburg and Esterhazy, as well as five dukes, six duchesses, and a number of other titled persons. The costumes ranged from various foreign princesses, to Hamlet, Mary Queen of Scots, and assorted occupations like haymaker and warrior.[8] The assembly rooms were decorated in a similar fashion to other masquerades, with festoons of artificial and real flowers around the columns and on the walls and the addition of more chandeliers and lamps to light the scene. Two bands were also provided for the occasion and it was reported to be one of the most agreeable balls of the Season.[9] There was very little difference in the general form of the masquerade when compared with other venues, except for its smaller scale and subsequent exclusivity.

Another event would be held at Almack's in July 1820, with many of the men appearing in full military uniforms, and the ladies in fancy and character dress.[10] Lady Caroline Lamb appeared at this event dressed as Don Juan, accompanied by devils as attendants,[11] although the devils were too numerous to create the intended effect, and instead seemed intent on carrying the whole of the crowd via coup de main to Tartarus, or so the paper reported. A Robin Hood and Woodman of Arden sung catches and glee to the amusement of the crowd, while a dog merchant carried two rowdy poodle puppies, and an unidentified woman represented widow and bride, with one side in white and one in black. Milanese minstrels played along with the band, and overall the combination of character, fancy dress, and dominoes gave every impression of a successful event.[12] As with the Argyll Rooms, the smaller size of crowds plus the frequent attendance by aristocracy and gentry meant more thorough reporting on the costumes and praise for creativity while detailing the fashionable and famous in attendance.

Throughout the 1820s and 1830s, Almack's would have Highland or Caledonian Fancy Dress Balls, often for the benefit of the Scottish Hospital or Caledonian Asylum, where attendees were required to appear in fancy dress, military uniform, or highland garb. In May 1835, a fancy dress ball was held at the Rooms for the Adult Orphan Institution, under the patronage of the queen and Princess Augusta.[13] Willis's Rooms hosted another grand fancy ball in March 1836, without an announced theme or cause but in the tradition of Wellington's mask-less event.[14] Arguably, the Almack's events set the fashion for the type of costume ball that would become standard in the Victorian era.

Masquerades were generally not common at Almack's or the Willis's Rooms, but they nonetheless had an impact on the overall culture of masquerades. While it did not diverge much from the décor, music, and supper of other venues, its curated guest list and preference for unmasked fancy dress was significant. The infrequency of these events, combined with the exclusivity, catered to a more reserved and distinguished set likely loathe to patronage the more risqué venues. Almack's masquerades, based on the accounts in newspapers and other publications, were comparably tame events for those seeking a bit of the high life, as the expression went, and represented a late Regency venue for a more exclusive masquerade. However, it was not the only venue in the late Regency to provide masked entertainment to Londoners, albeit it was definitely the most subdued.

The Lowther Rooms opened in 1833 on King William Street in the Strand and had a succession of masquerades in the 1830s. The building had been constructed in 1830 in a late Georgian style, and was often thought to be a seedy establishment with access to gin[15] and a reputation for attracting the hey-go-mad young bucks looking for a lark. Evidence suggests the Lowther Rooms masquerades began in November 1833, with a failed event intended to be a benefit for Polish exiles. The newspaper article complained that the rooms were not decorated and were likely opened prematurely.[16] The following year, the 1834 *Leigh's New Picture of London* guidebook listed the Lowther Rooms alongside the Opera House as the primary venues for masquerades as their production began in earnest alongside the exhibition of Madame Tussaud and Sons waxwork figures. Despite rumblings and dismissals, most of the London guidebooks continued to promote the Lowther Rooms as one of the main masquerade destinations for the decade.

The Lowther Rooms masquerades generally happened in November through to February, but on occasion a spring or summer event might occur. Tickets to include supper were usually one guinea. A character ticket could be purchased separately for ten shillings and six pence, with a la carte supper for six shillings and wine for five shillings. Like the other venues, the supper rooms opened at one o'clock. A fancy dress ball in February 1834 offered a two shilling discount from the seven shilling subscription fee for guests appearing in character dress, and offered supper, wines, and quadrille dancing.[17] Lowther were following the successes of other venues to incentivise wearing a costume by offering discounts for those appearing in character dress.

However, the Lowther Rooms did not strictly follow the lavish guidelines of predecessors; the productions were not over the top and supper and wines were seldom distinguished as unique or over-abundant. This wasn't to say there was no décor. A December masquerade at the Lowther Rooms in 1835 boasted of festive evergreens and seasonal emblems for decoration, as well as a variety of talent engaged to entertain.[18] An 1837 review of a Lowther Rooms masquerade pronounced the venue was well-adapted for the type of event, being spacious, well-lit and in neighbourhood that would be unbothered by late night revelry.[19]

Yet reviews were often mixed and the Lowther Rooms struggled with a less than savoury reputation. In addition to its more simple production values and access to gin, there was a lack of real curating of the guest list that attract a true mixed crowd, rendering it unappealing to more discriminating parties. The Lowther Rooms was not as exclusive as Almack's, and the *Chronicle* called it a refuge for destitute vagabonds and horrible drunken bad characters. The newspaper found the half-hundred women at one event in near nudity and the only music a jingling piano that offended as not only dreadful but lewd and in keeping with the depravity and indecency of public masquerades.[20] Other reviews of the masquerades were less severe, finding them well-managed events with a capital supper, and good attendance that was satisfied with the amusements on offer.[21] Yet Blake's Masquerades, as they would be known, were particularly popular with young bucks[22] and this helped hasten the notoriety of the establishment, so that reports would recall the bleak offerings attractive to London youth.[23] Masquerades would continue at the Lowther Rooms into the Victorian era, and the contemporary reviews were often less severe than the nostalgic accounts once the venue had gone. By 1855, it would do a stint as the Polygraphic Hall, then the Charing Cross Theatre, Folly Theatre, and finally Toole's Theatre in 1881.

Other London venues would host the occasional masquerade, typically dependent on their ability to secure the appropriate license and often in honour of a person or event. The London theatres, in particular, would host the infrequent masked event. Two examples of this were the Drury Lane and Lyceum Theatres. Both were established entertainment venues, familiar to both the haute ton and the middle class, as respectable locations with quality offerings. Masquerades for both of these theatres would be diversions from their normal fare, but nonetheless represented that masquerades were present and continued to flourish throughout the long Regency.

The Theatre Royal, in Drury Lane, was opened in October 1812 in its final location where it remains today, with seating for just over 3000 people. Rebuilt after an 1809 fire, the theatre would be home to Edmund Kean, who took the ton by storm. The 1812 building was designed by Benjamin Wyatt, and featured many grand chandeliers, a domed and ornate ceiling, friezes on the wall, and columns between the boxes. It was grand, but slightly smaller than the original theatre. Wyatt would publish, in 1813, his observations on the design of the building coupled with eighteen etchings. There seemed to be some accusations about Wyatt's design being similar to a Mr George Wyatt's design, as he would present his case in the publication before expanding on the logistic considerations of the theatre's design. The theatre held eighty boxes, with a large pit in varying tiers, and a large stage opening to enhance the public appetite for spectacle. Wyatt also took care to design the lobbies and entrances to separate what he called the rational and respectable company with the unsavoury and disreputable people frequently engaged in acts of disgusting indecency, at least by Wyatt's estimation.[24]

The Theatre, often known as Drury Lane Theatre, would have gas lighting by 1817. Management would start holding public masquerades in the 1820s. A June 1821 masquerade would see the theatre dressed in variegated lamps, wreaths of flowers, and transparencies while the stage was occupied with performances in the early hours of the event, followed by a series of other acts in honour of the coronation.[25] In June 1829 a masquerade was coupled with a *Festa di Ballo* and featured a variety of entertainments including Indian jugglers and acrobats, the Antipodean Pedestrian, a ballet, glee singers and several bands. The Antipodean Pedestrian, Richard Sands, was an American acrobat and circus owner named for his ceiling walks that were achieved through hanging feet from rings. The event allowed individuals to hire a box for the evening for seven shillings to view the masquerade without participating, while the lower gallery was just two shillings and six pence for admittance. Supper cost an additional seven shillings and six pence.[26] The event would be repeated on occasion throughout the next decade, into the Victorian era. There would be some debate in the 1840s as to whether or not the Theatre Royal had permission to host masquerade balls[27] which effectively ended the theatre's foray into masked events.

The Lyceum Theatre, originally constructed in the mid Georgian era, would be converted from Astley's circus venue to the English Opera house around 1816 until 1830. It would suffer a fire and be rebuilt in 1834. Occasional masquerades were introduced to the theatre in the off season around 1817, along with scholarly lectures, Caledonian dancing and music exhibitions, and other amusements. The original building was well suited for a variety of entertainments, having not only a theatre but also a large saloon, and several, smaller apartments. The façade included a stone portico, with Ionic columns, and generally featured Neoclassical elements popular and familiar to Regency audiences.[28]

The early masquerades at the Lyceum would follow the familiar formula, including similar costumes, military music, dancing, dinner and an early morning ending. One event in February 1817 reported between 800 and 900 people in attendance, with nobility and fashionable people amidst the throng.[29] The grand saloon was often used for the supper banquet, while the theatre stage could be fitted using various scenery for refreshment and entertainment. Music was situated throughout, with a band stationed to accompany dancing as well as entertain or greet guests as they entered. Tickets were, for most events, one guinea, with supper and wine an additional cost at ten shillings and six pence.[30]

The masquerades would continue at the Lyceum into the 1830s, and meet frequently with mixed reviews. An 1835 event opened with a farce, small concert, and other dramatic presentations before the masquerade ball kicked off.[31] Overall, masquerades at the Lyceum were infrequent. On occasion, like in January 1836, the Lyceum would serve as a backup venue to previously scheduled masquerade balls.[32] While not having a significant footprint in the history of the Regency masquerade, the Lyceum nonetheless was another theatre that found these types of specialty and diverse entertainments could be financially beneficial if a license could be obtained.

Other venues would hold a rare masquerade. Cumberland House would play host to the Union Club's May 1802 Grand Masque and Fancy Dress Ball.[33] This was the ball that preceded a well-attended masquerade at Ranelagh. The former home of the Duke of Cumberland was sold by the bank, who had seized control in 1800 for mortgages owed, to the Union Club in 1801. The Union Club would own it for five years before it was purchased by the Board of Ordnance. A few weeks prior, Martindale's on Bond Street hosted a masquerade ball, with a temporary building used for a ballroom. The temporary structure was fitted up as a greenhouse with an elaborate display of flora and fauna.[34] The Egyptian Hall in Piccadilly would play host to a May 1837 grand masquerade that featured 5000 lamps arranged into various emblems, Weippert's band, and a variety of characters and fancy dress.[35] There is also some evidence that unlicensed masquerades catering to middle or lower classes would occasionally appear, particularly in the later years of the Regency, as reported in June 1820 about a venue in Little Guildford Street catering to servants, tailors, waiters and other professional people.[36]

These additional London locations occasionally attracted masqueraders to their rooms. In many cases, these events marked special events or an attempt to diversify the income of the place by introducing different types of entertainment. Rather than going extinct in the Regency period, masquerades still had the impact of bringing crowds to different locations to engage in risqué or pseudo-risqué, as the case may have been, behaviour. Almack's was undoubtedly a place to indulge in the fashion of the masked ball without the risk of rubbing elbows with lower classes or the type of indecent behaviour maligned by architect Wyatt. Conversely, the Lowther Rooms represented an opportunity for the young bloods to cut loose away from the watchful eyes of the rest of the ton. The Theatre Royal would build on the spectacle baked into its design, to offer masked fetes meant to marvel and awe.

Other venues would use the masked and fancy dress ball to elevate their cause or in celebration of war time victories. The particulars of these events generally matched the foundational elements of the more traditional public masquerade venues. Music, dancing, supper, and spectacle were the primary entertainments. Profit, whether for charity or business, was the main motivation encouraging the attention to detail that would assure pleased crowds and a good report. The cadence of the masquerade evening was surety of success. Even private masquerades would follow the agenda, albeit with a more curated guest list.

The private masquerade, whether held in the hostess and host's home or in a hired venue, represented a similar novelty as the occasional masquerade venue. Although the private masquerade had little to no pecuniary interest, many hostesses and hosts during the long Regency were often awarded the prestigious sobriquet of masquerade celebrity. Landing a diverting and successful event, like a masked ball, would assure not only rave published reviews but also some recognition for their ability to entertain the ton. It is interesting, then, that a review of the private masquerades of the long Regency show marked similarities in the tempo and general foundational elements of the public masquerade. Fashion, doubtless of the epicentre of these repeating refrains, would carry these similar, private events through the bulk of the long Regency until the Victorian era.

## Chapter Five

# Private Masquerades

'The Fashionable World' section of the 3 June 1801 edition of the *Morning Post* provided a review of Mrs Alethea Walker's masquerade. She was noted as a tasteful and elegant masquerade hostess whose event belied the notion that masquerades were incompatible with the English character. Furthermore, she attracted crowds from the most exalted higher circles of society, including normally reclusive peers like the Duke of Gordon. Mrs Walker's Mayfair home on Stanhope Street hosted some 700 people for the occasion under brilliant stars and festoons of lights, a fancy dressed band at the entrance, and rooms well decked in roses, honeysuckle, oak, and laurel leaves.[1] The press coverage was effusive with compliments and honours, in much the same tenor and tone reporters would cover similar events throughout the long Regency. Mrs Walker had held a masquerade the prior year, in May, to a similar sized, fashionable crowd and knew the formula for success.

But Mrs Walker was not the only impressive masquerade hostess able to draw a crowd or to know what was on trend for the masked affair. Every year throughout the long Regency at least one private masquerade was grand enough to deserve thorough dissection by the newspapers, who faithfully reported the illustrious guest list, the elegant decorations, choicest wines and foods, and the tasteful music. Like the public events, private masquerades had many of the same features and lavish spending to the events: quality bands and dancing; décor heavy on patriotism or romantic greenery; every delicacy of the season; and an insistence on costumes over dominoes which would result in praise from the attendees and the newspapers.

Yet the private masquerade had the benefit of being free from commercial demands, so that exclusivity reigned supreme. The most exclusive masquerades of the Regency were those held at the private homes of the fashionable and the gentry. A private affair allowed for careful curation of the guest list, and also promised safety from the motley crews of the public venues in London. Private masquerades were most often held at the London homes of the Beau Monde during the traditional Season, between spring and early summer. As many of the hostesses and hosts preferred to throw open their gardens for the evening, the preferred month was May. The homes were decorated in much the same style as the venues, and often had many of the same features including two bands, a rich supper, and wines. An occasional country estate or winter masquerade also made the newspapers as a prominent fashionable event.

It was not uncommon, for those hostesses and hosts wishing to make a splash, to also hire a venue for their masquerades and fancy dress balls, particularly if the size of the event compared with their London home was of concern. The Hanover Square Rooms were a particular favourite, as was Burlington House. Beyond hiring a venue, hostesses and hosts would also seek out some of the resources of the venues, including scene painters, decoration, and lamps. Alternatively, they were able to hire décor from various warehouses or directly from the London theatres. That the source of décor was often limited, it makes sense that the private masquerade should be dressed similarly to the public masquerade. Likewise, the taste of the crowds would demand a similar high calibre of music, food, and wine. However, how a hostess or host sought to distinguish themselves was often revealed in the press coverage.

The private masquerade and fancy dress balls were as well reported as the more commercial ventures from the period. Appearing in the 'Fashionable World' section, or a corollary, the newspaper would share a blurb or sometimes a full length column on an event. Mrs Walker's 1801 masquerade merited a full column. The author focused on the setting, the decoration, and a recount of costumes of the fashionable and titled people in attendance. The full party list, the newspaper explained, would have to wait for the next day as its list of nearly 700 people was too much to print in concert with the descriptions.[2] Apologetically, the *Morning Post* was only able to devote a column to Mrs Grey Hunter's masquerade in May 1802. The account largely covered the guest list and costumes at the event, highlighting Grey Hunter's prohibition on dominoes, and waxing generally on masquerades and the importance of novelty.[3]

Mr Thellusson's masquerade in June 1802, credited as one of the first of such entertainments to be given in a private home, merited a column and half. A temporary passage was constructed to support entry to Foley House, in case of rain, and grandly illuminated. Guests were then ushered toward the South Garden arbour that was lushly decorated with foliage and had on offer every type of imaginable refreshments. The floors were detailed with crayon, and the great hall was made up to appear as a village to which the guests were invited into around two in the morning. The set up was very like similar schemes at the public venues where friends were engaged to represent the different shopkeepers. Gentlemen staged the stations, in character, and revived the party until supper.[4] Mr Thellusson himself was dressed as the elder landlady of The Feathers Inn, and sparked some excitement with an exchange with Sir Wynne who was dressed as a young man intending to take over the establishment. The postman delivered letters to a number of different characters, highly entertaining the guests, and Lord Longford invited them to share their good cheer at the taphouse across from the inn.[5] At three, the party made their way to the eight supper rooms for an elegant and luxurious banquet. Guests included the Prince of Wales, the Duke of Cumberland, and Prince William of Gloucester, alongside a long list of other nobility and fashionable people.[6]

Mrs Thellusson's Masquerade in May of 1804 warranted a column and a half in the *London Courier* and *Evening Gazette*, with a detailed list of attendees and their costumes, as well as an account of the controversial entertainment Mr Thellusson had originally planned. He had proposed of a mock staging of Bonaparte's coronation and a stage was erected in the Thellusson garden, with scenery borrowed from Drury Lane Theatre, for the purpose. However, the controversy caused Drury Lane and several actors to resign from participation, so that Mr Thellusson had to find a new company to stage the act. After an appeal by a lord the plan was abandoned and Mr Thellusson arranged for a different entertainment. Specifically, a play on the immorality of masquerades was staged which was well received.[7] The irony was likely part of the charm and seemed fitting with the mischievous personality of Mr Thellusson.

Peter Thellusson, the first Baron Rendlesham, was a merchant, banker, and politician who would die in 1808, at age 46, bringing an end to his masquerade antics. His name would be remembered as one of the beneficiaries of his father's controversial will that was talked about for years and that brought a suit that lasted half a century, impacted Chancery law, and inspired Charles Dicken's *Bleak House*.[8] The Baroness Rendlesham, Elizabeth Eleanor Thellusson, would pass away a year later, in 1809, at age 48. While masked balls were not their legacy, the Thellussons should be remembered as particularly impressive Regency event organisers and fans of the Regency masquerade, whose names were frequently in the list of highlighted attendees for both private and public masquerades.

Many other gentlewomen and gentlemen tried their hand at throwing the Season's grandest masquerade during the Regency era. A key feature of these events were their exclusivity, which was often more selective than even the Argyll Rooms or Almack's. Miss Morgan's Masquerade at Kensington Gore in 1801 accommodated a party of 400 people and was described as elegant, with the characters represented being the highlight and well described. Shakespearean characters, Greek gods, witches, ghosts, and other usual costumes made up the party. While the inside was filled with joyous celebration, outside a group of people tried to gain admittance but were found to have forged tickets and thus denied entrance.[9] A party crasher warranted a similar reporting at a Mrs Panton's masquerade in 1808.[10] Even under the cover of a mask, interlopers were denied; the private ballrooms were closed to uninvited guests.

Mrs Morton Pitt used the masked ball as a debut for her daughter, with a veritable list of who's who in the haute ton including the Prince of Wales, Lady Bentinck, Lady Greville, Lord Forbes, Lord Newburgh, the Duchess of Devonshire, and Mr Skeffington.[11] The June 1801 event had most attendees in costume, some creative, and many playing gender bending roles or as people from other countries. Although it was clearly outshone by Mrs Walker's masquerade, it nonetheless was highlighted as a successful event. The following year, Mrs Orby Hunter's May 1802 masquerade saw her home dressed in variegated lamps and artificial flowers, with a room for dancing and four supper rooms. Her masquerade was praised for the diversity of character, beauty of guests, and that guests did not depart for home until eight the next morning.[12]

The Duchess of St Alban's opened the doors of her Aldborough Square home, Stratford House, for a masquerade in July 1804. The home was noted for being spacious and commodious, with three elegant apartments on the ground floor and three on the first floor that were illuminated for the occasion in crystal and lustre lights. Transparent alabaster vases with wax lights decorated the ante-chambers and a band was stationed at the foot of the stairs while another set for dancing in the middle drawing room. A cold supper was offered, with delicacies complimented by fine wines. The masquerade had in attendance the Prince Regent, Lady Haggerstone, the Marquis of

Hartington, Lady Cavendish, Lady Morpeth, Lord Ossultston, and the Duchess of Devonshire among many other fashionable and titled persons. Dominoes were prevalent alongside an array of many common costumes as well as a few highlights including Lord Foppington and Mother Shipton.[13]

In June of 1805, the Countess of Barrymore gave a masquerade at her home at 29 Sackville Street. The Countess was married to Henry Barry, the 8th and final Earl of Barrymore, and often called Cripplegate for his club foot. It was a play off his older brother's nickname, Hellgate, who was also known as the Rake of Rakes. Three rooms were appointed at the Barrymore home for the event, hung with white gauze garlands, fragrant flowers, and a variety of lighting including variegated lamps, lustre lamps, and chandeliers.[14] One newspaper described the distinguished hostess as more fascinating than ever in a purple sarcenet and silver fancy dress with diamond headdress. While it was noted that the Duchess of Devonshire and the Marquis of Stafford were not in attendance, many other peers were including the Prince of Wales, the Duchess of Gordon, the Duchess of St Albans, the Duchess of Rutland, the Earl and Countess of Harrington, and Mr Sheridan.[15]

A month after the Countess's masquerade, Lady Louisa Manners would open her Pall Mall doors in July 1805 to a crowd of 450 people in character or fancy dress. The house was well lit by bell lights, chandeliers, and lustres, with the garden similarly illuminated in variegated lights, and artificial flowers were liberally interwoven to create a beautiful scene. A military band from the first regiment of the Guards played, and four supper rooms were laid with premier food. One of the supper rooms was set aside for and welcomed the Prince of Wales, who attended in domino with Mrs Fiztherbert. There were other titled and fashionable people in attendance, including the Duke of Sussex dressed as a German cavalry general officer, Lord Foley as a Quaker, Colonel Maitland as Don Quixote, Lady Douglas as a country girl, and the Countess of Jersey and Lady Villiers as Greek slaves. Supper was served at four o'clock while Mr Phelps and Mr Kennedy sung several glees, and the party soon followed the prince's retirement at five in the morning.[16] The following year, Lady Callender would host a grand masquerade, with her home in Mansfield Street decorated as an enchanted palace, with medallion painted ceilings, patent green painted and panelled walls with gold detail, large mirrors and chandeliers, crystal bell lamps, and a garden dressed to be a miniature Vauxhall with the prince's plume and stars in variegated lamps. The prince was in attendance, alongside the Duke of Cambridge, the Duke of Orleans, and Prince DeConde, alongside a list of other titled and fashionable people.[17]

The impressive guest lists, detailed décor, fine supper, and ready dancing both distinguished these private masquerades as well as demonstrated a marked similarity with public events. Every year at least one of the fashionable families of London would host a masquerade in their home or at a hired venue; throughout the 1810s, there would be masquerades thrown in the homes of Mrs Chichester, Mrs Boehm, Mrs Wheeler Milner, and Mrs Dottin. In 1811, at her home in Grosvenor Place, Lady Warburton opened her many apartments and delivered fine wine and excellent supper to the assembled masqueraders. Her home was lit through crystal lamps, chandelier lustres, and variegated lamps amplified by the strategic placement of mirrors, and the drawing rooms were draped in white and pink with the perfume of flowers and shrubs pleasing to the senses.[18] Lady Hyde Parker and Miss Onslow's 1819 masked ball was similarly decorated with sweet smelling greenery and flowers, with watercoloured painted floors. Paine's of Almack's and the Milanese Minstrels played to a company that danced and later dined on fine foods.[19]

In 1814, Burlington House, which was at that point in the ownership of the Duke of Devonshire, hosted a masquerade ball in honour of the Duke of Wellington. Sponsored by the Waiters Club and held at the end of June, the masked ball had an early arrival from some guests at half past nine with the company being full by eleven. The newspaper noted how well the carriage traffic was managed, which was frequently a complaint of tonnish events. The mansion's exterior was well illuminated by lamps, and the grand entrance was stationed with someone from the Committee of Management there to ensure guests had invitations. Rented chandeliers from Hancock's glass warehouse in Cockspur Street lit the twelve fluted pillars of white and pink silk, leading attendees towards the orchestra. At the other end of the ballroom was a temporary stage by which a ballet performance was followed by Grimaldi and other assorted amusements. The Duke of Wellington arrived, received by the Duke of Leinster and the Duke of Argyle, and proceeded to bow to the masqueraders while the song *See, the Conquering Hero Comes* from the band celebrated his presence. Notable attendees included Lord Byron, Lord Petersham, Mr Kean, and the Duchess of York.[20] The event was subsidised by subscriptions, and featured a Lottery of Bijoux where a variety of prizes were given including jewellery, ornaments, and other trinkets.[21]

While most of the private masquerades were held in the London or provincial homes of the titled and fashionable, on occasion a hostess or host would deem their own London abode too small or unsuitable for a masked ball. Luckily, there were several venues on hire. One in particular, the Hanover Square Rooms, was a favourite. The Hanover Square Rooms, or Queen's Concert Rooms, were established in 1774 in apartments at the corner of Hanover Square in London. For most of the nineteenth century, this was the main concert venue in London for Ancient Concerts, singing, top composers and performers including Haydn, Liszt, and Lind. It was also used for a variety of other events including lectures, exhibitions, and occasional balls and was available for hire for events like masquerades. The grant concert room was 90 feet by 35 feet, and able to hold up to 800 people with delated ceiling panels painted by Cipriani and space for an orchestra at the west end of the room. Transparent glass paintings produced by Gainsborough also decorated the rooms, and from the ceiling hung grand chandeliers. Portraits of famous musical composers, and a royal box draped in crimson were in keeping with its reputation as an elegant, commodious venue. This made it a prime location for hostesses and hosts wanting to make a splash in the ton.

The haute ton was familiar with the venue as a concert and lecture hall, but the transformation of the masquerade or ball undoubtedly leant a special feeling to an evening. That blend of familiarity and flirtation with exoticism would be a reoccurring refrain of the Regency masquerade, from the venues to the décor to the costumes and attendees. Masquerade celebrity,[22] Mrs Powell, would hold masquerades at Hanover Square Assembly Rooms. An April 1802 event made up a party of as many as 800 people, requiring non-transferable tickets. No dominos were permitted.[23] Mrs Dupre's Masquerade in May 1805 at Hanover Square Assembly Rooms resulted in a fracas which would later move through court.[24] This involved a dispute between Lord Reay and Mr Baillie while at a game of cards, with Baillie attempting to strike his lordship after Reay had tried to pull his nose. The matter first was suggested to duel, but then made its way to court where Reay promised to keep the peace. The conversation after suggested Lord Reay had been acting out a comic element of his character, but Baillie's supporters did not see it that way.[25]

Near to the Hanover Square Assembly Rooms, Mrs Coke held a well reported 1807 masquerade at 23 Hanover Square. Elegant lamps and diamond cut glass Grecian chandeliers lit up the grand hall, staircase, gallery and drawing rooms. Sprays of fragrant flowers filled the rooms, and the garden was also lit by variegated lamps where his Royal Highness the Duke of York's band in full uniform played. Several royals would be in early attendance but by eleven the masqueraders began to arrive.[26] Mrs Coke was the mother of Thomas Coke, the first Earl of Leicester and was also called by one newspaper a masquerade celebrity.[27] She had also given masquerades that were reported in 1805 and 1808. The 1805 Coke masquerade was blazing with light and filled with the fashionable and titled of London. Although no supper was provided, refreshments were on offer at two in the morning to the crowd of over 200 people.[28] An 1810 obituary would announce Mrs Coke's departure from her mortal coil at the age of 78, over 30 years past the death of her husband politician, Wenman Coke. Remembered over the years for her excellent parties and lively engagement in many of the ton's events, Mrs Coke well-earned the sobriquet of masquerade celebrity.

In 1819, the Countess of Darnley would give a masked ball at the Hanover Square Rooms where over 1000 people were in attendance, and were serenaded by the Band of the Coldstream Regiment of Guards upon entering the rooms.[29] The event merited only a brief mention in two different newspapers. A Grand Fancy Dress Ball in support of the Royal Academy of Music in June 1835 warranted a full column. Weippert's band played to well illuminated rooms. Costumes representing foreign nationals were the most popular among the fancy dress costumes shared, which were called splendid, and were listed as just one of the many reasons for what was measured to be a near perfect party.[30] Such effusive praise was certainly owing to the many titled and fashionable partis at the event.

Whether at a hired venue like the Hanover Square Rooms or their own London address, the private masquerades of the Regency era were exclusive, glamourous parties where the fashionable circle could indulge in both masked and unmasked costume balls. The opportunity to dazzle peers in fancy dress or character costume would continue throughout the long Regency. Though the crowds were typically smaller than the commercial events, enterprising hostesses and hosts often engaged the décor, music, and themes of their public counterparts. These trends and themes of the masquerade, however, were not reserved only for London, inspiring other masquerades throughout Great Britain and beyond.

By the Regency, private masquerades not only followed the trends of public masquerades but were also developing a reputation of their own; the private masquerade was often featured as a setting for intrigue or set up for comedy. The play *Fashionable Friends*, which debuted at the Theatre Royal in April 1802, made the joke that a private masquerade was an excuse to open a private residence more than was normally acceptable, including receiving partis ordinarily not acknowledged even as an acquaintance. A comedic Drury Lane Opera, *False Alarms*, performed in 1807 used the private masquerade as the setting for a woman to be engaged in flirtation by her friend's husband, which unleashed a comedy of errors set to music.[31] Conversely, one critique found a public masquerade the most vulgar of activities, while the private masquerade perhaps the dullest with hostesses and hosts aiming to be clever but falling flat.[32] The frequency by which masked balls were part of a broader cultural conversation made it clear they were not only fashionable, but a phenomena worthy of emulating.

## Chapter Six

# Masquerades Around Great Britain and Abroad

Beyond the venues of London, masquerades and fancy dress balls throughout the long Regency appeared in popular destinations. Summer resorts, colonial strongholds, country estates, and distant cities would assemble the local or visiting fashionable families for an event mirroring the most glorious masquerades London had on offer. Public masquerades would, naturally, be less exclusive than private events. Masks were sometimes encouraged, and in other cases left off. Enterprising local businesses and clothiers would advertise their ability to support these events. Whether to celebrate the holiday or tourist season, or to break the routine of events with a special costume party, masquerades outside of London would appear in the newspapers throughout the early nineteenth century.

Margate was a particular hot spot for masquerades outside of London. In part, it was ushered in by Dent de Lion and its Georgian rebirth as a pleasure garden. Dent de Lion, or Dandelion as it was known, near Margate in Kent was the site of a manor house constructed in the thirteenth century. In the eighteenth century it was converted to a pleasure garden with a hotel and tavern and served as a popular destination for Margate visitors. Cricket matches were often held at the Dandelion Paddock bowling green. The pleasure gardens had flowers, shrubs, a platform for dancing, an area for an orchestra, and spots perfect for drinking tea or enjoying special events.[1] In August 1798 a masquerade was held at Dandelion to closely mirror a recent masquerade at Ranelagh, including nearly 2000 lamps and a transparency on loan. Performers were also brought in, to be in character and entertain the guests. The hotel and home were open for accommodation and tickets were sold for ten shillings, six pence.[2] This was one example of several successful masquerades that would be held at Dent de Lion. By 1838 the manor house was gone and the property was turned back into a private residence. But it would not be the end of masquerades in Margate.

By the early Victorian era, Margate was an established destination. Dent de Lion's early success with masquerades helped introduce them to Kent along with the general traditions of the London public masquerade. Although on a significantly reduced scale, masquerades and fancy dress balls would proliferate in Margate over the long Regency, particularly in the summer months as London families sought holidays outside of the city. Margate, as an upcoming seaside resort in the late eighteenth century, would see development in the early nineteenth century in support of tourism. Described in an 1820 guidebook of Margate and the local area as having peculiar advantages, sea-bathing, beaches, a mild climate, and easy access from the Thames, it made this an idyllic summer retreat. A market town near Dover, prior to the rise in tourism it was a fishing town.[3] But the wealthy flocked to the area for its sandy beaches and the manifold health benefits of sea bathing, so much so that it would become the site of the Royal Sea Bathing Hospital, constructed in 1791. What followed was rapid construction of large brick homes and numerous buildings, paving the way for a continued history as a tourist destination.

This rapid redevelopment included many special events, like balls, musicales, and masquerades. In August 1801, Kidman's Assembly Rooms in Margate was host to a well-attended, described as tolerably so, masquerade.[4] The Assembly Rooms were well established in Cecil Square, decorated with girandoles, mirrors, chandeliers, and an orchestra box in an 87-foot-long by 43-foot-wide room.[5] It was known to be, at the time, one of the largest assembly rooms in Great Britain. In addition to the main ballroom, it also had a coffee room, parlours, and a billiard room, and was part of the Royal Hotel. The hotel was a large box structure with an Ionic façade, including a colonnade, Venetian windows, and decorative cornice. The Assembly Rooms were accessed at the colonnade's west end, passing through a vestibule and then up the staircase.[6]

Another Neoclassical venue in Margate would also deliver the occasional masquerade. Bettison's Rooms in Hawley Square in Margate hosted a masquerade in early September 1803.[7] Bettison's was a library and shop situated on the northwest corner of Hawley Square, separated by Corinthian columns, and under a large dome. It was said to have one of the largest collections of Georgian and Regency journals. Morning and evening promenades were hosted at Bettison's, which included vocal and instrumental music for the admission fee of ten shillings.[8]

In September 1805, the Master of Ceremonies ended partying at Dandelion at an early two o'clock in the morning to prepare the company for the masquerade ball being held at the Margate theatre later that night. Temporary flooring was laid over the pit, equal to the height of the stage, to allot enough space for characters and dominoes to mingle. Variegated lamps, festoons of flowers, and lit chandeliers brightened the packed room.[9] The Theatre Royal, as it was known, was at the northeast end of Hawley Square in a simple brick building modelled after the old Covent Garden theatre. Constructed in 1787[10] it provided another source of entertainment for fashionable people on holiday in Kent. The following year a masquerade at the theatre opened the Margate Season in August. Spectators filled the boxes, and many attendees assembled at eleven o'clock in character costumes.[11]

In a busy summer season of 1808, described as thronged and full, with a wide variety of carriages rolling through the humble streets, the Theatre Royal would play host to a masquerade open to all characters.[12] This was an improvement from a September masquerade that was poorly attended. That summer the Assembly Rooms hosted another masquerade that was said to be more brilliant, although the reporter wryly observed that in a town so small where everyone knew everyone else, few bothered with donning a mask or domino.[13] In September 1817, an Almack's style fancy dress ball was hosted at the Assembly Rooms while the Theatre Royal hosted a masquerade. Rich dresses elevated the Assembly Rooms éclat, while the Theatre Royal required masks and therefore enlivened the festivities through the element of surprise. For the event, the Theatre Royal was decorated al fresco, with many variegated lamps.[14] By 1833, the Theatre Royal promised three masquerades for the season, occurring early in January and February.[15] Throughout the long Regency, and with the participation of many of the entertainment centres of Kent, Margate would be a good summering locale for masquerading enthusiasts. With three of the primary entertainment locations offering masked and fancy dress events, Margate was one of the most proficient masquerading destinations in the early nineteenth century.

Another popular seaside destination, Brighton, would also have the occasional masquerade during the long Regency. In October 1801 preparations were being made in Brighton by well-known London caterer Waud, with the hopes of improving on the two previous masquerades that were poorly attended.[16] With no after event reporting or advertisements in the record, it is hard to know if Waud was successful. There were mentions of a Brighton masquerade at the theatre sometime in 1829, employing local actors to circulate among the crowd in character costume. Yet the reporter showed a gimlet eye to the manager's protestations of wanting to offer amusement rather than merely pocket the admission money.[17] In August 1828, a masquerade was held at the theatre in Brighton and another at the Royal Brighton Gardens.[18]

It is evident that the theatre in Brighton was the main masquerading venue for the destination. The theatre in Brighton in the New Road was constructed in 1806 and opened in 1807 with a production of *Hamlet.* In September 1828, another masquerade was held at the Royal Brighton Gardens, with roughly 500 people present.[19] The theatre, the same year, also had a second masquerade that was deemed to be much improved over the first, with many lively characters including Scaramouch, Hamlet, Paul Pry, and Sylvester Daggerwood. A performance by contortionist, magician and juggler Ching Lau Lauro was paired with several theatrical scenes before the opening of the masquerade ball. The ending conclusion of the review was that masquerades offered good variety for the theatre and should be repeated in the future.[20] A few years later, the officers of the King's Dragoon Guards held a grand fancy dress ball in February 1834 where guests dined on the choicest dainties and danced until six in the morning.[21]

Other popular destinations would also host the occasional masquerade. A February 1826 masquerade in Bath saw most area families attend, and almost all of the fashionable young men from the region, the *Morning Post* reported. However the result was judged flat as the characters lacked performance.[22] The port town of Yarmouth would be home to a March 1831 fancy dress ball and supper at the New Hall, where approximately 500 people from the vicinity as well as distant parts of Norfolk and Suffolk were in attendance. The floor was chalked and painted with various designs and mottoes, the hall rooms were awash with light, and the party appeared in both character costumes and fancy dress. It was judged to be a successful event.[23] Generally, masquerades were not as frequent as in London, but the summer time retreats obliged their tourists with amusements in the style they were accustomed to in Town.

Beyond the tourist locations, many cities would host the occasional masquerade at a local venue during the long Regency. Liverpool gentlemen revived the masquerade in February 1803 after an eighteen year hiatus, dressing the venue as the Temple of Mirth with a barrister at the front examining tickets and detailing masquerade law as an added amusement.[24] A Liverpool fancy dress ball in October 1833 merited three and a half pages in a local paper detailing every guest in attendance and what costume or fancy dress they appeared in.[25] Similar coverage was given to a fancy dress ball held in Manchester in September 1836. A follow up article shared additional costumes, but also that 4600 people had been admitted to the theatre for dancing, supported by two bands.[26]

Derby's New Assembly Room was put to use in February 1826 for a fancy dress ball that warranted three columns in the *Derby Mercury*, with a list of attendees and their costumes.[27] The same year, the Black Lion Assembly Rooms in Cumberland was well attended by rank and fashion of the area, despite poor weather. The place was brilliantly lit, with evergreen, artificial flowers, plants, and variegated lamps. Dancing began after most of the guests had arrived at nine, and a good time was had by the attendees.[28] Leicester would have a dress and fancy dress ball in September 1827 that included much of the local nobility, in character and fancy dress costumes.[29] Newcastle's Assembly Rooms played host to a masquerade ball in February 1828, with a wide array of guests in various fancy dress and character costumes.[30] A group of lady patronesses would host a fancy dress ball on 14 January 1836 at Batt's Royal Hotel in Torquay.[31] Throughout Great Britain, similar events would pop up. Grand masquerades, as they were styled in London, were more popular in the early Regency while toward the end of the era, fancy dress balls became more common. The fancy dress balls were still costumed, but masks would be less common by the Victorian era.

Dublin would be the site of masquerades during the long Regency, in the style of those frequented in London. The Dublin Castle would frequently be the venue of choice for grand fancy dress balls.[32] A May 1808 Dublin masquerade had all the usual character and fancy dress costumes, and while the rooms were said to be intolerably hot, a splendid supper and good attendance marked this a popular event.[33] In May 1817, the Theatre Royal in Dublin hosted a masquerade complete with many performers, including singers, actors, and a board sword and shield combat team.[34] Other cities in Ireland would also have masquerades and fancy dress balls; Limerick's Assembly House would also have several masked balls in the first decade of the 1800s.

Colonial strongholds would also be influenced by the fashionable London events. Madras, in India, would also see masquerades at Moore's Rooms, the theatre, or private homes in the early 1800s as would Calcutta. A subscription masquerade was presented at the Calcutta Theatre in January 1795[35] and again in 1796. Mrs Oakes' mansion in Madras in November 1811 was the location for a masquerade ball and supper, lit brightly with lamps to welcome assorted nobility, company people, and the Madras fashionable.[36] Masks were left behind for the fancy dress ball at Mr Stirling's in Calcutta in December 1827. The most popular costumes, according to the reporter, was a group of bodies including Lord Somebody, Mr Nobody, Mrs Busybody, Ensign Anybody, and Mr Everybody.[37] Masquerades in other British ruled places, like the West Indies and Jamaica, were either underreported or seldom occurrences during the Regency.

Beyond venues, masquerades would crop up in private, country estates throughout Great Britain and beyond during the nineteenth century. These events were notable, well-reported occasions. Mr Champney, a popular masquerader, opened up his Orchardleigh mansion, near Bath, to his fashionable neighbours in February 1803 for a masquerade. With two bands, one military and one for dancing, and extensive paintings by Mr Charles Davis, painter of Bath, made to resemble a vast grove of foreign trees and plants meeting at the Temple of Harmony, the crowd of 250 people enjoyed themselves until seven in the morning. The supper was notable for its bounty, and included hot soups, game, lamb, turkeys, and a variety of sides. The whole was served with Port and Madeira. Arches of artificial flowers and a mix of lamps completed the festive environs.[38]

The Duchess of Bedford held a Twelfth Night masquerade party in the early days of 1804 at her Bedfordshire home, Woburn Abbey, that attracted nearly 800 guests, including many fashionables who journeyed from London to attend. Flowers and evergreens, both real and artificial, served to dress the Abbey. While only a few characters appeared, with most preferring fancy dress or a domino, it was an overall success for the Duchess.[39] The Duchess, Anna Maria Russell, would later serve as Lady of the Bedchamber in the first four years of Queen Victoria's reign. Another Twelfth Night masquerade ball saw more than 150 guests in 1814. Sir Charles Morgan opened up his Monmouthshire mansion to entertain for a fortnight around sixty fashionable guests, capping the Christmastime festivities off with the masquerade that boasted more than one hundred servants dancing on attendance. The South Gloucester Militia Band supplied the music for the party which did not end until five the next morning.[40]

Lord and Lady Boringdon gave a masquerade ball at their Saltram House in Devonshire in 1814. It was likened to the last masquerade given in the region, at Lord Courtenay's Powderham Castle, and was given a glowing review for its humour and engagement of the guests.[41] Willingham Hall in Suffolk was the site for a masquerade in April 1810, welcoming neighbouring guests into the home decorated with lamps, white and red roses, and a temporary building for music and dancing.[42] Lord Dungannon's home, Brynkinalt, would host guests in costume in January 1816.[43] Mrs Sadlier gave a masked ball at her Bath mansion in Upper Church Street in April 1824. The gas lighting in her home made the first floor brilliantly illuminated, while the ground floor was dressed up to serve as a ballroom. The *Bath Chronicle* and *Weekly Gazette* highlighted many of the costumed guests, as well as the overall enjoyment of the party.[44] Mrs Mainwaring opened her Watergate, Chester home for a masquerade in January 1823. Her home was opened at nine to receive the sailors, broom girls, gods and goddesses, and various other character costumes. It was noted that several guests were so well masked it was difficult to uncover identities until the unveiling.[45]

These examples illustrate that by the beginning of the nineteenth century, masked and fancy dress balls were available to more than residents or visitors of London. Enterprising venues in smaller cities would leverage this style of event to diversify their repertoire and keep up with demands from residents and tourists alike. Country homes would be thrown open, particularly in winter, to entertain families both distant and local. And further afield, in other countries, masquerades would be hosted for the entertainment of the expats and military personnel stationed abroad. The masquerades would continue across the British Empire well into the Victorian era, albeit with limited regularity except for in locations like London or popular destinations like Margate. Creativity and performance could make or break the evening, in the eyes of the reporters and guests. This was near identical to the praise and criticism of London events. The biggest difference, according to a survey of reports, seemed to be that these masquerades abroad tended to start earlier, at nine or ten in the evening, than London events. Assembly rooms, theatres, and other local venues would be transformed into grand rooms for dancing, supper, and performance. The entertainment, including the usual array of character and fancy dress costumes, consisted of bands and sometimes paid performers. Emphasis was placed on spectacle, novelty, and people playing their part.

Despite sentiments that the Georgian masquerade was vanquished by the rising nineteenth century, a survey of the record demonstrates that masquerades were alive and well throughout the long Regency. While the venues would rise and fall out of fashion, often due to management issues, fires, or competition, throughout the Regency there would consistently be two to three primary venues providing annual masquerades. Coupled with at least one, but in reality many more, private masquerades for the titled and fashionable a year the upper class had a myriad of opportunities to engage in cosplay. Throughout the next chapters, themes of national identity will be teased out as similarities in décor, spectacle and entertainment, and costumes demonstrate a remarkable formula for a successful Regency masquerade. Despite significant differences in the public, exclusive public, and private events, the Regency masquerade record demonstrates a sameness that will later support analysis of national identity, cultural appropriation, and an influence into masquerades into the next era.

# Chapter Seven

# Décor and Decorations, Themes and Demonstrations

The Regency masquerade was a ball and a theatrical production, advertised as both grand and unique. The spaces in which these events were held, both public venues and private homes, often had Neoclassical architectural features promoting the sense of tradition while still featuring events, like masquerades, that critics found subversive. Many of the public venues had been designed specifically for performance, whether musical or theatrical, playing a critical part in the relationship between performance, spectators, and the space. Blažeković (2017) discusses theatres as quasi-religious spaces, museums of historical memory, and a marketing tool. This is particularly relevant for the long Regency, as venues were used to convey cultural messages, both of the past and contemporary, but also enact performances like the masquerade that had a religious tradition at its roots. Masquerade locations were sites of consumption, not only feasts for the senses but also the cultural at play. The grandness and pomp of the buildings were enhanced by lavish decoration to strengthen this interconnectedness between performance, spectators, and the space.

Despite the myriad of venues and private homes offering masquerades during the Regency era, there was a marked similarity in the design and execution of décor for these events. Well-lit, an emphasis on nature, and many spectacular accents highlighting the military, the royal family, or other national treasures were elements that would appear at masquerade after masquerade during the early nineteenth century. Themes of Romanticism, Neoclassicism, or imperialism were woven in to the symbols and signs of most masquerades. Beyond trends or what was fashionable, these decorations served to enhance the mood and meaning of the masked ball. From its origins in Italy, to the consumption sites of the Georgian masquerade in Great Britain, there would be a constant interplay between the elite and burgeoning middle class teetering on the exotic and dark places of both imagination and culture. Yet, ironically, many of these events were lit brilliantly. The only hiding was in the costume. But while costume was important to the overall masquerade theme, the décor would elevate the masked or fancy dress ball beyond the average event to something more luxurious and other worldly. Simultaneously, the themes of the décor would emphasise the symbols that united guests under one national identity.

Most masquerades in the Regency era, both public and private, played on nature, the ethereal and magical, or harkened to the Carnival and Italian history of the masquerade. These themes were achieved largely through the décor and decoration. The quasi-utopian Carnival was underscored by spectacle, invention, and conventions of the Beau Monde[1] in a near hyper-real, sanitised play of the everyday. Many of the tricks and techniques of the theatre would be critical to setting the stage for these events in which a duchess could play a milkmaid and an earl a chimney sweep. The similarities between both public and private masquerades, at homes and at venues, in London and outside, in part is owing to the conventions of décor utilised by impresarios, hostesses and hosts during the Regency period. Bright lights, artificial flowers and greenery, chalked floors, and transparencies were foundational elements of the Regency masquerade.

Through examples in the record, it will become clear that many of the designs and symbols employed to set the stage for these masked happenings would have ties to national identity. Monarchy, military, and prevalent themes like Neoclassicism would be exploited by promoters, hostesses and hosts to reproduce not only a sense of place, but likely a sense of belonging. Without attention to detail of these elements, critics would lambast a masquerade or venue. And more often than not, great pains and expenses would need to be undertaken to ensure every element worked together harmoniously to welcome, entertain, and to understate the broader themes of luxury, spectacle, and national identity explored by the décor, entertainment, and costumes of the Regency masquerade.

From advertisements to descriptions, one of the highlights of the Regency masquerade décor was the lighting. With the designs, novelty, brightness, or number of lights being mentioned as integral to the masquerade, it was almost a given that public and private masquerades would be awash with lights; the quantity and quality of lights were paramount to the perceived success of a masquerade not only at the venues like the Pantheon or the Opera House, but also at private homes and rural venues. Contrary to the idea of masquerades being an obvious place for dark doings and assignations, the trend was to brightly light the halls and gardens for the masked assemblies. Thousands of lamps would be employed to create the effect of near daylight, a luxury that also had a biological connection. Light has been shown to be a general arousal agent, increasing the levels of human activity and communication.[2] Given the length of these events, usually from ten or eleven at night until the early dawn hours, artificial light was essential for tricking the biology of party goers and energising them for the festivities. For an event centred on connection and engagement, lights helped to stimulate the crowds to interact. It was also likely helpful from a safety perspective, as masks would darken a person's vision and create a hazard were it not for the well-lit rooms.

Beyond biology, an abundance of light was also a symbol. As scholars have pointed to in their examination of spaces of consumption in the nineteenth century, lighting was one of the techniques to signal luxury, exoticism, and excess.[3] Most households were largely lit by candles and fire light, and that would have been proportionate to the wealth of the home; primary sources suggest that the price of candles was volatile, often based on the cost of tallow, and it was not uncommon for a dozen pounds of tallow candles to be over seven shillings. The sense was that those who could afford to be bathed in a blaze of light should, and the brighter the ballroom the better.[4] The implicit extravagance, then, of lighting hundreds if not thousands of lamps and saturating the environment with brightness likely filled the revellers with the sense of being bathed in wealth. Just as architects like Wyatt were trying to engineer a separation between the haves and the have less, commercial enterprises were, in a very theatrical homage, trying to create a space where consumption was prized.

In many modern depictions of Regency masquerades, the emphasis is on hiding and darkness. In romance novels, the masquerade is often a setting for intrigue or assignation, relying on the cover of the mask and dimly lit spaces to carry out said deeds. However, just as a modern tourist destination like Las Vegas boasts anonymity as a benefit, similar to masquerades, it also revels in the spectacle with over the top theatrical effects like music, smells, lighting, and set design. The idea that darkness was critical to the success of masquerades in the early nineteenth century is belied by the emphasis often placed on lighting as a key component to their success. As a review of an August 1820 Argyll Rooms masquerade suggested, the many wax candles provided an unmatched brilliance to the scene and added to the overall mood of the evening.[5]

Rather than shadows and darkness for assignation, masquerades were described as fully ablaze, showcasing the beautiful costumes, intricate décor, and the general merriment of the party. The idea of seeing and being seen, or in some cases participating as a wealthy observer, are evident in the accounts of masquerades from this era. Faithful reporting often listed the names of the titled and fashionable, sometimes with notes on their costumes. And several of the more public venues rented out boxes to wealthier guests so that they might observe the events without participating in potentially risky mingling with lewd and lascivious behaviours. This was clearly called out in numerous ads for box rental. From all indications, the visual spectacle was an important part of the British masquerade and lights were a critical factor in enhancing that experience.

In addition to the act of looking being supported by light and its stimulating effects on the crowd, the ambient effect wax lights and oil lamps created was described as enhancing the magical atmosphere, transforming venues and homes to what was oft described as a fairy land. Descriptions in reviews and memoirs emphasised the fantastical, larger than life experience of the masquerade. More often than not what was highlighted was the brightness, the shapes, and the types of lighting used by the venue or private home. The shapes, or devices as they were referred to, were a critical part of the décor. Cementing themes, celebrating honoured guests, and generally providing an air of festivity, the lights could be mounted or hung in a variety of styles to complement other décor elements.

Throughout the Regency, and despite whether at an established venue or private event, most masquerades relied on a combination of variegated lamps, chandeliers, and other types of lights. While wax lights were common, one of the most frequently emphasised lighting at Regency masquerades in newspaper coverage or memoirs were variegated lamps. The small, globular lamps were easy to arrange in pleasing forms that would help establish the tone and intent of the hostess or impresario; variegated lamps, often in festoons, were popular not only at masquerades but at a variety of sites of entertainment, including clubs, museums, and parties. Beyond garlands, other popular shapes for variegated lamp displays were the sun, stars, constellations, wreaths, and crowns. Some of these shapes played on national emblems, and others were taken from more broad, natural world motifs. On occasion, variegated lamps would be employed to spell names, initials, or mottos and to highlight architectural features of the various venues. There were also caricatures of guests of honour fashioned in lights at a few long Regency masquerades.

The variegated lamps were small, glass, and fashioned in an array of colours. From gold, emerald, rose, and blue the festoons would feature a broad mix of stained glass to enhance the fairy quality of the lamps. Some reports emphasised jewel tones, and for other events the colour of the lamps corresponded to the shape or initials to help the viewer understand the shape. The coloured lamps at all the venues that employed them would give the evening a magic touch necessary to increase the entertainment and satisfaction of the masquerade that, at the end of the day, was by in large a commercial venture. A Vauxhall ad for an 1804 event stressed that many thousand additional lamps would be brought in to add to the brilliancy of the scene, and that the variegated lamps would be entwined, like ivy around trees.[6] Another ad promised the addition of lamps would enliven all aspects of the gardens, and be displayed in rich groups and various shapes.[7]

Vauxhall, which had thousands of lamps by the Regency era, was known to have a linked fuse system that could light the lamps that stretched across several acres within a matter of minutes. Vauxhall's lights would be fired at dusk, accompanied by music of the orchestra, to dizzying effect and one account described the romance of eating supper by the light of variegated lamps. Lights were one of the most remarked about features of Vauxhall, and one early twentieth-century writer argued it was one of the few places where people could see artificial light at its most effective and radiant.[8] Another account remarked that as Vauxhall started to wane in popularity by the mid-1800s, a marked symbol was the dimming or disappearance of the brilliant lamps.[9]

Vauxhall's number of variegated lamps had an influence on the other venues. The Pantheon was known to have at least 10,000 variegated lamps, arranged in various shapes for masquerade events including phrases and initials.[10] The variegated lamps, combined with scenery and foliage, would be said to make a King's Theatre masquerade in 1829 of such grandeur that it surpassed similar events in Europe.[11] The Argyll Rooms employed variegated lamps at various masquerades. From Taunton to Leamington Spa, Hampshire and Margate, assembly rooms would include variegated lamps in their masquerade design. Variegated lamps were also a common highlight of Royal Jubilee celebrations, where businesses, households, and even the lamp posts would be strung with variegated lamps interspersed with foliage and flowers.

Variegated lamps were by and large fuelled by oil. The oil in this era was typically animal based, likely whale or seal blubber, and would give off a distinctive fishy smell that would have been familiar to the Regency era socialite. Housekeeping books from the era would recommend a pure oil to reduce the smoke and smell, but it was nonetheless a feature of oil lamps that would help spur invention for a cleaner fuel. A wick would be placed in the oil, much the same as a candle, to be lit. By the Regency era, the Argand lamp was the most common. Some venues, like Vauxhall, had clever set ups that allowed almost instantaneous lighting, much to the awe and amusement of the crowds. At other venues, the lamps on display would have to be hand lit by staff. The lamps were naturally susceptible to the elements, if out of doors, as wind and rain could easily snuff the flames and leave behind a smoke and smell.[12]

Prints and paintings from the Georgian and Regency eras show some of the coloured lamp displays at venues like Vauxhall, the King's Theatre, and the Pantheon. Highlighted in newspaper reports of the masquerades, the variegated lamps were a critical form of the spectacle that made masquerades popular. For instance, one description of a June 1804 masquerade at the Pantheon recounted the fanciful forms of the variegated lamps, including a star made from various colours which, the writer described, directed the crowd through a winding lane of traffic in the saloon.[13] More variegated lamps in star forms at the ends of the building combined with festoons of lights no doubt gave many revellers the same sense as the reporter, who spoke of the brilliance, splendour, and beauty of the décor with an emphasis on the light. An event at the Argyll Rooms in 1808 used variegated lamps to represent the Prince Regent's plume, motto, and star. Coupled with Chinese lamps suspended from the ceiling, the rooms were said to be ablaze enough to mimic daylight.[14] A celebratory masquerade in honour of Wellington's successes at Vauxhall in August 1812 had a variety of displays of his victories, the Prince Regent's plume, stars, pillars, a victor's wreath and a tremendous collection of bright, variegated lamps spelling out the Marquis of Wellington with two stars adorning it.[15] In addition to the transparencies, and other light displays, it was a magnificent tribute to the Regency hero.

Variegated lamps were so on trend that many private masquerades would also use them as part of the décor. The Countess of Barrymore's masquerade in June 1805, for instance, combined variegated lamps with chandeliers and lustres that were said to rival the splendour of afternoon.[16] Mrs Panton's home in Portland Place in 1808 was the setting for a masquerade with nearly 600 nobility and fashionable society. Her decorations included flowers intertwined with masks and lit by variegated lamps for an elegant and festive display.[17] And several years earlier, in June 1802, Mrs Thellusson's masquerade featured variegated lamps mixed with feathers and leaves in an arched covering of the garden that impressed with its brilliance.[18] Based on the record, the small glass lamps were ubiquitous for these special occasions, both a symbol of luxury, a biological stimulant, and a festive accent. Variegated lamps were available for hire at places like R. M. Harper, J. Appleton's Lamp and Oil Warehouse, or various glass manufacturers and warehouses throughout the United Kingdom. One ad from the *Reading Mercury* in 1802 advertised that B. Williams was available to wait on any lady or gentleman with a collection of plain, variegated, or transparent lamps in superior style with different devices.[19]

Variegated lamps were not the only type of decorative light to be used at a masquerade ball. Chinese lanterns and Grecian lamps[20] were occasionally mentioned at masquerade events, often correlating with a broader theme. Chinese lanterns, in particular, were used at larger venues like Vauxhall that had Chinese inspired pavilions or with events aiming to cover the exotic. One description of a Chinese lantern from an 1805 report on a gift from Lord Rivers to Princess Elizabeth describes it as made of ivory with three possible changes of transparencies.[21] Surviving antiques from the nineteenth century also show Chinese lanterns made of various metals, wood, paper, and linen, often with scenes painted or cut-out in metal on each side. They influenced the creation of magic lanterns, or early projectors, which would become a trendy item for upper class Victorians. Grecian lamps were seen with themes that emphasised the Neoclassical. At Mrs Pantone's packed house of over 600 fashionable people in May 1808, she had the rooms decked in variegated lamps and Grecian lustre lamps along with other tasteful and elegant accents.[22] A year before, the Argyll Rooms had set the tone with an impressive lighting display for their July masquerade, with variegated lamps, and six expensive diamond-cut Grecian lamps. The floor complemented the lamps with a Grecian-styled design in chalk.[23]

Other types of lights were also common and provided the true ambience for the space including chandeliers, crystal lamps, and larger glass lamps that could be suspended from trees or boxes or the ceiling to illuminate the party. Crystal lamps and cut glass lamps were often highlighted in advertisements or event reporting. In account after account, the comparison was made with daylight and the emphasis placed on how light created the ambience for the exclusive events. Such brightness was a luxury, a spectacle of wealth when ordinary people were limited by sunlight and tallow candles. There was also, on occasion, the mention of illuminated vases, and the use of mirrors to amplify light.

Towards the end of the Regency era, gas lamps began popping up at venues and private homes. King's Theatre was the first masquerade venue to have them. Drury Lane Theatre installed gas light around 1818. Mrs Sadlier's Bath home was ablaze with gas lamps for her April 1824 masked ball. The Theatre Royal in Cork, Ireland, advertised a January 1827 masquerade to include variegated, wax, and gas lamps.[24] Although it's cheaper cost would lead to widespread adoption of gas lighting by the late 1850s in Britain, gas was still considered advanced technology and a luxury during most of the Regency era. Advertisements and event reviews highlighted the gas lamps as a novelty in as much as particularly amusing costumes or lavish décor.

Advancements in oil lamps in the Georgian era, coupled with devotion for the theatrical and spectacle, no doubt increased the fervour for lighting. And, as these technological advancements, particularly when decorative, were largely only accessible to the very wealthy, it made incredible sense that masquerades, balls, and parties would display a dizzying number of lamps. It may be hard to appreciate, with modern sensibilities and conveniences, the true awe that these lighted displays likely inspired in even the most cynical breast. But it went beyond mere decadence, often into reverence or ritual as the themes and tributes were often repeated and devoted to strengthening the sense of national identity. This is apparent when the symbols and motifs created with lights were also apparent in other masquerade décor.

An example of this was the transparency. Another popular decoration for masquerades and other events, the transparency was used to celebrate an event theme or motif. Emerging as a craft in the late eighteenth century, venues and events would typically commission scene painters[25] to paint images of people, places, events, or mottos on large pieces of paper, silk, linen, or muslin. The images would be stretched on a frame, often with a coating of varnish on both sides, and then illuminated from behind to create stunning visuals celebrating the themes, patronesses, or guests of honour at many masquerades. Mentioned typically in the same sentence as variegated lamps, transparencies were equal attractions when promoting a masquerade and a feature often mentioned in newspaper coverage.

One celebrated artist, William Orme, painted several transparencies for the Grand Masquerade in February 1802 at the Pantheon.[26] Hung above the orchestra, the transparencies were bust likenesses of war heroes Howe, Vincent, and Nelson.[27] Another masquerade ball held in June 1802 at Ranelagh, and hosted by Boodle's members, featured two life-sized transparencies, one representing Britannia pointing to commerce on the Thames with London in the background, and the other a figure meant to stand for peace.[28] The June 1806 masquerade at the Argyll Rooms featured a disarmed Minerva, joined on the staircase by twelve transparent pillars inscribed with the names of the lady patronesses.[29] That same year in June, Lady Callender gave a masquerade at her home in Mansfield Street. Said to be one of the grandest masquerades of the Season with the appearance of an enchanted palace, the garden was added as an additional room with painted transparencies lining the interior of the temporary space.[30]

Another private masquerade held in January 1809 at Eglinton Castle boasted impressive transparencies. The gothic, castellated mansion in Scotland was finished in 1802, and the private masquerade was a Christmas season celebration. To welcome guests, the entrance hall featured a transparent painting of the Eglinton arms, the saloon held a transparency representing Britannia, and above the door of the breakfast parlour another depicting an Italian dance. The artist was Mr Smith of Irvine, and the transparencies were said to display real talent in both taste and execution.[31] The event was widely reported, as a notable and extravagant celebration. Transparencies were one of the highlighted features setting off the décor of the castle with a grandness that was deemed pleasing.

There was some variety in the scenes of transparencies. Though not a masquerade, a ball held in May 1802 by the Marchioness of Winchester featured gothic transparencies.[32] With the popularity of the gothic novel and the favoured Romanticism of the era, the gothic-themed transparencies were likely a showstopper. The influence abroad could be shown in a masquerade held in July 1810 in Madras, where the theatre venue was made to look like a gothic hall, with transparencies designed like gothic windows helped add to the sense of place.[33] The gothic theme was not unique to masquerades, appearing at various large society events during the long Regency, manifesting in décor like transparencies.

Transparencies also elevated aspects of the Empire. More pastoral views celebrating the Empire were a popular theme; a masquerade held in March 1810 at the Royal Hibernian Theatre in Dublin featured transparencies of views from Ireland, England, Wales, and Jamaica.[34] Mixing the romantic landscapes with underlying monuments to the Empire were easy emblems for the masqueraders to recognise and enjoy. Similarly, homages to art or famous figures would appear in the transparencies of masquerades. A masquerade event held in honour of Chevalier Bartholomew Pergami in 1820 at Brandyburgh House featured a transparency of the queen as Venus D'Arles. Additional transparencies featured Nero's Supper, Villa d'Este, and various other scenes.[35] A masquerade at the King's Theatre in 1829 was said to introduce a new life to the masked assembly, and featured a large, centre stage transparency of the king.[36] Over and over again, transparencies would be highlighted as standout masquerade décor. The latter feature on the aristocracy helped support greater themes of national identity woven through the décor.

Transparencies as masquerade décor were as ubiquitous further afield than London as they were in London. In March 1817, the theatre in Canterbury had a grand masquerade to follow a new three act comedy. Designed to resurrect a past Covent Garden benefit masquerade, the orchestra was fitted with variegated lamps and transparencies to illuminate the band.[37] A Leamington Spa masquerade in April 1830 was held at the Pavilion. To celebrate, many of the inns and public houses were decorated with transparent paintings, variegated lamps, and evergreens.[38] As with the arrangements of lamps and lights, the themes of transparencies hinged on sense of place, celebration of national identity, and honouring of distinguished persons. These transparencies emphasised icons and symbols that would have been familiar to the audiences and subconsciously and consciously strengthened ideas about community, duty, celebrity, and country. For instance, the frequent use of Britannia, a symbol of British power and unity, represented how masquerades were another opportunity for the ruling class to feel reinforced in the imperialism, war, and expansion of Great Britain's kingdom. Other frequent symbols were popular military heroes, fashionable people, and scenes meant to conjure a sense of belonging and place.

Transparencies were so fashionable they would become a popular do-it-yourself craft for the young Regency lady. Ackermann created a manual published in 1800 that described a new method for transparencies, comparing them to stained glass but more cost effective and durable. The transparency, he wrote, was particularly wonderful in fire and moon lights, and offered a fanciful effect for a variety of rooms and moods. His method recommended a mixture of one ounce of Canada Balsam and one ounce Spirit of Turpentine, which once combined should be allowed to rest for a day. The alternative receipt in the book was for four ounces of mastic and one pint of Spirit of Turpentine, with half an ounce of Canada Balsam gently warmed in water or sunlight and then allowed to cure over twenty-four hours. Naturally, his instructional came with it an advertisement for large and small prints on offer at his offices on the Strand. In addition to paper, gilt borders, and medallions, the inspired crafter might also purchase botanical paper, drawings of landscapes, bird, flowers, ornaments and insects, and fire screens or pasteboards for mounting. A young lady might paint or trace an image to be used as a fire screen or mounted in the window to delight her household and guests with her artistry.

Though not at the scale or with the expertise crafted by scenery painters for commercial events, the homemade transparency signalled the overall popularity of this decorative item. Many of the masquerades throughout the Regency would feature transparencies and these would be reviewed as one of the highlights of the event and décor. The art world, by contrast, would consider transparencies low art despite the arguable talent required to produce many of those on display at fashionable events.[39] This opinion was influenced by the fact that it was a popular ladies craft. Despite any beliefs that transparencies were low art, their presence at masquerades helped enhance the spectacle through sometimes near theatrical means. Vauxhall's Tin Cascade represented a storm at a watermill and miller's house, where hidden machinery enlivened the image with the crossing of a bridge by a wagon and horses or soldiers.[40] This more advanced transparency display epitomised the many fantastical elements venues like Vauxhall employed to entertain and amaze their guests. From the display of artificial icebergs, ship replicas, and assorted arctic life to mark the return of Ross' expedition in 1834[41] to the various balloon ascensions, the theatrical elements of not only Vauxhall but other venues were accentuated by elements like transparencies.

The Argyll Rooms' November 1828 masquerade featured transparencies that looked as if lit from the sky lending a varied lighted atmosphere that enhanced the gaze of attendees.[42] An April 1818 masquerade at the King's Theatre was decorated with a Grand Allegorical Transparency on the stage in honour of Princess Elizabeth and the Prince of Hesse Hombourg's marriage, painted by William Orme and meant to be the main decorative feature of the celebration.[43] A Vauxhall masquerade in August 1812 featured a transparency in front of the orchestra with the inscription, in Latin, of the Prince Regent and Britannia.[44] Just as many of the devices and arrangements of variegated lamps gave homage to the Royal Family, aristocratic heroes, or Britannia, transparencies were also a method to celebrate and exalt the people and symbols of the monarchy, the Empire, and more broadly, national identity. Unlike the home transparencies, that would undoubtedly be personal or decorative, these painted scenes conveyed messages about what it was to be British, at least from the prospective of the power elite. Yet transparencies and variegated lamps were not the only decorative item at masquerade events that would carry these messages.

Just as some of the light devices and transparency paintings would harken to Romanticism, other features of décor would set the tone for a more ethereal experience. Often mentioned in after event accounts in connection with lights and transparencies were flowers, both fresh and artificial, and greenery at masquerades. Some events were held out of doors, in pleasure gardens or household gardens and conservatories, while indoor events were often draped in boughs, wreaths, and floral arrangements to simulate a natural environment. Evergreens, oaks, and real and artificial shrubs would frequently make appearances, particularly in the winter months, while in the summer many venues would lay green baize over outdoor surfaces in imitation of grass. Sir Richard Plasket's grand masquerade in December 1826 impressed with the large yard covered with flowers, evergreens, lemon and orange trees for decoration.[45] Like many private masquerades of the long Regency, the outdoor space was incorporated regardless of the weather, and artfully decorated with natural flora and fauna.

The Argyll Rooms in 1806 held a masquerade, with its grand hall and staircase filled with shrubs, artificial roses and other flowers, in addition to variegated lamps and transparencies.[46] This was not a unique combination, with many variations on the theme throughout the Regency era, and appears to be also a common part of decorations for other significant events. The

Viscount Courtenay's masquerade ball in August 1801 featured a temporary room made to look like a long bower, whereby visitors passed through an arched alcove made of jessamine, roses, and honeysuckles on the roof and sides of rare shrubs in an enchanting display.[47] Waiter's 1814 masquerade at Burlington House featured a covered garden of orange trees, plants and shrubs that were elegantly lit, creating not only a cool temperature for party goers, but an overall ambiance of a romantic fairy story.[48] Mrs Walker's June 1801 masquerade had her staircase transformed into an alcove through the placement of oak and laurel leaves from which were nestled variegated lamps. The windows of the rooms were also decorated with boughs and entwined in them were roses and honeysuckles.[49] Roses harkened back to the Tudor era as a symbol of England and the monarchy, while also known to symbolise classical beauty, joy, and passion. Honeysuckles, with their strong fragrance, could be symbolic of innocence and joy.

On occasion, some masquerades fully embraced greenery and flowers as part of their broader theme. A White's Club masquerade in May 1802 made up their rooms to look like a greenhouse, bringing twenty-two wagon loads of lilac, shrubs, roses, and other flowers to decorate and transform the space.[50] The temporary building erected as a ballroom was designed to look like a greenhouse, and trellis work with roses and lilacs helped support the ambiance. Another room was fitted to look like a cavern grotto, with shell work on the ceiling.[51] Other masquerades built on the outdoor spaces of London or country homes to create a natural world environment for the events. Reoccurring were oak leaves, which according to floriography symbolise bravery, and roses which can be used to represent war but are England's national flower, so more likely used to represent national identity. Mr H. Johnston's masquerade at the Royal Hibernian Theatre in Dublin in 1810 featured greenery, artificial flowers, and lemons and oranges tied in with the transparencies.[52] Almack's August 1820 masquerade saw the ballroom decorated with festoons of artificial flowers, interspersed with natural flowers that provided a delicate perfume to the rooms.[53]

Green baize was sometimes laid down at outdoor venues to resemble grass, as it was for the June 1802 Ranelagh masquerade. A very tall canvas tent was erected, enclosing the trees, to provide an illuminated grove for people to walk and mingle under.[54] Ranelagh also laid down green baize the following year for the masquerade, well-lit by over 300 lamps in the trees.[55] The intermix of artificial and real flora and fauna was present at both private and public masquerades. Mrs Boehm's June 1810 masked ball was not only brilliantly illuminated, but also decked in a variety of real and artificial greenery and flowers. The balconies were filled with variegated shrubs and flowers, the hall and staircase with plants and arched bowers entwined with real and faux flowers as well as laurel and oak leaves.[56] Laurel leaves have traditionally been a sign of victory, while oak leaves represent strength and endurance, significant to the Empire as it was engaged in conflicts abroad.

National identity, war, and peace were not the only themes expressed through flora and fauna. A private ball in 1822 at the Shropshire home, Heath House of T. Beale, Esq. featured myrtle and flowers to accentuate the theme of Bazaar.[57] A fashionable interest in the imperialist exploits abroad was frequently woven into the designs and elements of masquerades. Beyond a fascination with other cultures, there were also elements of the romantic and natural in these displays. The practical benefit of flowers and greenery to treat the olfactory senses while also delighting the eyes also strengthened its presence at most masquerades; numerous stories about masquerades shared the sweet smell of flowers. One example was Almack's, decked with festoons of artificial flowers interlaced with real blossoms, so that the room was filled with a delightful fragrance as well as the lush beauty of the floral décor for an 1820 masquerade.[58] Frequent mentions of fairy kingdoms harkened to Romanticism and naturalism, and overall the emphasis on nature seemed synonymous with pleasure, entertainment, and relaxation. When combined with the sensory delighting features, like flowers and bright lights, it was easy to see why decoration emphasised the natural.

The cost would require some support by artificial flowers and greenery. Reports frequently mentioned the natural and artificial being artfully woven together to create the scene, and there was a sense of pride and elegance about even the artificial flora and fauna. Artificial flowers were generally a common accessory for décor and fashion. France was particularly famous, during the era, for artificial flowers and many instructionals on their creation referenced French materials or methods. Cambric, a light plain weave fabric originally from the northern France region, was often thought of as the main material for artificial flowers but linen, feathers, silk, tissue paper, and taffeta were also popular for construction.[59] Wires were used for the stalk and elements of leaves and petals to maintain a shapeable form that could be affixed to clothing, hats, or decoration. Gum paste was used to hold the items together and help give the flowers their shape.

Like transparencies, these were a popular Regency home craft with directions in several era books that suggested sugar, gum paste, and fabric as mediums for making them. Various pigments could be used to dye the flowers, and eggshells were used to shape the petals. Leaves were also made from gum paste, or fruit peels, and dried fruit could also be used to add to the homemade flowers.[60] Advertisements directed at women promised every colour and shade of India paper, ideal for making artificial flowers. Schools for young ladies would even advertise the making of artificial flowers in the list of arts and crafts taught at the schools.[61] Italy was credited, in one article, for originally creating flowers from ribbons and feathers, before graduating to cambric and silk.[62]

Advertisements suggest that artificial flowers were easy enough to come by in cities across the United Kingdom. Typical vendors were silk manufacturers, milliners, haberdashers, modistes, and wholesalers. The flowers were often promoted as of French, Italian, or English origin. There was a cluster of artificial flower makers in Westminster, with flower makers being both men and women.[63] Italy was recognised by most as the originator of artificial flowers, but by the Regency era there was a steady industry of flower makers across Great Britain. It was often discussed in trade guidebooks as reliable employment for women. In the large quantities needed to decorate a venue, rather than a hat or gown, artificial flowers could also be hired from theatre companies or warehouses specialising in décor rental. Doubtless many of the primary venues also had a collection of decorations available for a variety of events.

Mixing the artificial flowers with real flowers was cost effective while also providing the pleasing sense of smell and touch real flowers offered. But it also had the benefit of supporting a chosen theme. Flowers had their own language, so that a hostess, host, or impresario could send subtle but understandable messages through strategic selection of floral accents. Roses were the most obvious national flower originating with the Tudor era, and the oak had long been the English national tree, representing endurance and strength. Thistle is a national symbol of Scotland and the leek of Wales. These symbols would be repeated in other elements of the event's décor, including on the ballroom floors. Even today pastoral landscapes and nature are rooted in British national identity,[64] a sense of belonging deeply tied to the flora, fauna, and trees. Coupled with the romantic element of a natural fairy garden and the other aspects of symbolism, flora and fauna were a meaningful, luxurious addition to the masquerade décor.

The final common element for many masquerades was a chalked or painted floor. It was not unique to masquerades, but rather at many exclusive events for the haute ton. Chalk would typically be employed to decorate the floor with different shapes, dance figures, or other decorative features. In addition to enhancing the event décor, chalking was also useful to keep guests from slipping, given the often smooth leather soles women and men would wear to a ball. This replaced an earlier trend of individual dancers chalking the bottom of their shoes before dancing. Chalking also could be used to cover worn floors, particularly with the emphasis on bright lighting being the order of the day.[65] Preventing common slips and accidents and dampening any ill contrast with the luxurious chandeliers and other décor, chalking was both a safety feature and often a necessary cover up by way of embellishment.[66]

There are some current sources that cite 1808 as the year floor chalking began, but primary sources from the era suggests it occurred at least as early as 1790, with one example being at the Wargrave masquerade that happened in September of that year.[67] An article from August in 1790 stated that a new luxury was lately introduced into the ballrooms of great families hosting events. The article shared that once the carpets were removed for dancing, an artist was employed to cover the floor with flower garlands and other devices with French chalk, and this ingenious technique was not only beautiful but practical to hide worn, naked floors from view and keep feet from slipping while dancing.[68] It was a clever evolution from individuals chalking their soles, and a novel decoration when first seen that became a staple of the fashionable event. Another early example was the Duchess of Cumberland's December 1791 ball, which featured chalked floors, coloured foil ornaments, and artificial floral wreaths.[69]

Impresarios or private hostesses and hosts would typically employ a professional artist to design and chalk the floors. Some of the hired artists, based on evidence, were scene painters from local theatres, but others might be painters or other fine artists. Names of artists mentioned in reports on chalked floors included Mr Calton and Mr Glover of Brook Street. Beyond professional artists, there were other enterprising tradespeople who were available for chalking floors and also providing chairs, tables, and other items for parties including Route Furniture who advertised his services and supplies throughout the 1820s in London and a Shirley, in Great Marylebone Street, who also was responsible for the lighting of an 1809 ball. There were also reports of amateur chalkers, including people within the household, but it's likely that it would have taken a non-professional some time to accomplish given the scale of the rooms and often the intricacies demanded by fashion. In that case, it's understandable that a professional would be preferred.

Chalked floors would often smudge after the first dance, the designs lost. This had the benefit of encouraging early attendance for those who wanted to see the grand effect. The fleeting nature of these extensive and often expensive designs underscored the sense of luxury many masquerades aimed to achieve. For masquerades, both commercial and private, it is easy to see why investments in chalked floors were necessary to add to the ambience established through lighting, transparencies, and flora and fauna. While chalk was the most common of floor covering during the long Regency, there were a few other techniques artists sometimes employed on the ballroom floors.

The crayon floors at the June 1802 Foley House masquerade were said to give the scene a brilliance,[70] a sentiment that would be repeated throughout newspaper coverage of masked and fancy dress balls. Crayon is a French word that dates to around the sixteenth century and originally meant chalk pencil. The more modern crayon would be developed in Paris around 1828, but prior to that it would have been a mix of charcoal and oil or pigment and oil. Whereas chalk was largely white, black, or red, crayons could be made into reds, blues, yellows, browns, purples and blacks.[71] Doubtless a crafty artist could have also combined the pigments to make other colours like green or to meet the exact shade of flowers, fabric, or other inspiration. From primary research, it appears artists would use chalk, crayons, or watercolours to make their floor designs. White chalk, by the mid-1800s, was favoured because it created less staining on guest garments, but there is evidence to suggest coloured chalks and watercolours were not unusual to see on the floors of a masquerade or ball during the Regency period. Lady Carrington's ball in 1801 featured satin wallpaper, bright lights, and coloured chalk flowers with a flower motif.[72] The coloured floors for Lady Carrington's event were the main décor item, and much admired. Lady Lidell's ball in April 1816 would feature the artistry of Mr Glover, with chalked ballroom floors resembling bouquets of flowers and Etruscan scrolls, and appearing like crayon paintings.[73]

The designs could be practical but also often favoured common themes seen in the shape of lights, transparencies, and the selected greenery. In the 1790s, floral arrangements were most common. But by the turn of the nineteenth century, the designs would flourish. The Argyll Rooms' June 1806 masquerade had chalked floors, with dancing figures, the prince's feathers, flowers, and an Etruscan border. Described as novel, the floors represented some of the more popular elements of a Regency masquerade floor design.[74] Other common elements of chalked floors included coat of arms, the Union arms, symbols of peace, medallions of the admirals or other military insignia, mosaics inspired by exotic locations including Arabesque and Egyptian designs, shapes, and other symbols of meaning to attendees. Mottoes were also frequently mentioned in newspaper reports and other publications as making up the chalked floor design, as well as initials.

The Marchioness of Abercorn's 1805 ball had floors chalked in watercolours, with the Imperial Union represented as the centrepiece and surrounded by various national emblems including the rose, thistle, shamrock, crown, and the motto 'Tria Juncta in Una'.[75] An April 1827 masquerade had the floor chalked with mottoes.[76] Lady le Despencer's masquerade in 1805 featured an Egyptian-style chalking with Vandyke border in several apartments with the temporary ballroom in the garden surrounded by shrubs, laurel, and pots of fragrant flowers and the centrepiece of the floor in Grecian style was the ship, *Victory*, encased by trophies, music, flowers and mollusc shapes. Even the grand staircase was chalked with Egyptian designs leading to the upper rooms, one of which was reserved for the Prince Regent and his party.[77] An 1806 ball had Egyptian sphynxes circled by flowers.[78] Military symbols, the monarchy, flora and fauna, and exotic motifs were the mostly commonly reported chalked designs for masquerades.

Variations on chalk, watercolour, or crayon floors would continue to be a part of the overall pageantry of the masked ball. There were some hopes for a new variation; a report on an 1820 assembly at the Argyll Rooms proclaimed that the day of chalked floors had come and gone, sharing that the floors were instead rubbed with wax that was much cheaper and did not create dust or ruin silk hose and slippers.[79] However, it wasn't the end of chalked floors, and they would continue to be a favoured decoration well into the Victorian era. Indeed, the convention of decorated floors spread not only throughout Great Britain but to other Empire strongholds like Calcutta.

It is clear from a review of first hand reporting, most public and private masquerades had a well-established aesthetic that relied on brilliant and creative lighting, novelty pieces like transparencies, an abundance of greenery and flowers, and practical yet whimsical floor coverings. What brings all these décor elements together was not only their consistent presence across venues and private homes, and throughout the decades of the Regency, but also the familiarity of symbols used. Although the individual artist interpretation was different, often times the themes and symbols repeated themselves over the Regency. Some of the symbols were obviously alluding to and attempting to reinforce national identity: Britannia, the Union Jack, the rose, the thistle, the shamrock, military icons, country mottos, tributes to national heroes and royalty. The Prince of Wales's feathers alluded to the heraldic badge of the title, and would have been used in the Regency era in acknowledgment of the many discussions, bills, and final ascension of the Prince of Wales to Prince Regent in 1811. In 1820, when George IV formally ascended to the throne after his father's death, the plumes of the Prince of Wales would take a marked decline in use among masquerade decorations, replaced with other symbols of the monarchy.

There is evidence that, along with the combination of England and Scotland as states in the early eighteenth century, imperialism necessitated an emphasis on British, rather than English, national identity.[80] By the Regency period, the British State and its Empire were entrenched in an individual, particularly the elite's, praxis of national identity. It supported further expansion of the Empire, rapid industrialisation, and the development of a national character that emphasises Britishness; the engine of production that necessitated colonisation and industrialisation worked to tell a story of what it was to be British. The costumes at masquerades played with these concepts in more obvious ways, but the décor more subtly engaged with symbols including a sense of Britishness. There was still a reference, in many cases, to Englishness, but nonetheless the symbols underscored the significantly larger footprint of the monarchy and the British military.

The imperial footprint also introduced other cultures as part of the symbology. Egyptian Revival and its influences over architecture throughout the eighteenth and nineteenth centuries in England was strengthened by Napoleon's invasion of Egypt in 1798. Teams of over 100 scientists, artists, and others from France accompanied Napoleon's expedition to catalogue the artefacts and discoveries in Egypt, resulting in the publication of *The Description of Egypt* beginning in 1809. This series, brought to life with detailed engravings, pyramids, sculptures, hieroglyphics, and the scenery of

Van Loo, Jean-Baptiste, 'John James Heidegger', 1749. (*Public domain image, via Wikimedia Commons*)

John Bowles, 1701–1779, 'The Chinese House, the Rotunda, and the Company in Masquerade in Ranelagh Gardens'. (*Public domain image, via Yale Center for British Art, Paul Mellon Collection*)

Grignion, Charles, 'A View of the Canal, Chinese Building, Rotundo and Church in Ranelagh Gardens with the Masquerade'. (*Public domain image, via Yale Center for British Art, Paul Mellon Collection*)

Bowles, Thomas and Samuel Wale, 'A View of the Chinese Pavilions and Boxes in Vauxhall Gardens', 1751. (*Public domain image, via Yale Center for British Art, Paul Mellon Collection*)

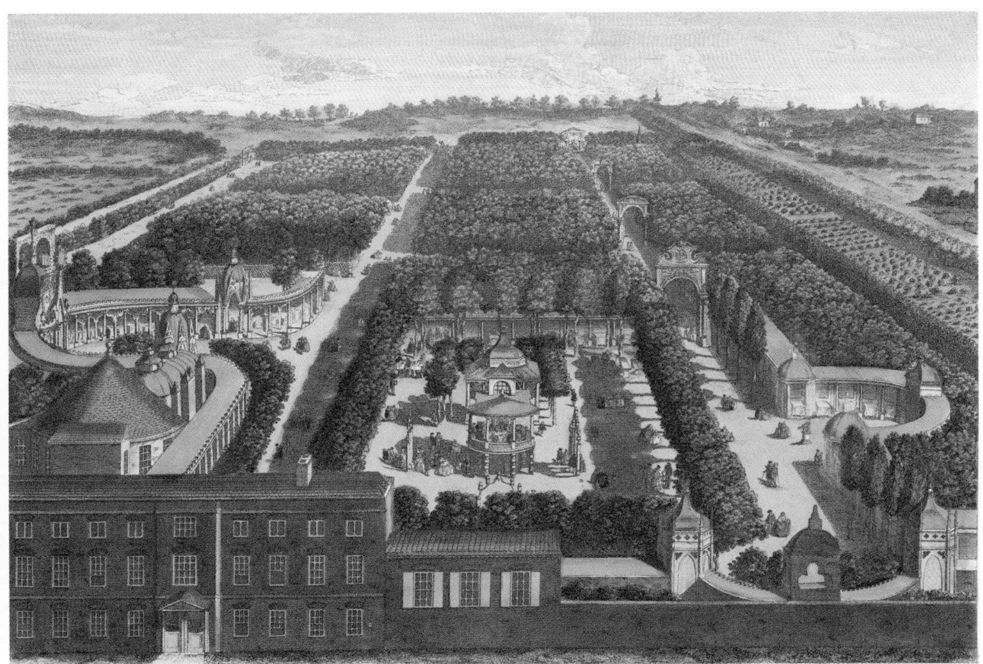

Muller, John and Samuel Wale, 'A General Prospect of the Vauxhall Gardens, Shewing at One View the Disposition of the Whole Gardens'. (*Public domain image, via Yale Center for British Art, Paul Mellon Collection*)

Wyatt, James, 'A Cross Section of the rotunda of the Pantheon', 1769. (*Public domain image, via Wikimedia Commons*)

Rowlandson, Thomas, 'Dressing for a Masquerade', April 1, 1790. (*Public domain image, via The Met*)

Williams, Charles, 'The Union Club Masquerade', 1802. (*Public domain image via Yale Center for British Art, Paul Mellon Collection*)

Burney, Edward Francis and James Gillray, 'The Pic-Nic Orchestra', 1802. (*Public domain image, via Wikimedia Commons*)

Bosio, Jean Francois and Anonymous, 'Bal de L'Opera', 1804. (*Public domain image, via The Rijksmuseum*)

Rowlandson, Thomas and Augustus Charles Pugin, 'A masquerade in the rebuilt and modified Pantheon, circa 1809'. (*Public domain image, via Wikimedia Commons*)

Rowlandson, Thomas, 'The Dance of Death: The Masquerade', 1816. (*Public domain image, via Wellcome Collection*)

Rowlandson, Thomas and Augustus Charles Pugin, 'Interior of second theatre (Haymarket) on the site, circa 1808'. (*Public domain image, via Wikimedia Commons*)

Rowlandson, Thomas and Augustus Charles Pugin, 'Vauxhall Garden from Ackerman's Repository', 1809. (*Public domain image, via Yale Center for British Art, Paul Mellon Collection*)

Almack's Assembly Rooms in King Street. (*Public domain image, via Wikimedia Commons*)

Alken, Henry Thomas, 'Masquerade, Tom & Bob Keeping It in Real Character', September 20, 1821. (*Public domain image, via Yale Center for British Art, Paul Mellon Collection*)

Wallis, Rober and Thomas Hosmer Shepherd, 'Argyle Rooms, Regent Street'. (*Public domain image, via Yale Center for British Art, Paul Mellon Collection*)

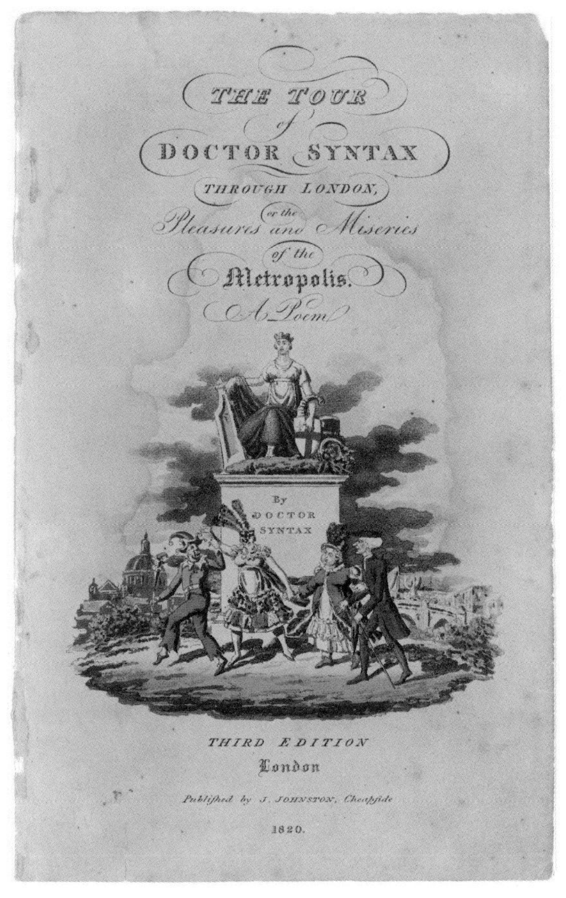

THE TOUR
of
DOCTOR SYNTAX
THROUGH LONDON,
or the
Pleasures and Miseries
of the
Metropolis.
A Poem

By
DOCTOR
SYNTAX

THIRD EDITION
London

Published by J. JOHNSTON, Cheapside

1820.

Cruikshank, Robert Isaac, Thomas Rowlandson and John Johnston, 'The Tour of Doctor Syntax', 1820. (*Public domain image, via The Rijksmuseum*)

Roberts, Pierce, 'Mr. Grimaldi as Joey the Clown', July 13, 1822. (*Public domain image, via Harris Brisbane Dick Fund, 1917; The Met*)

Hutchison, Joseph, 'Madame Saqui, the celebrated performer on the rope, at Vauxhall', 1820. (*Public domain image, via The New York Public Library Digital Collections*)

Cruikshank, George, 'London's High Society at Almack's', 1821. (*Public domain image, via Wikimedia Commons*)

Lane, Theodor, 'Masquerade, Argyll Rooms', 1826. (*Public domain image, via Wikimedia Commons*)

Shepherd, Thomas Hosmer, 'Drawing of the theatre (Haymarket)', 1827. (*Public domain image, via Wikimedia Commons*)

'Robert Isaac Cruikshank, 1789–1856', British, C. H. Simpson, Esq. M.C.R.G.V., 1833, Aquatint. (*Public domain image, via Yale Center for British Art, Paul Mellon Collection, B1977.14.18723*)

Lawrence, Thomas, 'Arthur Wellesley, 1st Duke of Wellington', 1815. (*Public domain image, via Wikimedia Commons*)

Lawrence, Thomas, 'King George IV', 1814. (*Public domain image, via Wikimedia Commons*)

Domino Mask. (*Public domain image, via Wikimedia Commons*)

'Duke of Gloucester's Band', 1811. (*Public domain image, via Wikimedia Commons*)

Lee, John, 'Instruments of Music, Pandean Minstrels in Performance at Vauxhall', 1806. (*Public domain image, via Wikimedia Commons*)

Larousse, 'Travestis Plate I', 1932. (*Public domain image, via Wikimedia Commons*)

TRAVESTIS

Larousse, 'Travestis Plate II', 1932. (*Public domain image, via Wikimedia Commons*)

Egypt inspired a new generation of interest in Egyptian culture. This interest would quickly have an influence on everything from furniture to fashion.

Thomas Hope, a Regency designer, opened his house on Duchess Street for viewing. It included an Egyptian room and an Egyptian influenced façade, which in turn enforced the designs of Hope's popular *Household Furniture* that included many designs of tables, chairs, settees and furnishings that included sphynxes, winged suns, and griffins. Hope had wished to influence the grand homes and people of the Regency, and was successful in creating an Egyptian trend although the style was a fusion of classical Egyptian symbols and modern British elements that were coined English Empire style. The title references the Empire style, named after Napoleon and representing the second iteration of Neoclassicism that rose in the 1760s in response to the then dominate Rococo style. The Rococo style was notable for emphasising ornamentation and asymmetry, while Neoclassicism reverted to simplicity and symmetry. The Empire style was most popular between 1800 and 1815, with the English Empire hitting London several years after.

Along with Egyptian motifs, Greco-Roman tributes were also popular and equally championed by influencers like Hope. In the posthumously published *An Historical Essay on Architecture,* Hope mused on Egyptian, Greek, Roman, Persian, and other classical cultures and their influences on architecture on art. As with Egyptian symbols recurrent in the décor of the Regency masquerades, so were Greek and Roman forms. From furniture and architecture to clothing and jewellery, classical elements were popular in the early nineteenth century.

Hope was not the only influencer bringing classical elements to the residents of Great Britain. Popular destinations in Regency England included the Egyptian Hall in London, the Egyptian Library in Devonport, the Egyptian House in Cornwall, and numerous other churches, lodges, monuments, mills, and industrial buildings designed in the Egyptian Revival style. Many furniture makers including George Smith, Thomas Sheraton, Augustus Pugin, and J. Stafford would use Egyptian, Greek, and Roman motifs in their designs. Well into the Victorian era, Egyptomania would proliferate into everything from jewellery designs to marketing on cosmetics.

Similarly, there was a devotion to Greco-Roman elements. Shelley stated in 1821 the belief that Greece was the birthplace of the civilised West, enlightenment being a gift from Ancient Greece that was further developed by British elites.[81] As trends of the time, Neoclassic elements were obvious choices for décor. Not only did many of the venues carry a Greek Revival style, with their Ionic pillars and Greco-Roman busts, but the tie-in with nationalism at the masquerades helped to express an emergent version of Neoclassicism of reserve that, despite conflicting with the bacchanalian roots, produced events that were orderly and celebrated the monarchy. Regency architecture, in this Greek Revival tradition, chose a more understated symmetry than Georgian Neoclassicism that spoke to similar trends in fashion, furniture, music, and art.

Beyond Egyptian and Greco-Roman influences, the emphasis on nature, including greenery and flowers, was representative of the very active Romantic movement that was, in part, a response of the beginning stages of the Industrial Revolution. As Romanticism spread through all facets of British culture, including poetry and literature, art, music, and architecture, its influence was evident in the gatherings of the haute ton. Some scholars have posited that Romanticism was itself a response to Neoclassicism, but in application it seems as often these two styles would be blended together harmoniously to evoke a strong sense of place and belonging. Hearts, flowers, and doves were easy symbols to weave into lighting, transparencies, and chalking to conjure the themes many of the attendees would have been engaged with in poetry, like that of Byron, in literature, like with Austen or the Brontës, and in art, like Koch.

Romantic nationalism is a newer concept that combines the two concepts of Romanticism and nationalism that became a force in the early 1800s. Leerssen (2013) wrote the technological advancements of industrialisation, including mass volume printing and investments in state-controlled libraries, archives, museums, and university systems as having given birth to both Romanticism and nationalism. International conflict, too, Leerssen posited, helped to reinforce broader socio-political trends. In turn, these socio-political developments including war had a direct influence on arts and culture. This manifested in masquerades, and other special events, that presented seemingly conflicting themes like patriotism, military pride, folk music, and nature in its most whimsical forms. Leerssen argued that both Romanticism and nationalism combine dynamic progressivism and nostalgia for permanence in a dialogue that seems contradictory, but yet serves remarkably to reproduce itself.

All of the elements, from bright lights to heroic transparencies, to an overabundance of flora and fauna and to chalked floors, leveraged these cultural symbols. Neoclassicism, Egyptomania, and Romanticism were coupled with other, more overt symbols of national identity including military and monarchy signs. With masquerades, the appearance of these themes served not only to underscore luxury, fashion, and national identity, but also to immerse the attendee in a cultural conversation. Without even considering the performance of costume or music, the masquerade milieu followed a well-worn pattern for expression favouring the power elite. The masked ball was an opportunity to escape the shackles of propriety and expectation by diving into anonymity, if only fleetingly. However, in as insular circles as these events occurred, the anonymity was more of a performance than in truth; the experience of the masquerade was in many respects curated to give a sense of risqué and risk, all the while propping up the themes, symbols, and sense of place and belonging within the aristocratic, gentry, and fashionable persons within Regency society. In some respects, it is an early form of the hyperreal where the consumption of a cultural experience was the drive for a repetitive production of Britishness, Romanticism, Neoclassicism, and more strikingly, a play on culture as performance.

Other performances elevated these sensibilities of the masquerade events. Spectacle, with paid actors and acrobats, fireworks, or other interactive elements heightened the experience for attendees and also reinforced some of the broader themes of the masquerades. In reviewing Regency masquerades, a basic formula for the event program is apparent. At least one band, but commonly two, were the minimum for entertainment and enabled dancing. For the larger commercial venues, paid performers and fireworks were added elements that enhanced the overall grandness. In the next chapter, we will review the spectacular elements of the long Regency masquerade and its tie-in to the other aspects of these events.

## Chapter Eight

# Fireworks, Music, Dancing, and the Spectacle of Masquerades

King's Theatre was brilliantly lit by lamps in a variety of devices, two bands playing as the attendees spilled through the rooms inhaling the spectacle and showcasing their characters until the one o'clock supper. What seemed like a pattern card masquerade would be enhanced by dedicated spectacle. A rope was suspended, in the style of Vauxhall Gardens, from which numerous fireworks were set alight. When the fireworks were not active, rope dancers used the ropes to display majestic feats of acrobatics for the busy February 1817 crowd.[1] The spectacle was not original, but it was nonetheless breathtaking for much of the audience, steeped in the spirit of the masquerade.

King's Theatre was not the only venue to ape the known theatrics and death defying feats commonly seen at Vauxhall Pleasure Gardens. The Argyll Rooms held a Bal Masque in February 1826 that featured Signor Antonio on the slack rope and two characters in Swiss costume on stilts wading through the crowds.[2] Waiter's July 1814 masquerade at Burlington House, described as one of the most brilliant amusements of its kind, featured a family of rope dancers, jugglers, and famous pantomime performers Grimaldi and Bologna. A ballet was performed, professional singers stalked the crowds, and a Lottery of Bijoux was announced at twelve thirty in the morning.[3] Each element was carefully orchestrated to keep the crowd engaged, amazed, and sure to return.

These three examples show the lengths promoters and clubs were willing to go to introduce novelty into masquerade events, entertaining the crowds with acrobatics, comedy, dance, and music. Spectacle was a significant part of the Regency masquerade. The crowds and media were not content with a mere ball and masked party, particularly for the larger venues, and even the theatrical performances of costumed characters did not suffice. Masquerades, from the very end of the eighteenth century to the middle of the nineteenth century became grander, with more exciting additions in performances, décor, and spectacle. Without these, the critics were ruthless and the crowds thin; even a good cause was often not enough to bring out the numbers needed to call a masquerade a grand success.

The scale of spectacle depended on the size and location of the venue. Large properties like the Pleasure Gardens had more opportunities for a diversity of entertainment when compared with the smaller places like the Willis' Rooms. They also had the pressure of needing to sell more tickets to make their events feel grand and interesting when compared with private homes or exclusive locations. However, there were common threads that emerge through a study of the Regency masquerade including music and dancing; dancing and several bands became nearly mandatory for a successful Regency masquerade. The larger venues would top these mainstay entertainments with exhibitions of fireworks and performers and sometimes enticements to special, celebrity guests.

Like other balls of the era, dancing was a standard feature of the Regency masquerade. Dancing was a popular form of amusement because it brought the sexes together in an activity that would allow them to be close and touch in ways that they ordinarily could not, due to propriety standards. At the masquerade, dancing would often be one of the main forms of activity over what usually spanned eight hours of night to early morning. Rust (1968) tracked the history of dance through the nineteenth century, from the popularity of country dances to the rise in the waltz and quadrille. Rust shared a theory that the waltz had an uncanny similarity to the rotary power of the steam engine, aligning bodily expression with the industrial rhythms. While there may have been a subconscious development of movement along the lines of manufacturing, what is more plain is that dance is a common expression of a culture and a way that supports community. The Regency was no different, in that the dance reflected both the precision, reserve, and organisation of the culture, but also helped to reinforce it. The masquerade would seem to offer a deviance from the rigid rules of dance, yet there were only minor divergence from what was commonly seen at any other ball during the long Regency.

Based on a review of advertisements, country reels and dances were popular at the beginning of the nineteenth century, following by quadrilles and waltzing in the middle to end of the long Regency; the Pantheon's masquerade advertisements usually promised reels and country dances, and reports of other masquerades indicated quadrilles and waltzes were not uncommon. These were familiar dances to the fashionable and wealthy Regency crowds, a chief form of entertainment at many social events and a way to provide interaction between the sexes. Country reels and dances would have been less scandalous than waltzes. Thomas Wilson, Dancing Master, published various titles on dancing in the middle to late Regency era, and described country dance figures as movements or directions performed in circular, half circular, serpentine, angular, straight lines and other patterns according to the music.[4] Wilson was also hired on a few occasions to give lessons to attendees ahead of the masquerade, ensuring everyone could participate if they wanted to. Country dances had an influence on the court that began in the fifteenth century, so that by the eighteenth and nineteenth century it was a familiar style of dancing to most people. The reel was a version of a country dance that is generally described as more lively, fast paced, performed with paired partners and set to a specific style of music called the reel. Quadrilles were contra dances performed by four couples in a rectangular formation, and was credited to be popularised by Lady Jersey in 1816. While even these classic and familiar forms could be exploited by characters performing their costumed part or for initiating lascivious contact, these dances were generally socially acceptable forms of entertainment.

More controversial and aligned with the risqué reputation of the masquerade was the waltz. The waltz was credited with being brought into fashion by another Almack's patroness, and initially was scandalous because it involved a clenched pair making tight figures across the floor. Waltzes were mentioned more often in the 1810s, which coincides with its introduction to the English ballroom around 1812 or 1813. While it had arguably arrived in England as early as the 1790s, it was not until it was endorsed by Dorothea Lieven that it became more respectable in the eyes of society. Princess Lieven was a leader in London when she and her ambassador husband arrived in Great Britian around 1812, eventually becoming the first foreigner to serve as an Almack's patroness. Known to be high in the instep, her approval of the waltz would naturally have made the dance fashionable. It would still be viewed by many as indecent as late as the 1820s, but was nonetheless expected at the more risqué masquerades or at the balls of fashionable people. If enough bands were hired for the masquerade, it was not uncommon to see waltzing in one room and country dances in another, capable of accommodating the large gathering's tastes and abilities. Some balls supplied up to four separate rooms for dancing.

Larger venues would often have the concert room or other rooms designated for dancing throughout the night and into the morning so that guests could go from room to room selecting which entertainment they wanted to engage in at any given hour. Private or smaller balls tended to have a schedule of events, with dancing happening in the early morning hours. At the Argyll Rooms, dancing usually preceded supper by about an hour, around one o'clock. Private balls were often subject to the whims of the hostess or host. Viscount Courtenay's August 1801 masquerade did not see dancing start until around three o'clock, after supper, although the heat was blamed for making the guests inactive.[5] The Willingham Hall masquerade in April 1810 had dancing early in the evening, unmasking at half past one, followed by supper and then more dancing into the early morning.[6]

Because dancing was an expectation for most balls or similar events, the record does not spend much time discussing masquerade dancing except in instances where dancing was part of the entertainment guests offered others while being in character. At Louisa Manner's masquerade in July 1805, Mr Bailey and Sir James Stronge were dressed as modern ladies, and amused the crowd by dancing ahead of supper,[7] while at Mrs Champney's masquerade in January 1801 one guest dressed as dancing bear.[8] Even abroad, in Madras, a December 1812 masquerade was entertained by the minuet dancing of Mr Ellis, Miss Spry, Mr Wayte, and Miss Emma Spry, who were all dressed in the fashions from the late seventeenth century.[9] Mr Wilson, Dancing Master, advertised in the late 1810s to instruct both individuals and groups for character themed dancing at masquerades.[10] Doubtless it was a popular service for those gentlemen and ladies wanting to impress others with their wit and commitment to character.

Again and again, newspapers would highlight these masked dancing performances by both actors and guests. Father Christmas danced around with his holly bush, surrounded by joyful companions at the February 1822 King's Theatre masquerade.[11] Drury Lane Theatre's end of season June 1829 masquerade featured a temple inspired by Neptune and the Tritons where a Pandean band played and inspired various characters to enter and dance true to form, including a Flying Indian, a flight of Cupids, and an assortment of costumed guests dancing the quadrille or waltz.[12] The uncharacteristic dancing of a Hamlet, and the contrast of French Dancing masters compared with a Gorgon was remarked upon by *The Star* after an April 1829 King's Theatre masquerade.[13] A party dressed in Highland garb appeared at the Argyll Rooms in December 1823 and performed several Scotch Reels.[14] The whimsical departures from the standard dancing helped enhance the alien and novel, while during the quadrilles the very appearance of characters adhering to the rules of the dance inspired delight.[15]

Masquerades offered the opportunity, not only for character based dancing, but also a comic influence into the traditional ballroom activity. Guests at Waiter's masquerade at Burlington House on Friday, July 4, 1814 were amused by Grimaldi and Bologna waltzing on their hands, with their heels in the air while the rest of the party featured strange but amusing waltzing partners.[16] Masquerades also gave the audience an opportunity to explore other cultural traditions, including dancing, or give dancing performances. The King's Theatre, in April 1818, advertised a grand masquerade in celebration of Princess Elizabeth's wedding to include national dances of foreign dignitaries, in addition to country dances, waltzes and quadrilles familiar to the British crowd.[17] A May 1818 Covent Garden masquerade featured the *minuet de la cour* and Vestris's gavotte, danced by Monsieur and Mademoiselle Simon.[18] As expressed by the critics, nothing was more dreadful at a masquerade than an individual not playing up their character, and conversely the crowd and newspapers were delighted when someone acted true to the form they chose to don for the evening. When a comedic element was introduced through actions like dancing, particularly with a comedic costume like harlequin, it stood out as a high spot of the evening among press reports. While these deviations from the common figures of dancing would be part of the festive air of a masquerade, it's worthwhile acknowledging the underlying thread of dances aligned with overall society expectations and trends; masquerades may have offered some unusual or fantastical dancing performances or opportunities, but on the whole the dancing was familiar to the British attendees. There is a broad sense that dancing is a form of cultural expression, reflecting the values and traditions of a people. In this way, dancing at masquerades was one activity which helped to re-enforce the culture and national identity of those in attendance.

But it was not the only component that suggests a cultural significance. Dancing was supported by the music, another key to the masquerade. The formulae impresarios and hostesses abided by typically included at least two bands; bands were there to greet guests and provide a pomp and circumstance to the occasion as well as provide the soundtrack to dancing. There would be some variety in how this was executed or what bands were hired. However, bands would be an important ingredient in the success of a public or private masquerade. The lack of enough music, or poor performances, could spell disaster for an event. One masquerade was criticised for the presence of only one band, as the music was not continuous. Twenty minute lulls, evidently, decreased the perceived activity and quality of the event.[19] Conversely, a Pantheon masquerade in 1804 was complimented on excellent music that played without breaks and led to uninterrupted dancing. As the ball had a lack of character dress, the music and dancing were seen as the principal entertainment.[20] While later Regency masquerades would up the types of amusements on offer, for the earlier era events music and dancing were key features. Advertisements typically broadcasted that two bands would be available for dancing in separate rooms, and in addition many events included a military band in the entrance to welcome visitors.[21]

In part, the presence of a military band was due to the surplus of military musicians. The British military, by the late eighteenth century, was the single largest employer of musicians.[22] The term military band was applied more generically to bands made up of wood, wind, and brass instruments.[23] However, in most of the mentions of masquerade military bands, their regiment was cited indicating they were in fact bands from the British military. Regimental bands for the Foot Guards were particularly popular, as a carryover from the Georgian era, with special notice often given for performances by the 1st Foot Guards, also known as the Duke of York's band, or the 3rd Guards band, known as the Duke of Gloucester's band. The performers would wear the bright red military coats, with golden buttons and frogs, and white trousers tucked into black boots. Typically they would be capped by a tricorn, and no doubt made a striking appearance for those entering the balls. The Coldstream Regiment of guards would provide the background music for supper at an April 1818 King's Theatre masquerade.[24] The Duke of York's band welcomed people at the foot of the stairs and played the entire night at a Martindale's 1802 subscription masquerade.[25] The Duke of Gloucester's Regiment band, alongside another band for dancing, played to King's Theatre crowds in June 1805.[26] Over and over again, from the beginning to the end of the long Regency, military music was woven into the masquerade.

By the Victorian era, the military would begin to influence many facets of the popular culture in Great Britain, in conjunction with imperialism, but the seeds of this development would be planted in the Georgian era and begin to grow during the Regency. The presence of these bands at popular events like masquerades that emphasised spectacle, underscored the importance of national identity in generating a sense of place and belonging. Particularly during times of war, the military band would serve as a symbol or connection to British armed forces abroad. That the sight and sound of these uniformed musicians evoked feelings of patriotism and pride was strategic.[27] Under the pretence of celebrating war efforts, the military was woven into many of the aspects of the Regency masquerade and the military band was one of the more obvious displays.

While one military band was fairly standard, it was not always the case. A grand masquerade at the Argyll Rooms had the Pandean Minstrels group in the hall and Gow's band, for dancing, in the ballrooms.[28] The Pandean Minstrels were a popular musical group that played a variety of dancing music styles and were known to simultaneously play the Pandean pipes and a percussion instrument, which was a novelty.[29] The Pandean Minstrels were commonly seen at Vauxhall Gardens from around 1802 to 1820 and included a troupe of five musicians that were known to dress in exotic, elaborate costumes.[30] Typically an alternative to the military band, they would often be stationed at the entrance or in one of the salons, although on occasion they would also provide music for dancing.

The other band at the Argyll Rooms, Gow's band, was also a popular choice for dancing. The Gow brothers, Nathaniel and John, were band leaders and publishers. Nathaniel was one of the most fashionable and famous band leaders of the Regency, comparable to Almack's James Paine. Because Nathaniel was largely Edinburgh based, it was more likely John, or Jock, who led the London based Gow's band.[31] Employing one of these very popular and fashionable brothers to play was a significant attraction for attendees. This combination of the Gow's band and Pandean Minstrels had been seen several years before at Mrs Egerton's masquerade in July of 1805.[32]

Other novelties or popular bands would also deviate from the standard selection. A masquerade in 1804 featured a full instrumental band on hire from the Opera House, while a band of Savoyards appeared in another part of the ball.[33] Mackintosh's band, along with a military band, and two Savoyard bands played for the Nelson Victory masquerade celebration at the

Pantheon in April 1801.[34] A year later, at a January Pantheon masquerade, Mackintosh's Band of Music, a band of Savoyards, and a military band performed.[35] A month later, Mr Mackintosh would lead the two bands at the King's Theatre masquerade.[36] Mr Mackintosh was a band leader that played at a variety of Regency venues including Vauxhall. An advertisement for Westminster and City Assemblies praised Gow and Mackintosh as two of the best ball music performers in the country.[37]

There were other popular band leaders that would also grace the orchestra stands of masquerades, including sometimes being hired for private masked balls. J. Weippert's band would play to the crowd at Mrs E. Goldsmid's fancy dress ball and supper in May 1828.[38] John Weippert was a composer, author, and conductor for many years of the Royal Quadrille Band, who would achieve fame and notoriety well into the Victorian era. While the Gow's band continued to flourish into the 1810s, introducing French quadrilles to London in 1817 and a variety of Scottish folk songs as reels and quadrilles to London throughout the 1820s, Mackintosh disappeared from the advertisements and other publications as a noted band leader. Gow's band continued to dominate the Argyll Rooms masquerades, while other unnamed band leaders took over for the various other masquerade venues. Gow's influence on the quadrille was notable. A Christmas time masquerade on 29 December 1829 featured the quadrille bands Litolff and Adam, accompanied by professional dancers, to entertain the crowds.[39] Quadrille bands would be particularly popular in the 1820s, being the primary dancing band while the military band would be stationed as a welcome near the entrance. This would continue into the 1830s, with venues like the Lowther Rooms hiring a Pandean band to entertain and a quadrille band for dancing.[40]

While most masquerades stuck to the two bands per event, on occasion a producer would splash out to provide multiple rooms for different styles of dancing; the Argyll Rooms provided a variety of music styles for attendees at His Majesty's birthday masked fete in April 1823. Military, Pandean, quadrille, country, and other bands were placed in separate rooms along with celebrated Dancing Master, Thomas Wilson, performing the tendue ballet, and Signor Antonio on a cloud swing.[41] There were also occasions, desirous of maintaining continuous music, that a venue or private event would have different bands playing at different points in the evening. While it was not notable, when compared with the superstar band leaders or pageantry of military bands, critics would certainly mention lulls or uninspired musical support to the masquerade.

In addition to bands, the event producers would also provide other musical acts. The Theatre Royal's May 1821 masquerade paid serenaders, ballad, and glee singers, and seventy instrumental performers sprinkled throughout the venue to play for the guests.[42] Professional glee artists, Savoyards, and minstrels strolled through Vauxhall Gardens on the occasion of July 1821's masquerade, in addition to a group of Morris Dancers.[43] King's Theatre's June 1828 masquerade featured a musical soiree with crowded orchestras throughout the theatre playing a variety of pieces and producing a pleasing result for attendees, who felt the promoter, Mr Wright, had achieved proximity to the Italian Carnival.[44] Bigger and better, the stakes for impressive musical accompaniment to the masquerades would increase until the end of the long Regency. While the Lowther Rooms would be criticised for its decided lack of spectacle and luxury, the expectation for many other venues was for it to top past masquerades in the imaginations of the public.

Beyond paid musical performances, it was not unusual for the attendees in character to entertain with catches, glees, and song. Two men dressed as ballad singers entertained the King's Theatre masquerade crowds in April 1818 with two or three songs including *The Groves of Poole*.[45] An 1804 Pantheon masquerade had a Muffin Man ringing his bell to the tune of *Who Wants Me* and offering his muffins.[46] The 1806 June Argyll Rooms masquerade kept the party going until half past nine in the morning, as a number of ladies and gentlemen sang glees, duets, and songs to the captivation of the crowd.[47] The Argyll Rooms December 1829 supper rooms were filled with music, catch and glee abound to the delight of guests.[48] In a well praised 1828 June King's Theatre masquerade, glee singers added to the overall pleasing effect of the event and helped set a cheerful tone.[49] Mrs Dottin's masquerade included a group of Banditti who sang a series of glees, as well as a ballad singer, and a blind fiddler and piper that played for the much amused company.[50]

Music and dancing were both an expected but often surprising element to the Regency masquerade. Clever hostesses and smart impresarios would not only supply the right amount of ceremony and overture to national identity by stationing a military band upon the entrance, but they would also introduce novelty into the otherwise pattern card elements of dancing and music. There are hints in the record that dancing at masquerades, particularly the public venues, would often be of a more licentious variety than would be seen in the private ballrooms of London town homes, but this also added to the expectation of the masquerade as a site of bacchanalian delights. With these basic elements masterfully executed at the more successful events, many public venues, and even some private homes, would seek out increasingly larger spectacles to wow crowds and underscore the luxury and pleasure pursuit of the Regency masquerade. This included paid performances of daring, amusement, and bombastic displays of ballooning and fireworks.

Fireworks were likely introduced in the late thirteenth century in Great Britain as a result of trade. Originating in China, fireworks were traditionally a blend of charcoal, sulphur, and saltpetre. The introduction of this mixture inspired the development of gunpowder. As gunpowder began to revolutionise armed conflicts in the fourteenth century, scientists were experimenting with different formulas and fireworks began to be used all over Europe for royal celebrations and events. Large celebrations like the 1763 Treaty of Paris on occasion resulted in casualties and a fire, but this did not discourage the use of fireworks into the Regency era.

Fireworks were most popular at outdoor venues, like the Pleasure Gardens, and would often be combined with music to inspire and amaze the guests. Ranelagh was one of the first public destinations to regularly give fireworks shows and featured the pyrotechnists Angelo and Son, who helped establish the popularity of fireworks displays.[51] The Vauxhall fireworks started in 1798 and would build up to a regular occurrence by 1813.[52] Vauxhall had a staple of well-known pyrotechnists, including Chevalier Southby, Signor Mortram, and Madame Hengler.[53] Sarah Hengler (nee Fields) was the second wife of circus performer John Michael Hengler, and had a successful career creating firework displays for Vauxhall, Astley's Royal Amphitheatre, the Royal Circus, and Surrey Theatre. After her husband's death, she remarried and ran her fireworks display business until her death. She was not the only woman in the fireworks business, as Madame Coton was another notable fireworks artisan who directed fireworks at Vauxhall for a time.[54]

J. Southby, also styled as Chevalier Southby, had his place of business at No. 8 Saville Place, Lambeth Walk and displayed his fireworks artistry at several venues, in addition to Vauxhall. Advertisements for Southby's services were published well into the mid-1800s, suggesting a long and successful career as a pyrotechnist. Signor Vincento de Mortram, whose factory was in Mead Place, St George's Fields, was forced to take a three year hiatus after his factory burned to the ground in 1818. There was some intimation that it may have been caused by a competitor, as Hengler was able to obtain near exclusive contracts at Vauxhall during those three years. However, while Hengler, Mortram, and Southby would often compete they also frequently collaborated on fireworks displays at Vauxhall and other venues.

Vauxhall would launch its display from a fireworks tower that contained atop the structure a large tank capable of 12,000 gallons of water, and included a painting room below. When a fire broke out in the tower in the summer of 1837, the water tank, with 8000 gallons contained, came crashing down but did not extinguish the flames that would burn the tower and the painting room to the ground.[55] Through the quick acting firemen and police, the fire did not spread to the nearby steam engine works and saw mills, likely saving many lives. The fire did burn between fourteen and fifteen trees to the ground, in addition to destroying the painted scenes inside the painting room.[56]

The fireworks tower had been indispensable to the fireworks displays, capable of achieving great heights. The structure was between 60 and 80 feet in height, lending itself to other performances besides fireworks like rope dancing and tightrope walking. Most famously, Madame Saqui summited the tower via rope in 1815 during the fireworks display.[57] The fireworks show typically commenced at half eleven or midnight. The show lasted about an hour, to be followed by dancing and then supper.[58] Vast and bright, the Vauxhall fireworks would light up the night sky regardless of the size of the crowds and be the high spot of most guests' evenings.[59] Popular configurations of fireworks included the cracker, serpent, sky-rocket, Catherine Wheel, or a variety of other wheel shapes.[60] It was not unusual to have several fireworks exploding at the same time. Various colours could be achieved by mixing various chemicals, including rosin, camphire, bloodstone, and sulphur.[61] Jane Austen herself was said to witness a fireworks display at Sydney Gardens and wrote that they were really beautiful and surpassed her expectations.[62] Fanny Burney described the crush preparing to view the fireworks at Marylebone Gardens, and also called them really beautiful but that the loud noise startled the crowd enough to jump and disperse.[63]

Vauxhall was not the only location to set off fireworks. Richmond would launch them over the gardens from a barge on the river, having done so for masquerades since the mid-seventeenth century.[64] Leicester's new cricket ground was the site of a masquerade and fireworks show in September

1827. The advertisement promised three days of fireworks to include rockets, Bengal lights, metamorphoses, rich wheels, Italian suns, six pointed starts, tourbillions, illuminated crosses, temples and more. Dancing in the Pavilion supported by a military band formed the other amusement, and the advertisement expressly stated that no admittance would be granted if guests were unmasked.[65] Similar events would occasionally pop up outside of London in popular watering holes like Margate and Bath.

On occasion, indoor venues would also have fireworks displays. The Theatre Royal in Covent Garden gave a masquerade for all the performers from all the London theatres, capped off with fireworks and balloon ascension over the pit. The balloon then burst to reveal smaller balloons along with a shower of mottos among the crowd and a rousing chorus of God Save the King.[66] This was not the first nor would it be the last of a balloon feature of this sort at a grand masquerade. Not to be outdone, the King's Theatre, in February 1817, had its impressive display of fireworks styled after Vauxhall, in combination with rope dancers.[67] Nonetheless, Vauxhall reigned supreme during the Regency when it came to fireworks.

The Vauxhall masquerade of June 1819 combined the fireworks with an identical scheme of smaller balloons and mottoes within a larger balloon, as featured four years previous at the Theatre Royal.[68] Vauxhall was also known for timing the fireworks with other performances, like the tightrope walking of Madame Saqui[69] or the flight of Mr Littleton from the top of the firework tower amid sparks.[70] Musical performances with the fireworks, too, would be a popular feature at Vauxhall both at masquerades and at other public events. This would also be an inspiration to other venues and events throughout Great Britain; the combination of masquerade and fireworks would expand beyond London to other destinations across Great Britain, including Brighton and the Shakespeare Festival in Stratford Upon Avon.

Fireworks had ties to national identity, as much as spectacle. There was a military basis for the field of pyrotechnics that arose with the introduction of fireworks. Artillerymen were more common in the field than lay pyrotechnics, but both worked together to continue to advance the art. An American Naval Officer, James Cutbush, would have his system of pyrotechny published in 1825, posthumously, which combined both fireworks for exhibition and military pyrotechny. It was not the only such book of its kind in the era, and the term was broadly understood to encompass both the science of gunpowder and fire, and also the showmanship of the fireworks spectacle.

The April 1830 masquerade at Leamington Spa's Pavilion would combine fireworks, music from the 2nd Regiment of Local Militia, as well as intervals of cannon fire and church bells in the day leading up to the grand event.[71]

In addition to the underlying theme of man's control of nature, fireworks in the eighteenth and nineteenth centuries were inextricably linked with imperialism, the monarchy, and the military.[72] The spectacle of fireworks at pleasure gardens and special events both excited and terrified spectators, in some respects desensitising them from the visceral sensations of more modern warfare but celebrating the beauty of the explosions despite the smells, noise, and violence of the bursts. In England, fireworks were also embedded in the consciousness, reinforced through the celebration of Guy Fawkes night which traditionally included bonfires and fireworks. The celebration of king's and parliament's survival with the very substance meant to assassinate them only served to strengthen the public imagination of fireworks and gunpowder as a triumph. The connection between the military and masquerades was not just in fireworks or décor, but would also present in music and costumes. Fireworks were typically combined with music to heighten the experience, often employing a military band to provide the soundtrack to the spectacle.

While fireworks could light up the night with colour and noise, other performances also served to enliven the masquerade atmosphere. Hired clowns like Grimaldi and Bologna, magicians, tightrope walkers, and a host of other performers would be brought in to the larger, grander masquerades to entertain the crowds. Ballets, farces, or dramatic scenes were, on occasion, also part of the evening's entertainment. Setting the space up as a makeshift market town happened at a few masquerades, as well as balloon shows, and other attractions. The most common addition were the appearance of paid costumed performers. While not typically distinguished from the accounts of the costumes at the events, a newspaper report would mention the presence of paid actors and actresses where it was either notable or part of the advertised attraction. The large venues, in particular, like Vauxhall and the Pantheon often hired Drury Lane or other theatre performers to attend in costume and act the part to amuse attendees. Paid performances included an assortment of character and fancy dress actors and actresses, often appearing as rehearsed characters or groups with songs or small plays.

There was a sense that without these professional characters, an evening might fall flat. Padding the crowd with skilled performers was a way to ensure for interaction and living theatre. Examples ranged from coordinated groups to individuals meant to melt into the crowd. A band of robbers, likely from Astley's, were conspicuous and amusing to guests at the August 1812 Vauxhall masquerade.[73] Notably, the majority of fancy dress attendees at the December 1826 Argyll Rooms masquerade were paid performers, and the guests were entertained by dancing and a ballet that wanted a few farcical songs.[74] An April 1823 the Argyll Rooms masquerade featured continental artists specifically engaged to appear in the costumes of various nations.[75] It was also implicit that the Pantheon and King's Theatre also had among the motley crowd an assembly of actors and actresses, although the newspaper coverage seldom named anyone in appearance by name. Whether this was due to the size of the crowd, or an effort to be discreet about these more risqué events, is unknown but it is clear from the record that impresarios hired characters for nearly every masquerade at the large venues. Mr Oxberry, from Drury Lane Theatre, appeared at an April 1818 masquerade at the King's Theatre as Doctor Snaggs, supported by Covent Garden actor, Mr Denning, in the role of his servant. The pair produced a wealth of mirth with highly caricatured costumes, comic talent, and extraordinary acting throughout the whole of the event.[76] At the same King's Theatre masquerade, Mr Conner and another man dressed as ballad singers and sang vulgar songs to the amusement of the crowd. Actors and actresses often provided the necessary comic relief to these events, a feat relying on their consummate skills as performers.

Costumed actors and actresses were not the only performers on hire for masquerades. Many of the popular acts of the era could also be seen at masquerades. The August 1812 Vauxhall masquerade featured a trained dog performing tricks, slack wire dancing and balancing, and other performances by Mr Daniel Gyngell and his company.[77] Gyngell was a well-known magician, sleight of hand master, and musical glass performer, who appeared at many of the fairs like Bartholomew to amuse the crowds. A rare Drury Lane Theatre masquerade featured slack rope vaulting, tumbling, sparring and the Fantoccini, in addition to the other standard amusements of dancing, music, and dinner.[78] The Fantocinni referred to a puppet or marionette show also known as the Great Public Puppet Show, which had been all the rage at least in early years of the Regency.[79] Other famed performers would be woven into the masquerades at Vauxhall and other venues, like the tightrope walking of Madame Saqui or the sword swallowing, juggling tricks of Ramo Samee and his troupe of Indian jugglers.

The January 1820 edition of La Belle Assemblee featured a biographical sketch of Madame Saqui, who was a sharp businesswoman best known for her Covent Garden and Vauxhall performances. Popular for dancing on the tightrope in defiance of gravity, Saqui would disappear from public view by the late Regency until she reappeared in Paris in 1852 to debut on the Hippodrome tightrope at the age of 75. Saqui was born to a noted acrobat and found her calling at the age of 9 or 10 when, in Tours, she witnessed the Spanish rope-dancer, the Beautiful Malaga, dancing on a tightrope. Saqui would perform several times for Napoleon.[80] While she had her own theatre for a time in France, her popularity in England came largely from performances at Vauxhall in the mid-Regency era that were memorialised by articles and print images.

Appearing around the same time in England, after a tour on the east coast of the United States, Ramo Samee and his troupe was said to originally have been brought to Pall Mall from India by Captain Campbell. Ramo Samee, or Ramaswamy, was known for swallowing beads on a string, and then pulling it from his throat, swallowing needles, sword swallowing, juggling, fire-eating, and magic tricks. He was popular for his flair for the dramatic, including wearing all white robes and a turban and, although he later died impoverished, during the height of his career was an in-demand performer who made considerable money. Ramo Samee mostly performed at theatres, but in 1822 had a residency of sorts at Vauxhall.[81]

Other performers commonly seen at theatres and other venues would be brought in to entertain guests at masquerade balls. Burlington Gardens' masquerade in July 1814 had Grimaldi, Bologna, and Farley performing along with rope dancing from a specially constructed platform and wires.[82] Grimaldi was English, and said to be one of the most popular entertainers of the Regency era, appearing at Theatre Royal, Drury Lane, Sadler's Wells and Covent Garden. His speciality was performing as a harlequin clown but he was also a noted actor and dancer. Grimaldi would make appearances at special events, like masquerades, at various venues in London. Bologna, or Jack Bologna as he was also known, was Italian but spent the majority of his career in England as a harlequin performing at Sadler's Wells and Covent Garden.

A performance by contortionist, magician, and juggler Ching Lau Lauro was paired with several theatrical scenes before the opening of the masquerade ball at the Brighton theatre in 1828.[83] Ching Lau Lauro would call himself

Professor Ching, and although not all of his performances were lauded, he was known to juggle, perform magic, and do acts of ventriloquism. Clowns, puppets, magicians, and high wire acts were some of the carnival spectacles seen at the public venues trying to increase the spectacle and entertainment of the masked events. Familiar to theatre goers, these entertainers were woven into the overall masquerade productions to provide an added incentive and amusement for attendance.

Theatrical productions were also not uncommon at the masquerades. Ballets, farces, or small stage productions would be woven in to the evening. The Argyll Rooms December 1826 masquerade had a ballet that was in need of a few comic songs.[84] At a King's Theatre masquerade and grand military fete in June 1824, in addition to the pit and stage set up as a tented field, with various military implements, a life-sized chess game recreating the same played before Bonaparte at Versailles added to the run of show. Men, dressed as the individual pieces, played out the game before the audience seated in boxes. This was then followed by a ballet given by the juvenile dancers of King's Theatre.[85] In February 1822, the King's Theatre brought small children to perform a miniature ballet that amazed the masqueraders and inspired a lively atmosphere for the rest of the evening.[86] Theatrical performances would occur ahead of supper and dancing, or be woven in to the event so that there were multiple activities and rooms attendees could move through in search of entertainment.

To help sell the spectacle, often a masquerade would rely on a theme. Venetian Carnival was a popular theme over the decades for masquerades. The May 1821 Theatre Royal event advertised a Grand Venetian Carnival-themed masquerade featured a slack rope vaulter, a warrior in real brass scale armour, as well as performances by the Duke of Gloucester's band, and seventy other musicians and singers.[87] In addition, the venue was dressed to represent Italian cottages, Swiss huts, Turkish and Chinese Pavilions and other architectural facades as the refreshment areas, with attendants in costume to match their appointed station.[88] The event was broadly advertised in most of the London papers of the day. This followed a similar event held at the King's Theatre in February of the same year as well as a Venetian Carnival and masquerade held at the Argyll Rooms that May in honour of the King's birthday. In June 1828, the King's Theatre would host a Venetian Carnival and Masquerade commemorating the Battle of Waterloo. Teased to be like a continental Carnival, adding to the usual entertainments of the masquerade, a musical soiree, combat in suits of armour, balancing, acrobatics, ballet, and a Mozart overture were planned to be capped off by a performance of the national anthem before dancing began.[89] These added performances were generally well received and complimented in memoirs and press coverage. A year later, the Theatre Royal would hold a grand masquerade and *Fest di Ballo* in June. The centre of the theatre housed a temple for the occasion, emblematic of the monarch of the sea and with a band of reed instruments to play to the seats arranged on the stage and pit. Planned for the evening was a new pastoral ballet, and a group of cupids were to distribute favours. Litolff and Adam's band were to play a new Masaniello quadrille, along with other music for dancing, and professional glee singers serenaded diners during a supper featuring the delicacies as provided by Mr Phillips of Steyne House. Also advertised for the event were Indian jugglers, the Flying Indian, and the Antipodean Pedestrian. As with the 1821 Theatre Royal event, no expenses were spared in trying to fill up the rooms to the maximum capacity of 1000 people for the cost of one guinea per ticket.[90] The event was packed with many characters and a noticeable plethora of young, fashionable men.[91]

If the promise of acrobatics, dancing, and other performances were not enough of an inducement for people to purchase a ticket, public masquerades would also, on rare occasions, offer door prizes and other gifts to delight those in attendance. The Ranelagh January 1803 event distributed raffle tickets to the first 400 masks, and 50 tickets were drawn and awarded a twelfth night cake.[92] Waiter's masquerade at Burlington House in July 1814 had a lottery of Bijoux that featured a wealth of prizes including gold watches, chains, broaches, pins, rings, boxes and other items featuring a likeness of Wellington, Alexander, and Parisian-inspired themes. The *Morning Chronicle* appreciated the variety on offer in the evening's amusement.[93] Yet it was not just the large and public venues that would reward their guests with gifts.

Private masquerades, like those of the Thellussons, were also known to feature elements like lotteries or faux market experiences to engage guests. However, for the most part the private and exclusive Regency masquerades needed no other enticement than a festive get-together with the fashionable and titled in London or farther flung locations. The private masquerades, judging by the evidence, took care with the décor, music, and food but left much of the spectacle, including fireworks, performers, and other entertainment to the large scale public events. Considering that most of the private, non-subscription masquerades were paid for through the host and hostesses' funds, it's perhaps not surprising that the smaller scale events left off with the paid performances and showstoppers of the public masquerade.

Combining traditional ballroom elements like music and dancing with the fantastic, including fireworks and paid performances, the Regency masquerade was a feast for the eyes and ears. Woven into these spectacles were elements of military regalia, national identity, the comedic and the exotic. Novelty helped to encourage attendance and drive the surprise and pleasure audiences craved at these events. While there were some differences, particularly depending on the scale and size of the event, generally there was a familiarity in the production and rhythm of these events as they reproduced year after year the most popular elements of their predecessors. Part of this formula for success included complimentary refreshments to sustain the long hours of masquerade. But beyond the obligatory beverages, the suppers were also a thing of luxury, spectacle, and excess.

## Chapter Nine

# Food and Refreshments

Regardless of the scale of entertainments, most masquerades in the Regency had one source of luxury in common. Supper, wine, and various refreshments were on offer at public and private events alike to revive and to dazzle those in attendance. From hiring superstar caterers to offering the choicest delicacies of the season, the supper table could make or break an event in the eyes of guests and reporters. While there would be some differences in the price, amount, and selection, all Regency masquerades had a supper, drink, and refreshments to serve their guests. Described in terms of abundance, and sometimes more critically of waste, the amount of food and drink would break up the events and allow guests some time to collect themselves before dancing the morning away.

In the nineteenth century, a ball supper at one, two, or three in the morning was becoming commonplace. By comparison, the Georgian masquerade more commonly had unmasking at midnight followed by a supper and then dancing. While there was a notion that dining late was unhealthy, given fashionable events ended the following morning, a late supper had become fashionable by the early 1800s.[1] Supper was a third or fourth meal for the guests, who would have dined before attendance either around lunch or early evening. The supper made an easy addition to a masquerade's schedule of activities, as well as being part of the early traditions. A buffet of various offerings could reanimate the party, offering an opportunity to sit and eat, visit, and rest before dancing commenced. On some occasions, dancing only commenced after supper, and at other masquerades dancing both preceded and followed the one or two o'clock supper time.

At most private and public masquerade balls, refreshments like tea and coffee were more readily available throughout the event at a separate table, room, or station for guests to stop and have a drink. When wines were served varied, as well as whether or not they made up part of the complimentary refreshments. There were occasions when the Georgian masquerade only supplied tea, lemonade, Orgeat and other drinks,[2] establishing a tradition for complimentary beverages at masquerades. By the Victorian era, some venues were experimenting with having the buffet and refreshments available throughout the entire event at stand-up tables. While this would be introduced at Regency events, the standard was to have the free drinks available around the clock and a designated supper time mid event, with wine available during a limited time for an additional payment, if required. Based on observations from first-hand accounts, alcohol access would be limited at many of the public events to reduce the levels of intoxication among the crowd.

Supper and refreshments were a compulsory mention in advertisements for the large public masquerades. On some occasions there was a separate cost to supper and wines. Although the particulars of the food were seldom detailed, the advertisements and after event reporting assured the supper had every delicacy of the season. It was a common expression during the Regency era, with its usage peaking in the 1860s, that hinted at a spread containing rare food stuff. Game, fish, poultry, exotic fruits,[3] and well cooked vegetables likely made up many of the supper tables, alongside jellies, ices, sweetmeats, and other sweet treats. A housekeeper's guide from 1809 suggested that a ball of twenty people should include the following: roast fowl, ham, prawns, lobster, cheesecakes, jelly, blancmange, roast lamb, raised pie, and savoy cake. For dessert, a selection of ices alongside pineapple, peaches, and grapes were recommended.[4] A bill of fare for a sixty-person ball listed prawns in a wax basket, jelly, savoy cakes, white soup, roast lamb, pineapple and grapes, torte, Italian salad, trifle, veal, ham, raised fowl pie, Dutch salad, blancmange, lobster, sweetmeats, strawberry cream, tongue, melon, asparagus, sea kale and small dessert dishes of almonds, raisins and fruit sweetmeats.[5] This type of menu could be scaled up accordingly.

One Pantheon ad for a masquerade in April 1802 mentioned a hot supper of poultry, lamb, and asparagus that required the supper rooms be opened precisely at one in the morning.[6] A piping hot selection was served after midnight at the Argyll Rooms in December 1829, prepared by the artiste Mr Grogan who was famous for his culinary delights.[7] The emphasis on hot was notable as some of the masquerades would only serve a cold collation. In the Victorian era, French Chef, Ude, would invent the stand-up supper, with easy to consume hand foods like sandwiches and fruit, and high tables where people could snack without a formal affair.[8] But during the long Regency, supper was still an event where royalty and their entourage would be given a separate supper room, and guests would be ushered in for a limited time to sit, be entertained by spontaneous and planned amusements like singing, and revive themselves with a meal, while flirting with other guests and enjoying conversation.

During the Regency era, the supper at a ball was defined by abundance. The best example of this was Vauxhall Gardens. Vauxhall promised a lavish spread, as one July 1821 masquerade confirmed with a one o'clock supper including shellfish, boiled and roasted fowl, ham, salad, roast lamb, pigeon and meat pies, jellies, strawberries, ices, pastry and sweetmeats. The spread was so large that the newspaper noted untouched delicacies left on the table and recommended it serve as a lesson for the less liberal provisions of in town masquerades.[9] Vauxhall advertised and was reported to consistently have one of the most lavish suppers and refreshments, offering a buffet of the meats and sweets favoured by people of fashion. Whether an enticement or expectation, the Vauxhall experience included dining on trendy food stuffs and beverages.

The Pantheon characteristically offered complimentary refreshments of tea and coffee, but sometimes charged an additional sum for supper. Exceptions, like the May 1808 masquerade charged one guinea for customers.[10] A May 1803 masquerade had supper advertised at seven shillings per person to be provided by Mr Waud of Bond Street.[11] The same was true for a King's Theatre masquerade in May 1801, where admission was a half guinea, and Mr Waud's supper and wines were an additional seven shillings per person.[12] By comparison, a Ranelagh masquerade in the same year provided not only the usual refreshments, but a supper in the boxes with chickens, ham, veal, tongue, beef, mince pies, jellies, blancmange, pastry, and fruit included in the half guinea price of admission.[13]

Part of the attraction of supper and wines were owing to the celebrity caterers. Mr Waud, for example, was a frequent caterer of masquerades and other events during the Regency period. He also frequently operated as a ticket agent for masquerades, theatrical productions, and other significant events like balloon ascensions. Waud was a popular confectioner, whose bon-bons and other sweets were popular with the Prince Regent and the Duke of York, rivalling the royal patronage of Gunter's.[14] An amusing review of his 1836 appointment to the queen as purveyor of turtle for Her Majesty appeared in a *Figaro in London*, in which the author was mystified as to why the queen needed a turtle purveyor in the first place, and second why a pastry cook of the highest order would be bestowed upon the honour.[15] The reality was Waud's was known as a superior location for turtle soup,[16] his talents extending beyond baking. His appointment would be three years after the *London Gazette* published a notice that Mr Waud, cook and confectioner, was bankrupt,[17] so it may have been a nod of royal support.

Waud's reputation as caterer, or proprietor as he was sometimes called, for early nineteenth-century masquerades was unparalleled. Because he was talented as a chef and pastry cook, he could produce a significant spread featuring all the delicacies of the season, craved by the fashionable set. For a masquerade he catered at Vauxhall, the delicacies of the season were listed as: 150 dozen fowls, 150 lamb dishes, 200 tongues and hams, 300 lobsters, 100 raised pies, 200 Savoy cakes, 250 pastry dishes, 300 jellies, 400 quarts of ice cream, 500 pots of strawberries, and 300 bunches of cherries, as well as a variety of other fruits and rare wine vintages.[18] Mr Waud was also known to cater other venue's masquerades, including the King's Theatre. One April 1803 masquerade promised an abundance of ice cream, tea, coffee, lemonade, Orgeat and more served by Mr Waud.[19] For another April 1807 Pantheon masquerade, Mr Waud was in charge of receiving applications for supper boxes, as the event planned for tea tables similar to the set up at Ranelagh, along with an upper end bar for ice cream, jellies, lemonade and other refreshments.[20] Mr Waud also provided a plentiful supper and excellent wines for a February 1803 Pantheon masquerade, but was criticised by the *Morning Post* for having sand on the floor of the supper rooms.[21] He was prolific in serving masquerade parties and seldom criticised by after event reports. No doubt, the sand was a one-time gaffe.

But Waud was not the only notable caterer serving Regency masquerades. Not to be outdone, Gunter's, under the auspices of Italian confectioner Mr Jarin, would cater an April 1823 masquerade at the Argyll Rooms that promised tea, coffee, ices, jellies, confectionery and more.[22] Mr Jarin was working for Gunter's in the 1820s, and the event was widely published in numerous London publications signalling the excitement and good reception the event had. Gunter's would also cater a July 1823 Argyll Rooms masquerade that featured an abundance of delicacies, including marinated chickens, pineapple, and an assortment of other fruits and dishes. Wine, on the occasion, was supplied by Mr Wright from the Haymarket Theatre.[23] It is perhaps the scathing review from a December 1821 Argyll Rooms masquerade, where a Cheapside confectioner catered with a cold collation and clumsy decorations, that drove the organisers to arrange for Gunter's to cater a few years later. While the *Morning Herald* was overall satisfied with the spread, the festooneries of coarse calamanco, pies, custards, cold chickens, and calf's foot jelly along wooden balusters resulted in the turn of phrase that the decorations were concocted in Cheap-side. The wines also failed to impress.[24] Gunter's would on occasion also provide supper for private masquerades; Lady Jersey's April 1815 masked ball was catered, both food and wine, by Gunter's.[25]

Beyond Waud and Gunter's, there were a variety of other caterers familiar to the Regency crowds, who served masquerades during the Regency era. Mr Parker of Compton Street provided a quality supper and wines for King's Theatre masquerades in April 1804,[26] June 1805,[27] and February 1806.[28] Mr Parker was the proprietor of the King's Arms in Soho. The February 1805 Pantheon masquerade was catered by Mr Escudier of No. 94 Oxford Street.[29] He was a well-established pastry cook, whose shop would be taken over by Mr Mera in the 1810s.[30] Mr Farrance of Ludgate Hill sold tickets and provided supper for a May 1803 Ranelagh masked ball[31] and a January 1800 Ranelagh masquerade in honour of the queen's birthday.[32] He was noted for frequently being responsible for the food and drink at Ranelagh's events. Farrance was a pastry cook who had his own shop, Farrance's, and was famed for his soups, tarts, savoury patties, pastries, confitures, and bon-bons. His shop also served seasonal fruits and ices and was known for its value and quality.[33] Dubourg provided a cold supper for the January 1834 King's Theatre masquerade, with jellies described as tooth-enticing and other confectionery treats that were quickly consumed rather than being thrown at the musicians. Although apparently, half-eaten birds and whole oranges were tossed at their fleeing forms.[34]

The caterers were not always named in coverage or advertisement, but the implications were clear that the food and drink were of superior quality. An unnamed, but celebrated caterer provided supper and refreshments for a December 1832 King's Theatre masquerade and Christmas festival.[35] There were few masquerades that did not have a traditional supper and refreshments on offer for guests, following the pattern of late night eating and drinking to encourage the party to linger until dawn or just after. A superstar chef brought the element of luxury and spectacle audiences demanded at masquerades. On the occasion when the food and wine were viewed as subpar, the newspapers would be sure to offer their critique. An Opera House masquerade in May

1824 served a tolerable supper and common wines that did little to redeem what was otherwise a run of the mill affair.[36] Conversely, a February Argyll Rooms masquerade of the same year was praised for plentiful and good quality supper and wines that disappeared almost supernaturally.[37] Most commonly, it was the amount of food and drink that inspired criticism from reporters. A February 1803 Haymarket masquerade was well regarded for its fashionable crowds and collection of costumes. While the supper was satisfying, wine was scarce. However, it seemed to have the impact of dampening the spirits so that the *Morning Post* observed that conduct was less improper than typically observed at similar occasions.[38]

Private masquerades, too, would on most occasions serve a late supper, generous and consisting of every delicacy of the season in ornamental abundance.[39] Because the late supper was a foundational part of both the public and private ball, it was paramount that it be in as good a taste as the rest of the event; the supper and wines could make or break a masquerade. Just as the décor hinted at luxury and wealth, the food and drink conveyed a message to guests of indulgence or economy. As neither commercial venture nor private party wanted to be accused of economies when serving the upper class, the spread must necessarily be overmuch and the wines of the best quality. In addition, the delicacies of the season meant costly fruits, vegetables, and meats should be on offer to impress the guests. The waste from ball suppers was known to be extraordinary, with food piling up in the kitchens and passageways after being removed from their serving dishes.[40] There was variability from private masquerade to masquerade, with some providing refreshments during the entire event for the leisure of guests[41] while others offered the traditional supper with a well-stocked banquet and most of the treats offered at commercial venues, albeit on a smaller scale.[42] For example, Mr Champney's masquerade in February 1803 at his country home near Bath had the supper rooms open between one and three in the morning. Guests were served hot soups, game, lamb, turkeys, and an assortment of other dishes with Port and Madeira to drink.[43] Supper of all the delicacies of the season, dessert of rare fruit, and an abundance of rich wines for the Eglinton Castle 1809 masquerade was accompanied by the sound of a gong announcing the ghost of the Governor from Don Juan stalking the rooms while four fiddlers who had been playing feigned shock.[44]

Regardless of when and how it was served, the expectation was that the food would be plentiful, varied, and consist of all the delicacies of the season. Like coverage of other private masquerades, Mrs Dupre's event was complimented for her plentiful and sumptuous food and choice, excellent wines which was set at side tables for the company to consume standing.[45] The exquisite galaxy of rank, beauty, and the fashionable at Mrs Sadlier's April 1824 masquerade was satisfied with a dining parlour filled with refreshments and illuminated by gas lamps in a showy embrace of new technology.[46] The private masquerade followed the pattern card of commercial events so neatly it was tradition and also in keeping with the more general rules that governed private balls. According to Walter Cox Green in *The Book of Good Manners: A Guide to Polite Usage for All Social Functions*, the ball supper was commonly a buffet because of the ease in serving and preparation. *The Etiquette for Ladies* (1838) also stressed that a well-regulated ball would customarily have a supper at the end of the evening.[47]

The supper spread was complimented by an early and continuous service of common beverages, and then highlighted and often limited service of wine. While coffee, tea, and other simple beverages were standard complimentary refreshment at the Regency masquerade, there was variability between events and venues when wine or other alcohol was included in the cost of admission. The Pantheon February 1803 masquerade had wines at a separate cost from supper and admission.[48] There was some variability in Pantheon events as to whether wine and supper were included. The Pantheon masquerade in May of 1808 advertised clearly that the wine bar would close at three o'clock, likely because the wines were that evening part of the cost of admission.[49] Similarly, the April 1802 Pantheon masquerade also offered wine along with supper included in the price of admission, but clearly stated that the wine bar would close at four in the morning.[50] The Argyll Rooms June 1810 masquerade did include supper, port, sherry, Madeira and claret to the admission cost, with gentlemen paying more than ladies.[51] The April 1818 Argyll Rooms masquerade ball included hot supper, wines, and admission for half a guinea,[52] half a guinea less than the April 1817 Argyll Rooms all-inclusive masquerade.[53] Admission went back up to one guinea for the masquerades the next year at the Argyll Rooms. The King's Theatre hosted a masquerade in April 1818, and allowed, with the cost of admission, one pint of port wine or sherry per supper ticket, with a variety of extra wines available for an additional, unlisted cost.[54] The pint of wine allowance was the same for their February 1811 masquerade.[55] This was a departure from the May 1810 masquerade at the King's Theatre, where supper, refreshments, and wine were included in the one guinea cost of admission.[56]

Ranelagh regularly provided wine as part of the ticket cost. The May 1803 masked ball cost one guinea, and included supper and port and sherry wines.[57] Farrance was the likely caterer for the April 1801 Ranelagh masquerade that served jellies, collared beef, blancmange, pastry and first quality wines at one o'clock in the supper boxes.[58] In comparison, Vauxhall's inclusion of wine in the cost of admission varied, sometimes only including supper as they advertised in August 1812.[59] A critical review of a January 1824 Argyll Rooms masquerade lamented the cost of attendance, including that supper tickets were an additional seven shillings, six pence on top of the one guinea admittance fee, and then wine was priced at between seven and seventeen shillings per bottle. Sherry and port were the most inexpensive at seven shillings, Madeira nine, claret ten shillings and six pence, and champagne the princely sum of seventeen shillings.[60] Regardless of the cost, wine for most was a necessary in enhancing the masquerade experience; one joke featured the suggestion to a would be masquerader to go to the event sober, for that was the one mask no friend would know him in.[61]

As with the selection and quality of food, wine too was expected to be if not of top quality, then at least good. In the early 1800s, the wine purveyor was either also the caterer or seldom mentioned. Mr Parker of Compton Street, for instance, provided both supper and wine for the 1805 King's Theatre masquerade[62] and Mr Waud was also frequently named as supplying food and wine, particularly between 1800 and 1809. Another purveyor mentioned was Mr Blanchenay of Pall Mall, who was noted as supplying excellent Burgundy and Champagne for a May 1824 King's Theatre masquerade.[63] M. Dubourg supplied the wines for the April 1834 King's Theatre masquerade.[64] Caterers would also team up with wine purveyors, as Waud and Wright did for the April 1822 King's Theatre masquerade[65] and the January 1825 Argyll Rooms masquerade.[66]

By the 1820s, Charles Wright was branded as the Champagne authority. Wine merchant Wright frequently supplied the wines for various masquerades during the Regency era, and if the newspaper coverage is any indication he was well established as an exceptional purveyor. One critical review of a December 1826 Argyll Rooms masked ball implicated Mr Wright's intoxicating juices, specifically Champagne, for violent scuffles including brawls and drama.[67] The June 1806 Argyll Rooms were complimented by the press for their Champagne and Burgundy, which were thought excellent.[68] The wines and food quickly vanished at the December 1825 Argyll Rooms masquerade under the auspices of Mr Wright.[69] A January 1826 masquerade at the Argyll Rooms also featured sparkling Champagne in large quantities to the delight of those in attendance who also enjoyed a capital supper, announced by a horn blaring 'O the Roast Beef of Old England'.[70]

Wright, as part of the Opera Colonnade, was also known to serve as host or promoter for the various masquerades, as he did for the King's Theatre event in February 1830. The guests were set to be so well soaked by the abundance and quality of Wright's Champagne that they would need a cure in the morning. The event had performances by Meinheer Von Klishnig and Ramo Samee, and the Siamese Youths were in one of the principal boxes. A tasteful supper was supplied by Grogan.[71] Wright produced a similar event with even more circus and acrobatic performers in July of the same year.

Champagne was sometimes highlighted as the premier alcohol, as it was for the February 1816 King's Theatre masquerade advertisement,[72] but most frequently a selection of wines was implied. The Martindale's masquerade in 1802 offered guests high quality Champagne, Burgundy, Claret and more.[73] Whether a separate cost, or included in the price of admission, wine was without fail mentioned in the advertisements, indicating a public interest in having access to alcohol at the masked ball. This was true for private masquerades as well, where wine was ranked alongside the other catered items as a highlight and mark of distinction. Tea, coffee, and other common refreshments like ratafia or lemonade were also a standard offering for the masked events and nearly always complimentary. However, they were so seldom mentioned in the press coverage that it is likely these beverages were an expected feature of any large private or public social event and therefore did not warrant comment. If wine was almost a requirement to lubricate the senses, supper served both as a refreshment for the night's activities and also another opportunity to surround the guests in luxury.

A few hours in to the masquerade, supper and wines were served. Suppers at commercial venues were served in separate rooms or in boxes. The number and size of the rooms varied according to the venue and overall capacity. A May 1810 Haymarket masquerade made accommodation available for parties of six or more in private rooms.[74] Newspaper coverage of a February 1807 King's Theatre masquerade noted that the boxes seemed to be taken only by couples, with some implication that it was being used as a place for lovers to connect.[75] The same year the Pantheon also advertised private supper boxes available upon application.[76] Ranelagh and Vauxhall served supper in either private boxes or on tables, variation depending on the number of attendees expected and taking a tiered approach to the cost. On occasion, the Prince Regent or other distinguished guests would be appointed their own supper rooms to dine or to rest.

Private balls, too, would often make special supper arrangements for the prince and his party. Mr and Mrs Thellusson's 1802 masquerade had a dedicated apartment for royal visitors to sup, described as appropriately fitted up with splendour.[77] Mrs Egerton's 1805 masquerade saw the library outfitted in a fabulous fashion for the Prince Regent's twenty-five-person party, with sweet scented floral arrangements, emblematic décor, silver candle branches with wax lights, solid silver plates, and a variety of other ornamentation.[78] The Marchioness of Lansdown's July 1806 grand masquerade had the royals sitting at one table for the two o'clock supper, with the Prince of Wales the first to seat, with the Marchioness on his arm.[79] On other occasions, either the newspaper account did not highlight special accommodations for royal guests or the prince and his party sat down with the rest of those in attendance.

Boxes or special spaces were not limited to supper time. Many of the large venues, like King's Theatre or the Pantheon, would offer private boxes for those who wanted to watch but not participate in the masquerade. Both large and small parties could be accommodated.[80] Even the Argyll Rooms on occasion offered a private box to view the masquerade safe from the motley crowd.[81]Alternatively, the boxes were on a few occasions set up as stalls or shops, or with tea tables as was the case at the February 1801 Pantheon masquerade[82] and the April 1807 Pantheon masquerade.[83] The 1801 Pantheon masquerade stalls featured whisky, confectionery, fruits, hats, and other items provided complimentary to attendees.[84]

Beyond delivering a unique experience, as in the case of the faux market street, boxes were an effective way to craft specific moments for guests, particularly if they had the funds to pay for them. Simply allowing a safe distance and privacy to watch, for instance, was an attraction for some. The King's Theatre boxes were filled with primarily noble and genteel ladies on the eve of the February 1817 masquerade, offering them separation from the motley crowd.[85] The *Morning Post* observed the same for the April 1826 King's Theatre masquerade, finding a goodly number of ladies watching the crowd's merriment from the safety of the boxes.[86] Creating spaces for experiences or voyeurism, based on the reviews, were a critical part of the theatre of the public masquerade. While private masquerades were already exclusive, having VIP areas for guests gave even the most innocent guest an opportunity to participate.

As one of the foundational elements of a masquerade, and indeed other types of balls or functions, the supper and refreshments on offer could result in positive or critical reception by attendees and the press. If an impresario or host or hostess stuck to the general formula for success, they were almost guaranteed rave reviews; abundance, liberality, exotic, and costly were the features that seemed not only anticipated but expected at masked events. Whether a small, private event or a very large commercial venture, the expectation was for all the delicacies of the season. This turn of phrase implied exotic fruits, choice meats, and assorted pastries. For public masquerades, a superstar caterer/pastry chef was also a la mode.

Like so many of the other features of the Regency masquerade, the refreshments and foods were both a selling point and a symbol of excess, luxury, and national identity. From the limited menus available, there was little variation in the types of dishes offered. What tended to be most remarked upon were the quantity and quality of the items. From champagne to ices, masquerade attendees could expect a meal fit for royalty. And for those seeking an even more exclusive experience, in some cases they could apply for a private box to sup and admire the crowds at a distance.

Food and drink were also part of the broader entertainments making up the general agenda of the Regency masquerade. Alongside music, dancing, performances, and general merriment, supper was a way to corral the party and revive them during the lengthy events that would typically last until the early morning hours. Alcohol played a large part in lubricating sensibilities to ensure mutual enjoyment, while the food served to emphasise the unique experience. Overall, the refreshments served helped elevate the overall tone of the Regency masquerade to a grand affair, worth the expense of admittance and hiring of costume to consume with the eyes, ears, mouth, and nose, all the delicacies of Regency life including food and drink.

## Chapter Ten

# Dominoes, Characters, and Fancy Dress

In June 1820, Orion stalked the crowds of the masquerade, armed with his hunting tackle and a star-be-speckled belt. A crowd gathered around the constellation come to life, bombarding him with questions while he struggled to imitate their language until he was able to speak. His light blue star spangled habit and white cloud cloak matched with the dog star on his helmet, star on his collar, and general air of alien. He finally greeted his audience with speech announcing his identity, and quickly and wittily telling a joke for which a nearby lady pronounced him very droll, indeed.[1] The account resembles the public attention when a masquerader arrived not only with a novel and well executed costume, but also a performance designed to awe and entertain.

Costumes, including the masks, were a direct reflection of performance and desire. Surveying the popular costumes over the four decades, it is clear that class, nationalism, nostalgia, and a variety of other motivations were a part of the cultural dialogue happening during this period in Great Britain. Combined with broader human desires to play the wit, the siren, the fool, and other archetypes, the character and fancy dress costumes from Regency masquerades provide a window into not only individual fantasies but also the broader sense of place and identity. The sleek lines and form fitting gowns, inexpressibles, and waistcoats of the Regency era could be abandoned, if only for a night, at a masquerade. The imagination was only limited by what was available at the costume warehouses, the attics, or what could be created in time. People are not so very different, that 200 years ago they did not like to masquerade as someone sexy, powerful, comic, or witty as is common with contemporary costumes. And how fortunate are we that many lists of costumes for fancy dress, as they were referred to, survive today along with drawings and prints to paint a picture of how Regency ladies and gentlemen dressed for the occasion.

Castle (1986) broke down the eighteenth-century masquerade costume trio, which based on primary evidence, was much the same for the Regency era. There were consistently three types of masquerade wear: the domino, the fancy dress, and the character costume. The prevalence of one type over another depended on the event and the individuals participating, but generally there appeared to be a good mix of the three represented at both public and private masquerades. Dominos were often lamented in coverage, while fancy dress and character costumers praised. Towards the end of the Regency, into the Victorian era, fancy dress would become more popular.

The domino was basic, not based on any character or theme, but rather a simple way to incorporate a hidden identity. Venetian in origin, the term domino could be used to describe just the mask or a simple dark, loose cloak that would have covered the clothing combined with a simple mask. On occasion the cloak may have been hooded, concealing the hair of the wearer. The domino mask was small, dark, and typically only covered the area around the eyes so that the nose and mouth were clearly visible, however shadowed by the presence of a hood. There are references to different colours of dominos, from golds to pinks, and trimmed with feathers, ribbon, or other decoration. Black or white were typically the colours of choice, with black being the most common. An 1803 account of an Opera House masquerade indicated that black dominoes prevailed, as usual, making the assembly gloomy. But a favourite was a man dressed in a rose domino with green trim, a cape, and Spanish hat with pink and white feathers. This article spent a paragraph describing the impropriety and even impertinence of attendees not wearing any sort of disguise, as it took away from amusement of all, and recommending the offences against the public be rectified in the future.[2]

The domino mask was often made of fabric, like silk or satin, sometimes cotton or brocade and tied around the head. A half mask, it was also referred to as a loo mask. Many of the larger public masquerades had dominos on the ready for guests who had not come costumed, and some insisted the minimum for entrance was a domino. Wearing a domino appeared to be the hallmark of a lazy party-goer, inspiring little enthusiasm and often being the source of complaint. Some masquerades even prohibited entrance if one was only wearing a domino. The domino mask could be combined with a cape with a hood that could hide identifying hair colours or styles, or add to the mystery in concealing the wearer's identity. Coverage of Lady Castlereagh's Masquerade Ball that took place in June 1800 called the non-assuming mien of the silent domino mask a contrast to character dress where the wearer knew little of that they were to be portraying. According to the listed appearances, many of the aristocratic crowd appeared in elegant dominos of varying colours, including yellow, black, blue, and white.[3] This was alongside character and fancy dress costumes.

Fancy dress was used commonly to describe when a person dressed as a type of person, a theme, or a similar element. Examples from the Regency include military wear, professional wear like a flower girl, judge, shepherdess or chimney sweep, court costume, harlequin, foreign dress like American, Spanish, or Chinese, and also caricatures of religion like Quaker or Muslim. More esoteric concepts were also explored like Night, or Sun, or Mother Nature. It was also not uncommon for fancy dress to include Georgian or earlier costumes from Great Britain's aristocratic history. Fancy dress was also used, in advertisements and other publications, as the general term for wear combined with a mask. Masked balls, for instance, were alternatively called fancy dress balls. The evidence suggests that fancy dress, costumes, and dominos were prevalent among guests at the fancy dress ball, making it a universally understood term meaning masked costume party. However, beginning in the Regency there would be a trend that would carry forward to the Victorian era of having a fancy dress ball without masks. Fancy dress could also mean elaborate dress and accessories without a theme, which would be more common into the Victorian era.

If the fancy dress generally explored themes, costumes, and caricatures, a character dress described someone dressing up as a specific person. The specific person could be historical or fictional. Common character dresses included the weird sisters from Macbeth, the Devil, Richard III, Winifred Jenkins, Falstaff, and various Greek and Roman gods and goddesses. With both the fancy and character dress, there was some expectation the masqueraders would also comport themselves true to character and in some cases, shops or other scenarios were set up to engage characters in mimicry of their inspiration. Singing, calling, performing, or acting were highlights of after event reporting. Generally, the press and the other attendees seemed to prefer a well-played character over fancy dress.

Some events had a specific theme for fancy dress or character costumes, such as the July 1823 Spanish fancy dress ball at Covent Garden Theatre to celebrate Spanish independence.[4] Military themes were common, and encouraged the men to wear regimentals or come in tribute to war heroes. The theme of people around the world was used on occasion as was Italian Carnival. Inevitably a reporter would observe, and often complain, that dominos dominated even themed masked events. The preference at most events, at least from the organiser and observer's perspective, was for people to appear in character. Some would even clearly state that no person would be admitted without a mask, character dress, or domino.[5] This would require some pre-planning and thought in some cases, particularly to acquire a ticket or beg admittance at the more exclusive venues, but there were also options for the parties who lagged behind in preparing their dress.

By the Regency era, there were a variety of costume warehouses to choose from and many venues would have a costumer set up on site the night of the event to, at minimum, supply dominoes. Costume warehouses also offered dressing rooms for both the night of, to get ready, and the morning after, to dress for home.[6] Mrs Lloyd's masquerade warehouse at No. 10 Old Lisle Street in Leicester Square advertised a variety of character costumes, dominos, and masks to be hired at reasonable terms.[7] Mrs Lloyd opened up her established in 1802, with ads appearing in 1803 and 1804 as well. In an 1818 ad for an April masquerade at the Argyle Rooms, tickets could be had at the following locations: Mr Milward's Masquerade Warehouse in Little Brook Street, Hanover Square; Mr Fentum's Masquerade Warehouse in the Strand; Mr Thresher's Masquerade Warehouse on Panton Street in Haymarket; Mr Lay's Masquerade on South Molton Street; and Mr Sizeland's Masquerade Warehouse on Vere Street and Oxford Street.[8] These were just a sample of the masquerade warehouses and other establishments that could provide costumes for masquerades. Other enterprising companies would offer accessories to compliment an ensemble. Dison, Wilson and Company, lace manufacturers, advertised in 1823 that they had a variety of accessories well adapted for masquerades or fancy dress balls including aprons, scarfs, gold figured nets for turbans, lace dresses, and a gold Circassian robe.[9] Similar establishments were available outside of London in places like Cheltenham, which in 1811 directed potential attendees to H. Ruff at the Cheltenham Library with a wide variety of character dresses, dominos, hats, masks and more on moderate terms.[10]

Fentum's would still be in business by the 1840s. It was given a nod in the satirical poems, *Dr Syntax*, written by William Combe in 1809, which included Rowlandson illustrations. The gentle, comedic commentary on the Regency era included a visit by Dr Syntax to a masquerade with dragons, harlequins, a sultan, and assorted fancy dress and Fentum's was where the hero and his lady companion obtained costumes for the masquerade ball.

Dr Syntax is now regarded as the first cartoon character and, accordingly, had a large following that included merchandise like snuffboxes, dinner plates, cane and swordstick handles, and a chamber pot.[11] Dr Syntax would also be a popular masquerade costume. Fentum's was clearly the most reputed of masquerade warehouses, but there were a plethora on offer and many would strike deals with various venues to serve their customers for masquerades.

For last minute masqueraders, the masquerade venues would often provide a space and a costumer on hand to outfit them in necessary mask and dress. Ranelagh Gardens April 1801 event provided a commodious room, by the admission entrance, where black and coloured silk dominos were on hire for five shillings to one guinea.[12] The Pantheon did the same for its February 1803 masquerade, having Mrs Richmand on site with wardrobe and masks to dress lest guests be prohibited entrance. Mrs Richmand's Masquerade Warehouse was in Oxford Street.[13]A few years later, King's Theatre had an attendant with masks and dominos in the lobbies to encourage last minute masking at the June 1805 masquerade.[14] Obbard's was on site at the King's Theatre in April 1834 to provide masks and dominoes, with a selection of fancy costumes available at their King William Street warehouse.[15] There were numerous examples throughout the long Regency of venues staging a costume warehouse at the entrance to ensure easy access to a costume on the night of the masquerade. The masquerade offices also commonly served as ticket offices for advanced purchase of an admittance ticket.

However, despite how many opportunities were created for the party to dress in costume, or how much a hostess insisted, there were still some that would fall back on the domino. At Mrs Orby Hunter's May 1799 masquerade, she had insisted all the company should appear in character dress, but the standard raft of disappointing dominos appeared despite her best intentions.[16] A critical reporter for the *New Times*, when writing about a masquerade at the Argyll Rooms in December 1826, summed up his assessment that the English were not of a theatrical bent and so that many of the characters were hired theatre or other actors, paid to appear and act in costume for the entertainment of the crowds. Threadbare stock costumes, he suggested, made it evident that the English had much less dedication to playing in costume than counterparts in France or Italy.[17]

While dominos were good for a last minute mask or for those who had little creativity or interest in donning a character or new persona, most events had a decent sum of attendees that opted for character or fancy dress.

Costumes, not unlike today, fell into several broad categories: nostalgic, exotic, comic, heroic, sexy, or scary. A January 1801 Ranelagh masquerade featured the following costumes: housemaids, footmen, shepherdesses, fruit girls, Quakers, tinkers, an Indian, mad Tom, Diana, and harlequins.[18] Sprightly country lasses, well-proportioned[19] goddesses, and pretty milkmaids[20] were the types of fancy dress attributed to pretty, innocent, and alluring women. Although it is hard to ascertain the motive of the individual, the result was an emphasis on the beauty and demureness of the lady wearing these types of costumes. By contrast, men would lean heavily towards the heroic or the comedic, preferring harlequins, farcical characters, and military figures.

Miss Morgan's masquerade, held in June 1802 at Kensington Gore, had 400 attendees in various costumes including flower girls, a primrose girl, mad Tom, Evelina in the Castle Spectre, Friar Lawrence, the apothecary from Romeo and Juliet, Prospero, a conjuror, Adonis, witch, weird sister, fortune teller, Highland officer, ghost, Blue Beard, French abbe, French refugee, Frenchwomen, envoy from the Sublime Porte, Mr Jones, tailor, old coxcomb, watchman, Don Roberto, Punch, rustic, Captain Fluellen, harlequin, and assorted gods and goddesses.[21] The Argyll Rooms June 1826 event had a ballad singer, Dame Quickly, parliamentary orators, Death, Don Juan, Spanish guerrillas, Roman bandit and wife, Jerry Sneak, Major Sturgeon, the Devil, German doctor, Falstaff, monks, countrymen, and assorted other character costumes.[22] This list of characters is representative of the costumes at masquerades that would be reported on throughout the Regency.

Although the broad categories are intended to be loose groupings based on a survey of the available record, as themes they can also hint at intent, trends, and popular culture at the time. Literature and theatre were two common sources for character and fancy dress costumes. Other sources included perceptions about other cultures, historical references, occupations across the classes, and abstract costumes. The representations were influenced by a variety of factors including access and availability. The sheer repetition of costumes reflect that availability, particularly from places where individuals could hire costumes, was important. But the repetition is also suggestive of the intent behind an individual's choice.

Scary costumes included ghosts, gothic elements, the Weird Sisters, the Devil, Falstaff, or other terrifying historical figures. The height of the gothic novel hit followed the 1799 premier of *Feudal Times* at the Theatre Royal. Notable to Nigro (2010) was the frequent criticisms of anachronisms in costuming around the Gothic medieval rival in the theatre. These limitations extended to the costume shop.[23] Regardless of the accuracy of these representations, the gothic and the horrible were common sources of entertainment for the Regency leisure class. The gothic was tied to Romanticism, and Winter (2020) argues, also tied to emerging capitalism. Anxieties about debt, property, and consumption were projected into the supernatural. The thematic devices of the gothic genre, mystery, haunted castles, intrepid heroines and villains represent the broader conflicts of duty and desire, past and present[24], and freedom versus property. As the contemporary reader and consumer of Regency media grappled with these concepts through the mechanisms of the fantastical, so too could the masquerader garb themselves in one of these frightening characters if not to scare counterparts, then at least to experience the sense of recognition. One example was at the Argyll Rooms June 1806 masquerade where Mr G. Robinson appeared in the guise of Romaldi from the gothic melodrama *A Tale of Mystery*.[25] The early nineteenth century play had the character Romaldi himself disguised for the climactic scene. No doubt many in attendance at the Argyll Rooms would recognise both the character and the history of the characters as himself a masquerader. Delightful double meanings and witty cultural references were often the most popular characters at the masquerades.

Scary or gothic costumes in many ways were less wish fulfilment than direct cultural engagement. Shakespearean costumes like the Weird Sisters and ghosts from Hamlet and Macbeth, would have been as familiar, if not more, to the masquerading audience as gothic characters. More abstract characters or fancy dress like the Devil would have relied on shared symbols of what the Devil looked like. Similarly, Bluebeard and Evelina from Castle Spectre might have needed some specific clues in dress or accessories to tip off others as to the identity. But these examples, costumes that showed up again and again in the record throughout the Regency, demonstrate that the gothic and terrible were top of mind for the Regency gentleman or lady.

Sloan (2017) argues that the gothic sartorial mode of dress was the expression of terror and anxiety those in the nineteenth century were faced with when considering an imagined romantic past and industrial future. Opening with the example of *Northanger Abbey*'s pairing of a dressmaker's errand and the enthralling text of Radcliffe's *Udolpho* and later the discovery of a laundry list in the trunk of her room at Northanger Abbey, Austen is parodying gothic sensibility with particular skill by tying in clothing to both scenarios.[26] Fashion, a critical feature of upper class circles during the early nineteenth century, was a perfect place to act out not only anxieties but also the mundane. Austen's juxtaposition between the gothic and the mundane suggests that with the lens of Romanticism, even the most tedious chores can be fantastical. In the more novel setting of the masquerade, the act of dressing mirrors the everyday social performance. But as with a mirror, the reflection is an inverse representation.

Romanticism centred individualism and the natural, challenging rising industrialisation and scientific advancements. These themes were opposites. Heroines and heroes of the gothic and supernatural stories, as free, natural, and good would challenge not only the elements but also villains. These villains, or characters of terror, often represented the tyrannies of property, economics, and consumer culture. Individuals appearing as stand-ins for these villains at a reputed bacchanalian event like a masquerade expected to elicit reactions from others. These representations depended on cultural literacy and engagement with the idea of Romanticism. Some, like Austen, parodied the gothic image while others might embrace it and find the future terrifying. On the whole, the scary costume embodied an individual's desire to shock, terrify, or amuse others who understood the symbols. Similarly, a masquerader disguising themselves as a known icon of heroic proportions also traded on cultural literacy to merit a response.

Heroic costumes most commonly appeared as military icons, military dress, fictional heroes and heroines, or gods and goddesses. Greek and Roman mythological characters were preferred, in keeping with the Neoclassical trends of the Regency era. The Graces were popular, as was Don Quixote, Corsairs, Robin Hood, and King Arthur characters. Representations of past royalty also frequently appeared at the events. One of the better costumes at King's Theatre in April 1804 was a man dressed at Hercules who displayed great dexterity in wielding his club.[27] Robin Hood and his merry Woodman of Arden appeared at Almacks in August 1820, amusing the crowd with catches and glees. The same night, half a dozen appeared in military costume.[28] Other enterprising masquerades, like Orion, would astound crowds with their creative costumes that were well coded and paired with quality performance.

In addition to many masquerades honouring living or recently deceased military heroes, it was common to see character and fancy dress costume portrayals of known warriors, idols, and ideals. The emphasis on the military, like other elements of the Regency masquerade, spoke to the identity of a nation at war. The Greek and Roman presence also represented the popularity of Neoclassism. Aristocratic and royal characters honoured both notions of the Empire and monarch and traditions. Those traditions, or fascination with history, had a quality of Romanticism as nostalgia for simpler times and was wrapped up in romantic ideals of nature and the individual. This often translated into costumes that were an expression of wish fulfilment, wanting to live out the romantic lives of those seen in novels, plays, and the newspaper, if only for an evening. The Prince Regent was notorious for a devotion to dressing up in historical and fanciful costume, enjoying the spectacle and luxury but also the idea of immersing himself and thus aligning himself with well-loved figures.[29] A big part of his play often involved the military. His 1811 Wimbledon Royal Review featured 20,000 soldiers parading in a two mile set of parallel lines as part of his over the top celebrations of his accession to Prince Regent.[30]

The military spectacle was well-matched for the heightened experience of a masquerade. With its military bands, national symbols, fireworks, and other nods to wartime, the masquerade enforced a nineteenth-century public fascination with military spectacle. This, in turn, improved public perception of the British military and strengthened patriotism. Yet these public displays of pageantry were not limited to masquerades. Military symbols and elements, like music, were woven through many experiences during the British Regency including public reviews, equestrian shows, literature, and day to day fashion. Wellington's boots, Hussar inspired headwear, epaulettes on pelisses, and brass buttons on livery were fashionable expressions of military influence on Regency life. As the military rose in prominence in the public imagination, so too did the popularity of donning military uniforms for the masquerade; while accounts of early nineteenth century masquerades might mention a sailor or solider among the costumes, by the time of Almack's 1818 Grand Fancy Dress Ball, around half of the gentlemen appeared in regimentals.[31] Whether in military uniform, or under the guise of a fictional protagonist, the heroic costume was a popular character and fancy dress option for masqueraders throughout the long Regency. As prevalent as a superhero costume is at a costume party today, Regency men in particular would appear masked as a popular figure or honourable service man. However, the heroic costume was not as well loved by audience and reporters as the comedic character.

The newspapers loved to report on the comic characters. That may be owing, at least in part, to masquerades being sold as the height of fun and frivolity, with many opportunities for amusements and wit.[32] These comedic characters helped to sell that experience, enlivening the crowd. Harlequins were common enough to seldom attract too much notice, but an enthusiastic masquerader could make any character deliver mirth and hilarity to the party. Such praise was heaped upon an Indian Chief and Dicky Gossip who gave support to their characters at an April 1801 Ranelagh masquerade.[33] Dicky Gossip was a well-loved character from the playwright Prince Hoare's *My Grandmother* that debuted on the stage in 1793. Performances of *My Grandmother* would regularly be staged throughout the Regency, and spin offs in the form of song, poetry, stories and even editorials would appear demonstrating the popularity of the character. From Mrs Owen's 1811 masquerade to an 1824 King's Theatre masquerade, the character would frequently appear to the delight of those in attendance. The 1802 Foley House masquerade even had Dicky Gossip's shop as part of the market town layout.[34]

It was not always the characters taken from farcical productions that were enjoyed for their comedic elements. Performance was a big part of what appeared to amuse the party; a Lowther Rooms masquerade report stated that laughter could be gained without wit.[35] At the Exton Hall December 1806 masquerade, an Old Beau could not be identified, but was well praised for his dedication to the role, and a Dr Spiccum, a Nutman, Country Bumpkin, and a Miss in her teens were part of a list of characters providing an uproar of joviality.[36] A baker threw flour on the party at the King's Theatre in May 1826, amusing the throng.[37] Even a character seemingly doing something typical for them, like a broom girl urging others to buy a broom was admired for an accurate, yet somehow humorous representation.[38] Two rival Moll Flagons at the June 1824 Argyll Rooms masquerade stole the show with a contest of who best embodied their character.[39] *Moll Flagon* was frequently performed on the stage in drag, to add to the comedic effect, and masqueraders loved to emulate this. These examples showcase that commitment to the part, with props, songs, or other catcalls to enliven the experience and helped to make the comic a favourite costume type.

Clowns with wit and harlequins with tricks and leaps filled the rooms at Haymarket for the April 1829 masquerade, with a wild man of the woods accompanying a dandisette that made a comedic splash.[40] Harlequins were most revered when actually acrobatic and animated and the odd pairing of the wild man and dandisette were also comedy gold at a masquerade. What was even more praised was when the masquerader brought the rest of the crowd into the performance. At Mrs Walker's June 1801 masquerade, the Honourable Mrs Walpole impressed the party in character as Goody Notable, dispensing good advice to the London fine ladies including recommending notable employments and works of all kinds instead of cards and idleness. It was done with such humour and commitment that the press found her to display a goodly amount of wit. The same night Lord Ashtoun was dressed as Sylvester Hortical, a gardener, and presented a comical bill to Mr Paul Methuen who was costumed magnificently as a dragon with wings and a tail.[41] The May 1799 Mrs Orby Hunter's Masquerade was made merry by the appearance of Doctor Moses Israel Funnidos, a quack who delivered handbills to the crowd competing with another character, Madame Commode who also distributed handbills of her wares. These two costumes were highlighted among a shortlist of those who amused the party.[42] The props certainly sold their costumes and increased the performance which, in turn, increased engagement and laughter.

The crowds favoured those who performed their part. A female lace smuggler alarmed several of the other ladies by dunning them at the Haymarket February 1807 event, surprising them for her close detection of what they had paid for their furbelows.[43] Brownlow North, a Church of England bishop who, at 40, appeared at Miss Morgan's masquerade in June 1802, led the charge to persuade the porter and Miss Morgan to let in twenty tickets she was convinced were forgeries.[44] His heroic deed was nonetheless described in comedic accents for his costume and appeal to Lady Warren to stand as his columbine. At the Marchioness of Buckingham's masquerade in May 1808, Mr Champneys, a regular masquerade attendee, appeared as Counselor Bother'em. With his pockets full of briefs, he was received with universal pleasure for his humour and dedication to his role.[45] Counsellor Bother'em was a general nickname to send up counsellors, and often described in opposition to Counsellor Bore'em. The characters would appear throughout the nineteenth century in poems, songs, satirical stories, and even in parliamentary debates.

Mr H. Johnson, dressed as a Scottish horse dealer, could be tracked throughout the room as bursts of laughter followed his journey in April 1818 at the King's Theatre. His affected accent, as well as sarcastic repartee were highlights, and he increased his popularity when teaming up with a half-drunk Irishman as a foil.[46] Robin Hood and the Woodman of Arden were a popular group theme, particularly for those individuals who liked to sing catches and glee, as such a group did at the Almack's August 1820 masquerade.[47] The newspapers would review these performances, highlighting those in particular that amused the party or those who failed to support their characters. The Haymarket's February 1822 masquerade had in attendance Father Christmas, who danced heartily surrounded by assorted other characters.[48] The Argyll Rooms January 1825 masquerade, according to the British Press, had a list of characters that while brilliantly dressed lacked in performance, including Monsieur Morbleu, Billy Lackaday, and Richard the Third.[49]

Popular farcical characters were consistent crowd pleasers. At the August 1820 Almack's masked ball, a well-concealed Mr Hamilton ably sported his costume of Dr Syntax, anxious to display his knowledge of men and manners to the crowd, in particular focusing on the domino clad persons of the Marquis of Tichfield and the Marquis of Worcester. It was only under the auspices of the clever Miss Wilbraham, disguised as a fortune teller, that Mr Hamilton was revealed to be the doctor.[50] Dr Syntax was often a highlight of the Regency masquerade, the humour of the performance emphasised over any particular fascination with the actual clothes or mask. An easily recognisable character that also had an entrendre-like affiliation with the masquerade, the cultural reference was surely made for comedic effect. Similarly, Mrs Guzzle's appearance at Viscount Courtenay's August 1801[51] masquerade ball harkened back to Fielding's 1734 comedy, *Don Quixote in England.* The play involved a series of misadventures Quixote is involved with in a tour of England, lampooning the legal system, the aristocracy, and literary culture of the Georgian era. Characters taken from theatrical comedies were often listed among the highlighted characters, as was Mrs Guzzle that night in 1801.

Another frequent costume guaranteed to inspire amusement was Major Sturgeon; Mr E Anderson was a favourite as Major Sturgeon at Mrs Boehm's June 1810 masquerade ball, his appearance peppered with noteworthy comic descriptions.[52] Major Sturgeon was a lead character of the farce, *The Mayor of Garratt*, written by Samuel Foote. During its debut in the 1760s, Foote played the Major who is discovered in a locked summer house with the main character's (Mr Sneak) wife. The Major and Mr Sneak appeared again at the June 1825 Argyll Rooms Grand Masquerade, mentioned alongside a list of other favoured costumes for the evening.[53] Mr John Gage paid homage to comedian John 'Jack' Bannister and highly entertained the party as the barrister in Weathercock with a gown covered with briefs at the May 1809 Argyll Rooms masquerade.[54] Another Bannister character, Colman's Sylvester Daggerwood, was also a popular costume. The farcical leads, particularly when supported by skilled presentation, were easy costumes for those seeking to make others laugh. As one critical review of a December 1823 Argyll Rooms event pointed out, dress alone was seldom enough to establish a character.[55]

Beyond the individual guests who were the object of praise or censure from the press, there were also several hostesses and hosts that would be favoured for turning their private masquerades into performance art. Thellusson's private masquerades were famous for their creativity and detail. The June 1802 event at Foley House had the great hall appearing as a village, with an assortment of peers and fashionables standing in as shopkeepers for entertainment and comedic effect. Mr Thellusson himself appeared as an old landlady, Mr Champneys as Doctor Brodum, Lord Grantley as Levi's Old Cloth maker, Mr Giles as Dicky Gossip, Mr Cox as Tiddy Doll at a Gingerbread shop, Colonel Fitzroy as Snip the Tailor, Mr Maddocks as Jobson the Cobler, Mr Wrottesley as Caleb Quotem Auctioneer, Colonel Armstrong as staymaker Jemmy Jumps, Lord Longford as a tapster at the inn, and Mr T. Sheridan appearing as a Methodist Preacher in a tub in the middle of the village decrying the immorality of masquerades.[56] These synchronised efforts supported the overall success of a masquerade, with respect to characters and costumes.

Forethought into a costume never ceased to earn the respect of the party and the reporters, as was the occasion for the Grand Masquerade at Argyll Rooms in June 1825. An unnamed talent appeared in the guise of a postman with letters addressed to the various members of the ton who were in attendance, astonishing and delighting them by delivering the letters to them even while masked. The same evening, a German doctor offered an antidote to swoons, melancholy, and despair alongside a stimulant to awaken joy and mirth, amusing the crowd so much that many ladies lined up to taste his potations. His elixir was so popular it attracted the attention of Mr Wright, who after a sip declared to a delighted crowd that the potion was none other than his own champagne.[57] The costume had made an appearance at Mrs Boehm's masquerade a decade and a half earlier when Lord Granville Leveson Gower dressed as a high German doctor, dispensing pills, bills, and potions[58] and something similar was warn at the October 1790 Wargrave masquerade.[59] Performances tied up in comedy reigned supreme at the Regency masquerade, but were also well complimented by more majestic and serious disguises.

Exotic costumes varied from foreign royalty to religious icons, or the more abstract costumes likely meant to inspire wonder or curiosity. A King's Theatre 1832 masquerade in December had court ladies, princesses and waiting women, immortals, Pharaoh's soldiers, and people dressed to represent different nations.[60] These costumes were praised for the opulence, detail, or authenticity in execution. A man dressed in Turkish costume appeared at the May 1826 King's Theatre masquerade, drawing significant attention as he walked solemnly through the crowd and about the room, while several Circassians pirouetted around him trying to gain his notice.[61] Fortune teller was a popular character for women, as displayed by Mrs Senate at the May 1802 King's Theatre masquerade. The *Morning Post* reported that she displayed real knowledge of fortune telling, a wealth of sarcasm, and witty repartee.[62]

At Almack's in 1820, Mr George Parkhouse appeared as a Persian Grandee, in a dress of pure gold and turban of linen, enriched with precious gems. He was not the only attendee appearing as a foreign aristocrat, dignitary, or national. The Earl of Bective and the Earl of Clare were both dressed as Spaniards, the Earl of Ancram as a noble Roman, Mr R. Spencer in the costume of a Cardinal, Lady Jane Lennox was masked in a beautiful Polish costume, Mr Charles Lane as a first class Grandee in blue and silver dress with towering plumes of ostrich feathers, accompanied by a party of Spanish Donnas, and Mr Alexander Bax displayed great dignity and grace as a Polish Grandee in the time of Stanislaus. Mr H. Kemble appeared as the Chief of the Banditti from the Alps, and the Earl of Blessington led a group of Irish peasants as an old Irish priest.[63] In July 1804, the Duchess of St Alban's masquerade saw Madame Gramont and Miss St Julien as Cherokees, Countess Harrington, Lady Stanhope, Lady Bligh, and the Misses Colman as Spanish Donnas, Miss Johnstone as a sultana, Mrs Duff as a Highlander, Mr Manners as the head of a banditti tribe, the Marquis of Hartington as a Chinese man, and a collection of men in Turkish costume including Lord Ossultstone, Mr Sneid, Mr Johnstone, and the Earl of Ormond. An abundance of Romani costumes, referred to as gypsies, were sported that night, including those worn by Lady Manners, Lady Perth, Miss Drummond, Lady Halliday, Mrs Butler, Miss Blackwell, the Misses Fieldings, Lady Melbourne, Lady Wombwell, and Miss Lambe. There was an equal abundance of Spanish-styled costumes, including those donned by Mr Robinson, Mr Greville, the Earl of Aberdeen, Mr Forester, Lady Harriet Cavendish, and Lady Morpeth.[64]

In contrast, when a real foreign dignitary was actually in attendance, they would appear unmasked; at Mrs Boehm's 1810 event His Highness the Duke of Gloucester and the Persian Ambassador appeared in their real ceremonial attire without masks. By comparison, that same evening Mrs O'Brien received much attention in her embroidered gown of black velvet and silver as a sultana and Lord Hawarden warranted notice in his costume of a Spaniard.[65] The Honourable Mr Lamb would dress as an Italian at an 1809 masquerade, while the Honourable Mr Blight would dress as a Highlander; meanwhile another guest dressed as a rich Turk in a mask while a real Turkish ambassador attended mask-less.[66] There was a clear divide between the marginalised and those in power, and costumes were clearly one way of reproducing the hierarchy.

The exotic, or culturally appropriating, costume was sometimes underscored by exaggerated performances. African or Indian dancing, for example, were described as highlights for several masquerades. Without details, it's difficult to assess whether the dancing, singing, or other acts performed were accurate or pure fiction concocted by those in costume to amuse and delight their counterparts. Lady Blacket's masquerade in April 1809 was well attended by many of the fashionable names of the era. That evening Miss Millman was dressed in Spanish costume and danced a Spanish fandango with castanets that impressed the crowd as did Mr Stewart, who as a Highlander, performed the Highland Fling.[67] The Highland Fling was performed eight years earlier by the Marquis of Loro and Mr T. Sheridan at Mrs Walker's masquerade ball.[68] It would also be performed at the Argyll Rooms in June 1825 by an unnamed group in costume.[69] A group of gentlemen dressed in Swiss garb performed a series of difficult, technical dances followed by elegantly dressed nymphs making up the bulk of the quadrille and waltz sets at the King's Theatre in January 1829.[70] We can speculate some of the dances were accurate, or close, and others were fabricated, but generally they were not performed with the same level of respect or care or in service of meaning as might be done by their native dancers.

The exotic costumes were commonly representations of ceremonial or royal attire, rather than everyday wear. Lavish and detailed costumes, although doubtless more stylised than authentic, would feature expensive jewels or their paste equivalents, rich silks and other fine fabrics, and expansive headdresses. Like fancy dress, the object seemed to be to impress. At the Hanover Square Rooms in June 1835, Lady Londonderry appeared as Cleopatra, wearing a host of costly gems in a gown embroidered with emeralds, diamonds, and pearls, with a detailed tiara on her head. She was said to outshine even herself.[71] A report from the 1802 Union Club masquerade suggested that the unrestrained excess of expenditure of not only décor but on clothing was as if the nobility and gentry resolved to display all the war time resources that should have been exhausted instead of celebrating peace.[72] Another category of costumes seemed to have similar leanings in implicit intent. The historical or nostalgic costumes often had individuals dressed as great historic figures including royalty. Whether convenient to raid their own attics for these costumes or driven by the desire to place themselves in the narrative of the past, nostalgic costumes, like exotic costumes, were most commonly lavish, detailed, and well accessorised.

Nostalgic costumes, particularly those that harkened back to bygone eras of England's history, were frequent at the events. At the May 1809 Argyll Rooms masquerade, Mr Champneys wore a very ancient court dress of brown velvet embroidered with silver frogs borrowed from the wardrobe of the late Sir William Pultney. Mrs Hoare graced the Rooms that evening as a lady of fashion from the reign of Queen Elizabeth. Her scarlet satin dress was ornamented with point lace and pearl beads, and likely had the puffed skirts, cinched waste, and bell sleeves of the Elizabethan era. Her husband, Mr Hoare was considered well dressed as a baron of ancient times in blue velvet dress with gold embroidery.[73] An old school Lord Chesterfield was highlighted after appearing at a May 1824 King's Theatre masquerade, alongside many of the standard costumes of the motley assembly.[74] With the exception of instances like the raid on deceased friends and relatives wardrobes, the historical recreations were fraught with anachronisms. As many of the detailed costumes were hired from theatres or warehouses, they were made with more readily available materials and techniques common to the Regency era rather than one of the past.

Queens, kings, courtiers, and ancient historical homages were popular themes also requiring some concessions for function over form. In other words, the representation was more important than the actual practical application so that an individual might give the impression of their character without having their movements restricted. Lord Lake and his party appeared as crusaders for the Almack's August 1820 masquerade, joined by the Earl of Ancram as a noble Roman.[75] Knights in armour were stationed along the staircases of a June 1828 King's Theatre masquerade, then later marching through the house with their chainmail breasts reflecting the brilliance of the well-lit theatre.[76] It is not known if these costumes actually included real chainmail and armour, or theatrical magic. Whatever the case, the nostalgic costume was popular, with these appearing in late Victorian fancy dress costume guidebooks.

Occasionally nostalgia would blend with the exotic to feature Greek and Roman gods and goddesses, or Pharaohs and their military. Typically described in detail, the costumes were rich representations of the past, based on a shared understanding of the symbols and elements expected to typify those slices of time. In most cases these costumes were on loan from theatre companies or masquerade warehouses, owing to the careful construction and embellishments. Indeed, in the hype leading up to the event it was not unusual to see a blurb suggesting the high demand for theatrical character dresses.[77] It's likely these were seeded articles meant to whip up interest in the events and promise novelty in the form of characters in abundance, but it nonetheless indicates the common practice of hiring costumes from the theatres for a masquerade.

Beyond the lavish and exotic, there was an element of the nostalgic in the rustic costumes that peppered the Regency masquerade. Farmers and yeomen, shepherdesses, country girls, and other rural representations conjured life not only away from town, but also the rapidly industrialising nation. One of the standouts at Viscount Courtenay's masquerade in August 1801 was a fiddler at a fair, who offered a lottery with wit displayed on the tickets he dispensed.[78] The appearance of a shepherdess at a Ranelagh masquerade in June 1802 caused the reporter to reminisce about a time past when wealthy, aristocratic daughters still tended to flocks.[79] Newspaper coverage of Almack's August 1820 masquerade highlighted Colonel Johnstone's Jolly Friar, a popular costume, and Mrs Hamilton's market woman,[80] two common examples of nostalgic costumes conjuring up a past away from the metropolis. These simple costumes were described as charming, enhancing female beauty and sometimes played to comic effect. With Regency slang being overrun with insults referencing a rustic or country person, humour and fantasy underlined the rustic character or fancy dress.

There were also more urban professions being mimicked at these events: the February 1817 Lyceum Theatre masquerade, in addition to sailors and soldiers, also had firemen and watermen in the crowd.[81] Fruit girls, fishmongers, and other market characters were also common costumes at most masquerades. Brownie (2013) calls the trans-status disguise the act of abandoning one's pressures and responsibilities in a performance of ordinariness. Her argument is that performance of ordinariness is the means to enable behaviour otherwise inappropriate or impossible according to the societal bounds of one's own class.[82] This intent best aligns with the Castlean idea of the masquerade, a pursuit of pleasure in defiance of propriety and expectation. Whether as comedic fodder, opportunity to best showcase personal attributes or to temporarily occupy a different status the rustic or occupational costume would be present at nearly every masquerade throughout the long Regency.

The country character represented just one opportunity to fully embrace a different lifestyle. Animals were sometimes introduced to the company. The November 1828 Argyll Rooms masquerade featured a small elephant that was tormented by a baboon while several monkeys enjoyed the event.[83] Monkeys were at the grand masquerade at King's Theatre in January 1826, including Monsieur Gouffe.[84] Monsieur Gouffe also made an appearance at the Argyll Rooms the same month and year rivalling with an imitator from Covent Garden. A Mr B., dressed as Beast from Beauty and the Beast, was also present and entertaining the crowd with his gruff pronouncements.[85] Just a few years after the Regency era, in 1840, the Reform Club would host a zoological masquerade, whereby menagerie animals were depicted in costume and mask.[86]An owl was a prominent costume at the Champney's January 1801 event, along with a dancing bear.[87] Beasts of the field, birds, and fishes were all in attendance at the King's Theatre in December 1832, with bears being pronounced the best for English masquerades.[88]

Although not commonplace costumes, animals represented another opportunity to abandon a person's identity and expectations to behave wildly. Comic in performance, the examples showcase the humans embodying mischief and mayhem as if real, untamed animals were let loose into the room. Even if the costume was not enhanced by performance and the wearer obeyed social strictures, the mask and attire alone could achieve an otherworldly effect. According to Klapp's (1954) social type theory, animal costumes are closely aligned with the fool, or the comedic type. Less important than realism is a caricature that builds in deviance with limited punishment.[89] There is an implicit understanding that the representation is fictional, and therefore the immediate idea of agency for the individual reduced if not eliminated. Purely fictional characters, whether anthropomorphised animals or the products of literature and theatre, gave wearers not only a sort of script to guide performance but also a license to completely abandon themselves.

Among the fictional inspiration sources for costumes, Shakespeare ranked high, with frequent appearances by mad Tom (of King Lear), Ariel, Prospero, Orlando, Romeo, Juliet, Rosalind, Hamlet, the Weird Sisters, Friar Lawrence, and Macbeth. These would have been familiar characters to the Regency audience, and therefore more readable to other guests, as well as likely an easy costume to acquire from a rental company. One author argued, in the 1930s, that no great drama was written in the nineteenth century owing to an overemphasis on Shakespeare, in part a sign of the Romanticism of the times.[90] Macbeth, Hamlet, King Lear, and other Shakespearean dramas were frequently on the stage in London and other cities throughout Great Britain, making a trio dressed as the Weird Sisters as ubiquitous as the stereotypical witch costume is today. However, not everyone dressed in pairs and groups when donning a Shakespearean fancy dress, as often the newspaper would recount a forlorn Rosalind or Romeo looking for their match.

Lublin's (2016) survey of the traditions of Shakespearean costumes in early modern England focuses on the visual codes offered by these costumes, which in turn, influenced the costuming practices. He highlights that even for those plays set in far off locations and in the past, performers often wore contemporary English clothing. This was not just a practical choice, Lublin argues, but a way for audiences to quickly gather information about the characters before they even spoke: their class, occupation, and gender were all discernible given clues in the costume.[91] This tradition of coding in theatrical costumes would have made the characters easy to figure at a masquerade. Whether the individual masquerader's intention was one of recognition, fantasy, or some other motivation, the Shakespearean costume was steeped in theatrical tradition and visual coding.

While some individuals may have chosen to showcase their beauty by dressing as Rosalind, or emphasise their wealth by dressing in rich fabric and jewels as a sultan, other costumes appeared to be the opposite of who the person was in real life. Lord Mansfield appeared at Mrs Walker's 1801 masquerade as a poor soldier, Lady Susan Hamilton as a Dutch housemaid,

Lady Ashburnham as a country girl, Lady Charlotte Lindsey as a kitchen maid, and Mr James as a farmer's wife.[92] The Marquis of Huntly and the Duke of Manchester were in the character of watermen at an 1809 event.[93] Rustic or trans-status costumes such as these were so run-of-the-mill as to only provide reaction in being diametrically opposed to the wearer's identity.

This may have been why the newspaper reports of these types of costumes were so cynical and quick to report it. For example, the Argyll Rooms in December 1825 was said to welcome Drury Lane actresses dressed as Quakers and vestal virgins, sailors who had never made it beyond Greenwich, rustics who had never ventured further from London than Primrose Hill, aging school boys, and Cockney Frenchmen.[94] Haymarket's April 1829 event saw friars with unholy attitudes, impure nuns, and urbane knights nonetheless in bulky armour.[95] These costumes were commonplace, the usual style as referenced by the newspaper reflecting the types of costumes readily available at the various costume warehouses; columbines, clowns, waggoneers, haymakers, maids, barbers, sweeps, tomboys, bubs, and friars were all listed as the standard characters witnessed at a masquerade by the end of the eighteenth century.[96] The response was more to the lack of novelty in the costume than the engagement of the masquerader with the category of costume they chose to don.

This refrain would appear over the years of newspaper coverage of masquerades, the writer drawing the contrast between costumes and the individuals who chose to masquerade as something opposite their own identity or experience. A May 1835 King's Theatre event was host to flower girls who could not name the content of their baskets, sailors who never had seen a frigate, and schoolboys who knew nothing of cricket and taw. But the author judged it justified for the crowds were entertained.[97] Humour was unlikely to be the intent of so mundane a costume, no matter the result. While it is hard to import the motive behind a costume donned by people from the Regency era, the *London Courier* and *Evening Gazette* suggested, with few exceptions, that people chose the costume and character most in step with their own spirit, nature, and disposition.[98]

*La Belle Assemblée* from November 1819 described fancy balls as all the rage in England and argued that it was of benefit because it highlighted the unique beauty of young ladies from various ethnicities. It went on to describe four costume ideas for young ladies, including the dress of a young sultana, fancy French dress, South American Indian dress, and Spanish fancy dress.[99]

This inclusive piece, albeit still smacking of cultural appropriation, suggested that costumes could be utilised to enhance one's personal attributes including colouring. This was not a unique perspective. Multiple editorial accounts would suggest that costumes were frequently chosen to emphasise positive attributes of a person including humour and wit, beauty, and strength.

Conversely, costumes represented the opportunity to embody the opposite of one's ordinary persona, as Castle suggested.[100] There are readily available examples of this in the record, some which will be explored with respect to national identity, cultural appropriation, and gender. This included young men masquerading as elderly women, white people masquerading as other ethnicities or races, Christians masquerading as Muslim, but also people dressing as animals, concepts, scary characters, and fictional characters. The opportunity for play outside of the confines of society was a powerful lure. Whether as wish fulfilment, subversion, or some other intent a masked costume could temporarily relieve social pressures and allow a person to explore another reality.

If costumes represented either the chance to enhance a person's identity or oppose it, then the domino must be read as a rejection of both of these things. While, more simply, it could have merely signalled the lack of preparation on the part of the masquerader or the significantly lower cost and therefore accessibility of the domino, its broad acceptance, albeit begrudging and often the subject of criticism, suggests that there was some understanding that certain people would not want to play. While the mask and hood would offer some disguise, and therefore surprise to others in attendance, it did not offer the same level of engagement. What developed as a strong preference for character costumes and performance at the British masquerade was soundly rejected by a non-descript anonymous silk mask and hood.

Despite the preference, it was not uncommon for dominoes to be the dominate costume. Ranelagh's masquerade in April 1801 had a few notable characters, but the crowd was largely garbed in dominos.[101] That August, Viscount Courtenay's lavish masquerade was said to suffer from the solemn show of domino dullness, although the author speculated the hot weather may have also resulted in wilting performances.[102] Almack's 1820 masquerade had many of the noble lords in attendance in dominos.[103] The domino-ed guests for the Argyll Rooms April 1823 masquerade were judged to be as indifferent spectators, rather than participants.[104] Two years later at a January Argyll Rooms grand masquerade and carnival, a sprinkling of nobility and fashionable persons were spotted in dominos among a crowd with little novelty.[105] When dominos prevailed at an event, as they did in February 1803 at Haymarket, it was said to give the assembly a gloom, dragging down the crowd for lack of novelty and entertainment provided by character costumes. Over and over, the newspaper coverage would represent the position that the domino was lazy and unentertaining. This, along with direct commentary, clearly indicates that more than ritual or an opportunity to anonymously mingle with others of different walks of life, by the Regency era the British masquerade was mainly an opportunity to entertain and be entertained.

This was never as clear when considering commentary of people attending masquerades without any mask or costume. The *Morning Post* described the act of appearing mask-less as a near impertinence, but certainly improper.[106] It was a common enough problem that masquerades, like the one held at the Pantheon in 1803, barred entry unless guests were dressed in domino or character. The reporter observed that those who were allowed to be mask-less, except when appropriate for their character, excited neither wit of others or among themselves.[107] Other events would go so far as to charge a premium for people appearing in dominos or without masks. Mrs Champney's January 1801 masquerade banned dominos, insisting on character and fancy dress costumes among the 200 guests to increase the hilarity of the masquerade.[108] Both incentives and barred admittance were frequent tactics both private and public events employed to maintain the festive air.

Much can be inferred from the festive efforts. The record of Regency masquerades points to the significant nuance when considering costumes. The categories of character and fancy dress costumes offer insight into trends, availability, and possible intentions behind donning a specific persona for the evening. Beginning in the early 1880s, a variety of titles were published that provided descriptions and even some plates showing characters or fancy dress ideas for balls. This helped industrialise the costuming world in an early form of what we see today. But during the Regency era, masqueraders would have to rely on their financial or other resources and imagination to create a costume that was visually coded enough to generate their desired reaction from others.

Costumes represent the true dialogic centre of masquerades, where everyone was expected to participate. Beyond the machinations of the promoters or hostesses and hosts, who invested heavily in décor, food, venue and spectacle, the costume was one of the primary, novel entertainments of the masquerade ball. Although the impresarios would hedge their bet by providing paid character performers, it was clear the preference was for organic showcases of talent, wit, and humour. Costumes will make a central part of the discussion on gender, race, class and culture, because they were so centred not only in the namesake and intent of the masquerade, but also as the vehicle for individual participant expression.

## Chapter Eleven

# National Identity, Class, and Cultural Appropriation

In the preceding chapters there have been hints and indications of national identity and its influence on the Regency masquerade. Overt homages to military heroes and the monarchy and the use of national symbols like oak leaves and roses were frequent. More subtly, the long Regency masquerades were filled with a reproduction of the social hierarchy, othering foreign nationals, religions and the working class through costumes and keeping exclusivity through high admittance fees or the use of private boxes. Even the repetitive refreshments and supper played to popular notions of luxury and elegance. The entertainment, too, played on what was culturally popular and also represented further opportunities to both exploit the other and strengthen a sense of belonging.

National identity is generally understood to be a sense of belonging to one or more states or nations. That state or nation is generally represented by specific language, culture, traditions and these markers tend to be dynamic. Smith (1991) suggested that national identity is a complex construct including ethnic, cultural, territorial and legal-political components that create solidarity in the community and are supported by symbols, values, and traditions. Symbols are an important touchstone of nationalism and national identity, ranging from obvious like a national flag or anthem, to more subtle and subjective, like a shared belief or attitude. It is the reading, reproduction and reinterpretation by members of a nation of these patterns of symbols that facilitates the sense of belonging and identity critical to national identity.[1] Smith (1991) posited that nationalism developed, according to modern understandings, in the eighteenth century, in a process of differentiation that enforced characteristics of ethno-nations. Even if the characteristics it enforced were negative.

Hutchinson and Smith (1994) suggested that this early phase of nationalism was dominated by Neoclassicism, developing in the later part of the eighteenth century, and then subsequently followed by Romanticism. Coupled with these broad cultural movements was an increasing sense of ethnicity, in some respects as a response to the American and French Revolutions. Global pressures, in this way, worked to strengthen the need for national identity rooted in nationalism. The presence of Neoclassical and Romantic themes during the long Regency, specifically as reoccurring motifs of the masquerade ball and other, similar celebrations, certainly strengthens the narrative that nationalism was on the rise in Great Britain at the end of the Georgian era into the Regency. There also is a more current sense that Romanticism and nationalism are two sides of the same coin, thus the development of the concept of Romantic nationalism. Masquerades were a perfect marriage of these elements, in productions that helped to produce and reproduce national identity. The sense of race and ethnicity, on the rise, was also being played out in the presentation of these identities through costumes and performance during the long Regency. Yet many of these elements had their start in the preceding century.

Beginning in the eighteenth century through the Regency era, British identity emerged as a concerted effort worked to unify the various countries of the British Isles and beyond, the broader Empire. Colley (1992) charted this formation by identifying four defining features that united Britain: it was a Protestant state, it was an island nation with a strong Navy, it was a metropole, and it was a direct rival to France.[2] Other scholars, like Barczewski (2000) have suggested that British national identity in the nineteenth century was a variety of competing points of view, including imperialism, nostalgia, duty, Romanticism, and competing values of the classes. Colley's four features, even with the added contrasts provided by Barczewski, offer a good overview for understanding the broad basis for national identity in Great Britain during the long Regency. Examined in the context of the masquerade, these themes become evident in the celebrations and even formula of these events. It also helps explains some of the seeming contradictory themes like Neoclassicism and Romanticism occurring at masquerades and how they played with nationalism.

It's helpful to first look generally at the relationship between masquerades and increasing commentary on the British character, or national identity. This tells us what contemporaries were thinking about the times they were living in, or challenging about the features they were seeing play out in real time. The criticism of masquerades, in particular, provide good commentary on not only what was ringing authentic for the target audience, but also what was not. Throughout the long Regency, the criticisms were remarkably similar and provide a pattern of critique centred on national identity. First, there was the argument that masquerades were a foreign invention at odds with British national identity; imported from morally liberal and licentious continental cities, masquerades were considered to be a strange fashion to adopt in Great Britain. This assessment was part of an overall 1814 guidebook and editorial on Bath, and the author judged the masquerade an unfortunate cultural import.[3] The implication was that Great Britain's people were more reserved, moral, and that the masquerade was encouraging people to adopt the more loose morals of European counterparts. In this way, masquerades were viewed as subversive. While the editorial focused primarily on morality and manners, implicit was the sense that masquerades essentially made the British sympathetic with Europe. Considering the backdrop of the Napoleonic Wars, this was an untenable idea.

This guidebook was not alone in such an assessment. Sermons lamenting the lack of shame the masquerade allowed for were delivered. Hand wringing over the loose morals of urban places allowing masquerades was written in editorials and tomes. For all that the fashionable set enjoyed the character and fancy dress balls, sumptuous refreshments and supper, and lavish decorations, there were critics on the fringe finding the events completely devoid of any moral or other value. Excess, particularly in light of war time, was particularly suspect and ripe for censure. In fact, some contemporary writers and clergy would suggest the masquerades were dangerous to Great Britain. Public masquerades, in particular, were seen by some as dangerous places to be exposed to criminal elements, including con artists, pickpockets, and sex workers. Even at the more successful events, like the Pantheon February 1803 masquerade, pickpockets were plentiful, taking advantage of the domino mask to conceal themselves among the throngs of people. That same event saw a small set-to between a naval Captain and a well-known brewer, who were overheard to mention pistols and dawn hours.[4] While not all events appeared to have this level of disruption, there was a general sense of danger in attending a public masquerade. The crowds were typically described as motley, implying a mixing of class that frankly was more imagined than reality. However, for the larger public venues, like the Pantheon, the safety of private boxes were on offer to segregate wealthy patrons wanting to observe the festivities but not participate.

Beyond mixing with unsavoury elements, there was the broader danger of intoxication to spoil a sense of peace. Drunkenness was a common complaint often resulting in fights or near deadly incidents as was the case at the September 1828 masquerade at the Royal Gardens in Brighton. Owing to the mixed company, or so suggested the *Brighton Gazette*, a fight broke out in the saloon between a livery servant and a High Street inhabitant. The livery servant, who the article hastened to add was a real servant and part of a larger group of servants at the masquerade, was said to toss a High Street person down the stairs hard enough to nearly break his neck.[5] This was a standout event, but seemed to solidify to the masquerade critics that intoxication was central to unsavoury behaviour and part of what made these events dangerous. Some venues limited the hours that alcohol was available to reduce drunkenness, and many reviews of events would mention the success of the event in relation to how intoxicated people were. The Lowther Rooms, in particular, had a terrible reputation for being mainly visited by young bucks intent on heavy drinking and partying.

It's likely these types of incidents helped further support criticism that masquerades were incompatible with British identity. It is also why public masquerades were discouraged for unmarried ladies, and often more broadly elegant ladies. Private masquerades, where the guests were on a strict invitation list were more acceptable for varied company, including fashionable ladies, likely because it restricted mixing with unknown persons; some works of fiction or tomes of etiquette advised that no gentleman should bring his respectable wife to a public masquerade. As even the favourable reviews shared, more genteel ladies tended to stick to the boxes of the larger events at venues like the Pantheon to avoid mingling with the motley crew. Beyond the drinking, carousing, and wild behaviour, the events were also described as dirty, noisy, and unbearable in temperature so as to assault all the senses with significantly less refinement than gently reared people were used to. At least that was the implication. The more exclusive venues were also not immune to these criticisms, particularly when alcohol was freely available and likely to enliven the spirits of the party to such an extent as to become unseemly and wild.

Not every criticism focused on the danger and immorality of the masquerade. Some criticisms centred on a perceived mismatch between British character or national identity and the essence of a masquerade. A comedic essay called the English masquerade flat and unprofitable with the very nature of the masquerade requiring witty repartee and liveliness, in opposition to the national character which was more commonly blunt and taciturn. It stated that a public masquerade in England was little more than a dull game of dominoes.[6] The suggestion that masquerades were contrary to the English character was not a fresh perspective, having been argued in past editorials. Some were likely said in loving jest for their fellow countrymen, while others judged masquerades too fanciful and risqué for the British temperament. An 1835 masquerade was roasted for offering noise and vulgarity in the place of wit and humour,[7] while a scathing send up of young bucks and older gentlemen attending an 1824 Argyll Rooms masquerade labelled masquerades motley and insipid events.[8] On occasion, a reporter would lament about the bygone era when masquerades were a novelty, a new thing, compared with the stale and repetitious spectacle they had become in the nineteenth century. In some cases, masquerades were so commonplace that they had become trite and dull. Rather than a ritual, as with their continental counterparts, they were manufactured experiences that emphasised spectacle over substance.

Masquerades were also judged harshly when they failed to meet the basic standards established for the entertainment, including décor, refreshments, and a large attendance of people in costume. Dominos were found lacking and unimaginative, and even the presence of character or fancy dress was not enough to delight if the wearer was not fully engaged in performance of the person or thing they deigned to represent. An 1803 King's Theatre masquerade was judged to be dull and monotonous despite the majority of the attendees never having been at a masquerade before. While the lack of character dress, in part, was held to blame, the undercurrent of this report was that masquerades were entirely incompatible with Britons.[9] A year later, a scathing brief on a May Pantheon masquerade called it a satire to the memory of elegant masquerades of the past, featuring miserable characters.[10] The short blurb highlighted little but the seeming misery of attendees. Whether those in attendance did not understand the expectations for their own performance, or that the novelty was too thin, these occasions highlight a not uncommon refrain.

Even the Argyll Rooms was not without critique. After a December 1825 masquerade, the *New Times* published a punishing review that suggested the only females attending public masquerades were notorious and in love with notoriety so that their main interest was in the revealing of their identity rather than concealing. Worse still, was that a guinea admission was a low enough bar to prevent exclusivity, so that the party was a mob, and stupid at that, leaving only broad humour and forced joviality to enliven the atmosphere. While the December Argyll Rooms event was saved from this more contemptuous rumination by having a larger number of genteel and fashionable men on hand, the general concept of a masquerade was put forth as flat.[11]

A year earlier, following a November Argyll Rooms masquerade, a reporter mused that masquerades were inevitably the domain of the idle and dissolute, seeking to be entertained rather than participate in the general entertainment of others. The only highlight, according to the review, was the supper which was of excellent quality and plentiful.[12] In December 1823, the *Morning Herald* also lambasted the Argyll Rooms masquerades, particularly for its use of the word Carnival, which they suggested foreigners abroad in London doubtless laughed at the misapplication of the word, having no connection to Lent. Furthermore, while there was a good mix of the usual character costumes, there was little performance from the people who had dressed up and almost all the women who appeared were Cyprians, albeit the more exclusive of the set, signalling the general encouragement of masquerades to citizens to engage in vice. They suggested while masquerades abroad naturally involved the intermixing of classes, in England it would be unnatural and embarrassing to everyone involved.[13] These refrains would not be unique to particular venues or events, and would make up the main body of critique against the Regency masquerade.

A few decades later, the perspective would shift again. A Victorian survey of London life proclaimed that masquerades had never acquired stable popularity. While this is arguable, considering the tremendous number of masquerades that occurred over the long Regency, there is some familiar critique in the rationale on offer. The author's argument was that the masquerade was the very antithesis of English national character. Specifically, it was posited that the English do not have fast enough wit or sufficient animal spirit to sustain a masquerade. Furthermore, when the theatres were enlisted to provide the necessary entertainment, like paid actors and actresses dressed in character costumes, the proceedings would ultimately devolve into vulgarity and indecency. An exception was made for private masquerades and Vauxhall Gardens.[14] This scathing assessment echoed other contemporary criticisms of Regency masquerades that suggested the

British nature was contrary to the spirit of a masquerade. Whether likened to a dull set of dominoes or a flat and unfanciful affair, it was clear some felt masquerades were not supported by the British character.

The continental cities, critics would suggest, were more interesting locations for masquerades as the qualities of such assemblies better aligned with the overall character of the nations.[15] However, the travel memoirs and reporting from the era on continental masquerades suggest there is some nuance in understanding this comparison. One diary stated unequivocally that an Italian masquerade was duller than one in England, although the author admits that he based the conclusion off attendance at one masquerade ball held in Florence.[16] Another travelogue suggested that rather than repartee or dialogue, the chief amusement at Neapolitan masquerades were in opportunities for secret intrigue.[17]

An 1802 report from Paris on the three weeks of Carnival held that district police paid individuals appearing in mask and dress, but at many of the venue balls gentlemen wore neither a domino nor mask, while the ladies appeared predominantly in fancy dress with dominoes.[18] Dominoes were portrayed as the ultimate affront to the spirit and intent of a masquerade. This was so similar to many of the laments of the London masquerade. The distinct difference was really in incentivising people through payment. London venues typically took a more punitive approach, barring entrance without a mask. One travel account argued that the Italian masquerade costumes were less varied than those of Haymarket, and that there is an implicit lack of intent with respect to humour in dressing for the Carnival.[19] Another travelogue recounted experiences at Carnival, stating the masks infrequently attempted any character, were insipid, and not backed by any attempt at performance.[20]

A detailed account of an Italian masquerade in 1816 listed costumes not dissimilar to those that appeared at British events. The author, James Sloan, described the complete abandonment of morals and gallantry at the events, and the build up after days of events to a crescendo where all public places were crowded with masked and costumed people. In an analysis of the Italian masquerade, Sloan first stated that the masquerade festivities were so subversive as to completely undo the virtuous foundation of places like America, and further suggested that the profligate manners across the social classes no doubt led to the fall of the Italian republic.[21] His hyperbolic assessment was perhaps giving masquerades more credit than they deserved in their influence on politics, but it did capture the sense that masquerades were wanton and gluttonous pursuits. In some cases both British and foreign masquerades were the target of censure; coverage of a June 1825 Argyll Rooms masquerade pronounced British masquerades a dismal display due to the lack of mercurial temperament to support the festivities, although it also pronounced modern Carnivals in Italy to be a pageant of heartlessness, showing a sentimental longing for the bygone era of masquerades, including a harkening back to Grecian versions and a masked ball in Stockholm.[22]

Whether the opinions of those British masquerade critics truly believed continental masquerades to be superior or the positive spin of continental masquerades was manufactured to serve as stark contrast to the British masquerade, it is clear from the available literature that there were both similarities and differences in the form and function of masquerades. On the whole these criticisms of British character with respect to masquerades emphasised the need for wit and a certain carefree attitude to embrace the testing of boundaries implicit in a masked event. This was not a universal sentiment, clearly, but likely a platform serving to largely critique the British rather than be favourable to other nationalities.

This harsh summation of British character, and masquerades, misses the point of how masquerades were adapted over the eighteenth century to support and further British national identity. It is the foundational elements that, by and large, seem to separate British and continental masquerades. On occasion, British events would have a Carnival theme, but in purpose and form what evolved in Great Britain was substantively different than the European masquerade. The Carnival of Venice, broadly speaking, used a series of specific masks, some grotesque and others simple, to hide their identity and allow the classes to intermingle for the celebration. Anonymity was the object, rather than performance. Religious overtones would have been present, even when by the eighteenth century pleasure was an important element of the celebrations. There was a deep tradition, a ritual, in the Venetian Carnival that held religious and socio-economic significance to the Italians.

Comparatively, the origins of the British masquerade were routed in novelty spurred by an entrepreneurial motivation for commercial success. Heidegger and Cornelys, the two main impresario figures of the eighteenth century masquerade, were not religious icons, political leaders, or the like but instead were a form of cultural influencer. Trendsetters that financially benefited from putting something into fashion, these promoter's fortunes were linked to the success of the masquerades. The motivation for these masquerades would set a foundation for them to develop over the century into something that intentionally looked very different from the continental Carnival. It's not surprising that wit and repartee would be emphasised, as well as the idea of amusing or entertaining others, when the primary motivation was to entertain people enough to come again, and spend money doing so. As one newspaper pronounced, referencing a June 1826 masquerade at the Argyll Rooms, the English masquerade is for those dedicated to amusement, enhanced by Champagne and a general mood of conviviality.[23] Spectacle heightened the novelty of the experience for the British Regency masquerade, deviating from earlier events and continental counterparts in large because of the pecuniary impetus behind these event productions. Luxury and abundance in décor, food, alcohol, and entertainment strengthened the sense of uniqueness, while also heavily relying on cultural symbols familiar and comfortable to the higher income people in attendance.

Everything was centred around the elite at a British Regency masquerade. Where the intermingling of classes was a pinnacle feature of the Venetian masquerade, even at the larger, public venues there were opportunities for the wealthy and fashionable to distance themselves from the motley crowd. Exclusivity reigned at the smaller venues, through the institution of patroness approval or high entrance fees. And private masquerades were limited to the rank and file of the haute ton. These events were less about the opportunity to mingle freely with people from other walks of life, and arguably more about maintaining a status quo. This becomes an important idea when we scrutinise how the masquerade was reproductive of national identity, using costumes, décor elements, and music to create a shared experience that further rooted a sense of place and class.

Some of the forced distance between the classes might have been engineered to save attendees the embarrassment of class mingling, as critics suggested. But it is more likely that, with the impetus behind masquerades being commercial success for venues and promoters, it was more profitable to do so. Although, for some of the larger venues, the reports hint at vulgarity and promiscuity among a faceless mass, the entrance fee would have barred lower classes from participating. The entrance fee alone would have been a significant barrier to egalitarianism at these events, if not for all the other expenses; an account following an 1824 Argyll Rooms masquerade figured the cost to be roughly three guineas to an attendee, including a ticket, costume, supper, and wine. The author suggested an Italian, French, or

Spanish masquerader would be hard pressed to spend one sixth of the sum.[24] And for those wanting to be even more exclusive, they would pay an even higher cost for entrance fees or box rentals. This, in turn, would generate more income for the venues and promoters.

Still, there was a need to manufacture some sense of risk and the risqué, a way to embody the spirit of the continental masquerade without the true risk and lack of profit associated with class mingling. Castle (1986) makes the argument for the Georgian masquerade being a bacchanalian pursuit of free love and class exploration. There may be some truth to this in the Georgian era, although recent scholars have taken issue with Castle's claims. However, by the Regency era, much of the class mingling was artificially facilitated by the promoters who paid performers to attend for the amusement of the paying customers. Actors and actresses would be hired to appear in character dress, meeting the expectation for wit and entertainment, all the while maintaining a safe distinction between performers and patrons. This was clearly evident at venues that required subscriptions and approval from patronesses, like the Argyll Rooms and certainly at private masquerades where reports would occasionally surface of attempted party crashers who would cause a scene.

At the Pantheon and Vauxhall where attendance would often rank in the thousands, it's likely that there was some infiltration of the fashionable crowds by the upcoming middle classes, although how much that occurred is up for debate. Current scholarship suggests that the cost of a season subscription and dressing appropriately for the various events at the more popular venues would have been too cost prohibitive for even the bourgeois.[25] This narrows the general population in attendance to those of the upper classes, those paid to be there, and those who obtained entrance by means foul or fair. Of note, critics often cited the abundance of sex workers and pickpockets making up the crowd. This separation of classes was a clear deviation from the Venetian Carnival origins. While the individual participants of a London masquerade may have enjoyed the masquerade for similar reasons as the Carnival goers, the forming tradition would be more about entertainment for entertainment's sake for those who could afford the novelty.

Entertainment in its broadest sense was an integral part of the British masquerade, woven into nearly all aspects. The formula for a masquerade, set in the Georgian era, focused on the décor, refreshments and supper, music, and band to the extent that these were viewed as necessary for success of an event. The décor, the music, and the various performances had a similar rhythm from event to event, but from the Georgian to Regency era the emphasis on spectacle would continue to create a sense of novelty for the masquerades. Whether in the form of awe-inspiring chalk drawings or transparencies celebrating the monarchy, or two or more bands, or fireworks, or balloon ascensions, the program of masquerades emphasised excess, luxury, and inspiring awe among attendees. The sheer number of lamps used at many of the venues, at a great cost, set a tone for the extraordinary.

While the entertaining spectacles were in a race to outperform one another, from event to event and venue to venue, a startling reliable repetition of the symbols used at Regency masquerades underscored national identity. Monarchy symbols in the light displays, flora and fauna of the Empire, military accompaniments, and homages to military heroes emphasised national identity so overtly that it was likely taken for granted by attendees. It would have been unremarkable to attend any number of these events in the forty year time span and listen to a military band serenade you upon entrance, to look up and see transparencies of the regent or king, and to find oak leaves and roses hung strategically on bannisters.

Coupled with the thirst for character dress and performance, the script for masquerades almost ensured for little authenticity in how these events played out. The character dresses and performances, too, had some repetition to hint at not only individual identity but also the broader national identity. While I will later explore cultural appropriation and how it may have been used in support of national identity, more broadly speaking the popular character costumes highlighted in press and memoirs were not unique but had some defining characteristics. First, they traded on a shared literacy of popular media like theatre or literature. This assumed other attendees had the wherewithal, both in time and money, to be well versed in both including being literate. Second, collective review of masquerades emphasised performance as part of the entertainment factor in the masquerade; it was not enough to dress cleverly or well, one was expected to also embody the character the individual was intending to portray. Third, despite the individual intentions or desires revealed by the character or fancy dress costume, or domino for that matter, there was an inherent social contract in masquerading as a play of presentation of self in everyday life.

The play was apparent when looking at coverage of character costumes and how the comedic characters, in particular, were often amusing because they were the opposite of how the individual ordinarily presented themselves. However, newspaper articles also highlighted how many chose costumes intended to enhance their natural features of power, beauty, acrobatics, or wit. Conversely, paid actors and actresses who appeared at events in costumes to entertain were seldom named or otherwise identified beyond the character they dressed as, in an acknowledgment that their attendance was true theatre rather than a play on identity. Both the theatrical guest and the guest playing off their own identity by masquerading as something different had a place in the overall London masquerade that, more than anything, sought to entertain rather than enact any ritual or rite. These origins and the importance of novelty and entertainment over ritual or tradition necessarily set the stage for the increasing levels of spectacle seen at the Regency masquerade.

Criticism about individual masqueraders, whether not acting the part or simply being unimaginative, had some merit. It was not unusual for a critical review of a masquerade to highlight how few people appeared in much more than a domino, if that, and that the celebrations would often devolve into debauchery. Debauchery, when described, seemed largely to consist of drunkenness, and loud, lewd behaviour rather than frenzied free love. However, this criticism tells us something about the British national identity, at least from an iterative perspective. In a sampling of critical reviews of Regency masquerades, there are several common refrains. The lack of costume, performance, and participation were frequent laments. Naturally, the expectation was that at a masked ball those in attendance would be masked. The performance piece is more subtle. The underlying assumption is that the act of donning a mask itself implies the commitment to adopting a different persona. In the case of the Carnival, the emphasis was more of being a part of a faceless mass able to act freely without fear of consequence. However, because the preference for the British masquerade emphasised character or fancy dress, the stress was on the masquerader becoming that person. Such a transformation, naturally, would depend on the talent of the individual. The mask and dress alone do not imbue magical powers to become a historical figure or an abstract concept. Yet, the expectation was for that performance, a desire for entertainment or amusement or delight in others being the opposite or something very different than how they appeared typically in society.

There were individuals named time and time again in press coverage and memoirs that delighted in the performance piece of the masquerade – the

Thellussons, Sheridan, Champney, the prince, and numerous celebrated masquerade hostesses like Mrs Powell and Mrs Coke. It was also notable that the tone of reporting for public masquerades and private masquerades very subtly hinted at the vast difference between anonymous performance and performance requiring some familiarity. The private masquerade often had orchestrated performances among the guests, intended to amuse the others much like an inside joke. Conversely, the public masquerade stressed less the notable difference between the authentic person and their performed character, and more on the overall embodiment of that which they intended to represent.

Several themes emerge with Regency masquerades based on an examination of contemporary sources. First, national identity was a foundational element to décor, guests, and the spectacle. Not only were military bands, dress, and symbols used commonly in masquerades, but homages to the monarchy were also prevalent in the songs, symbols, and exclusive spaces reserved for the queen, the prince, and others. The second emergent theme is that cultural appropriation, or at least the praxis of other cultures, focused on imperialism was a component that reinforced national identity. The contrast of the selected character and fancy dress is stark against the general sense of British national identity of reserve and formality. The cloak of an opposite persona would have been appealing to shed the mantle of more repressive accents. Yet, the appropriated culture also gives clues to national identity beyond mere dissimilarity.

National identity is generally understood as the sense of a nation as a whole, represented by language, culture, and traditions unique to a country or collection of countries. The Georgian and Regency British identity was, according to scholars, a war against powerful France, bringing with it religious undertones that pit Protestantism against Catholicism. Anti-Catholic rhetoric was frequently baked in to parliamentary and other conversations about the expanding Empire, even in the face of the 1829 Catholic Emancipation.[26] While British culture in the Regency was filled with Francophilia in its dedicated interest to French fashion, cuisine, and culture, there was also an ever-present acknowledgment of France being an adversary. In both European conflict, and conflict between warring imperial colonisation, Great Britain and France were the reigning super powers of the Western World, locked in a battle for supremacy.

However, British national identity during the Regency was not exclusively about its complicated relationship with France. McLeod (1999) identifies five national identity themes in the century following Waterloo: Christian, Protestant, prosperous, civilised, and free. In part, these identities developed in direct, stark contrast to French identities; the British were moral while the French were immoral, the British were serious while the French were frivolous, and the British were faith based opposed to French scepticism. But beyond France, these identity themes had their roots in a changing landscape moving towards urbanisation and industrialisation. Newman (1987) pointed to the Georgian rise in cosmopolitanism as the foundation to British national identity. Forged with the Anglo-French interchange of feeling intellectual and moral superiority to the rest of the globe, strengthened by an emphasis on the aristocratic culture, cosmopolitanism drove the elites of Georgian and Regency England towards the urbane and luxurious. The Regency era was the very embodiment of aristocratic culture obsession, even as individual families were coming to terms with globalisation, changing economies, and the rise of the mass production that would shift Great Britain away from a feudal and agriculture based economy.

Coupled with the nationalism that focused on defence against enemies and expansion abroad,[27] it is not surprising that the masquerades in Great Britain were a study in contrast. It was these contrasts that were raised by critical reviews of masquerades and the seeming dichotomy between the essence of masquerade and British national identity. The drive for variety, force, and originality in characters[28] was in direct competition with the need for sameness, reserve, and morality. Simultaneously, the promoters emphasised the war with France, including overt symbols from the military and monarchy, while the masqueraders delighted in caricatures of foreign nationals, different religions, and lower classes.

Meghan Kobza (2023) has examined cultural appropriation with respect to the Georgian masquerade, arguing that Enlightenment ideas of ethnicity and race were leveraged at the masquerade as a form of praxis to celebrate the Empire while othering colonised or other marginalised people. Like their Georgian counterparts, Regency masqueraders also frequently dressed in character or fancy dress costumes representing Africans, American Indians, and Indians. It was also commonplace to see masqueraders dressed to represent Muslim or Jewish people. The accounts from balls suggest not only did masqueraders dress in a style they thought represented different races, ethnicities, and religions, but frequently there was an impersonation or act along with the costumes that relied heavily on stereotypes. This cultural appropriation was not exclusive to communities of colour or marginalised religions, as it also included a variety of cultures across continents. There was also frequently a class element to the masquerade.

At the Grand Fancy Ball at the Hanover Square Rooms in June 1835, Lady Chesterfield was garbed as a sultana and her sister, Mrs Anson, in Greek robes. The *Morning Post* called them, and their companions who were similarly dressed, correct and sumptuous representations of Oriental gorgeousness. Lady Londonderry was Cleopatra idealised, wearing a profusion of jewels embroidered into her gown and on her person. That evening several gentlemen were dressed in the splendour of Oriental travellers, and the reporter observed that the contrast between genuine costumes and fictional ones was very obvious.[29] A 1791 masquerade appearance of a gentleman dressed as a Sandwich Island native was complimented for his striking figure[30] while a King's Theatre masquerade in February 1803 had one man dressed in black face and three or four women similarly costumed. At that same event, an Indian was said to be indecent in his dance and a Chinese man gave a speech that portrayed him as humbled by his experience abroad in England. There were also two people dressed to represented Jewish money lenders, performing the stereotype to the pleasure of the crowd.[31] These examples, which were not exceptional, highlight the types of presentation masqueraders would affect in appropriating other cultures, clearly objectifying the other while also seeking to promote something about themselves: beauty, wealth, and comic talent were compliments bestowed on these types of masqueraders to demonstrate a reporter and the crowd's pleasure.

The wealthy and elite would also fit themselves in finery meant to portray agricultural workers, lower class hawkers, and foreign peasants, ironic because the costumes were often of higher quality and ornamentation than those they would caricature. Stereotypes could be relied upon as symbols and signals to those in attendance, and were enhanced by performance from the subtle and shy to the overt calling out in song. Yet the goal was always unmasking, and as the *Newcastle Courant* described following a June 1825 Argyll Rooms masquerade, amusing acquaintances and friends with their wit, performance, and characterisations. On occasion, as was the case for an August 1802 masquerade, fellow peers would be lampooned but it was more common for masqueraders to select costumes that represented those outside of their class, religion, country, and race. If costumes, as Ermilova (2020) stated, are informational and sign structures meant to convey regional, national, and other affiliations, then perhaps it is their richness and difference that lent themselves so successfully to serving as a novel diversion from most attendees' norm. Kobza squarely places the practice of cultural appropriation on a subconscious need to perpetuate stereotypes about enslaved and other marginalised people, as a way to promote the sense of superiority and white supremacy.

Rogers (2006) identified four types of appropriation including exchange, dominance, exploitation, and transculturation. This framework is helpful to understand not only the nuances of the complex idea of cultural appropriation, but also how the examples from the Regency masquerade seem to differ in intention. Cultural exploitation, Rogers defined, is using elements of a subordinated culture by a dominant culture without permission, compensation or other type of exchange. Much of the Regency masquerade costumes are tied to this definition, because of the power dynamic at play. Most participants of the British Regency masquerade were white, wealthy, and Protestant. Their use of cultural symbols or costumes of marginalised or subordinated cultures served to promote their own interests, even if that was as simple as entertainment. Western culture now frames this as punching down, exploiting marginalised people to serve as the butt of jokes. Yet these stereotypical costumes were often unoriginal and relied on an already commodified expression of the other. Rogers stated that by fetishizing other cultures, the act of commodification is obscured and the justification for unequal power relations is preserved.

Cultural appropriation was not new to Great Britian. Scholars point to seventeenth-century figures like Lord Sherley, whose exploits abroad were packaged for a British audience into travelogues, and memoirs of Francis Bacon, who appropriated Chinese inventions of gunpowder, printing and compasses to try to make the claim for English supremacy. As the British Empire marched towards the first steps of globalism, it was not uncommon for art, invention, and culture to be first de-cultured then figured as transcultural in a complex system of appropriation meant to prop up British, and Anglo-Christian, supremacy.[32] Wild (2020) summarised much of the current literature on cultural appropriation that proposes it is an ongoing dialogue between self and social identities. His analysis suggests that intent is likely much more complex than simply to reduce other cultures as commodities.

Yet the commodification of culture was nonetheless part of these exchanges, centring the power elite's experience and objectifying others as a way to eliminate true cultural dialogue.

Whether culturally appropriating or transcultural, the Regency masquerade as a commercial, rather than ritual activity lent itself to privileging the perspective of the ruling class. Luxury, nationalism, and a fantasy of risk that was more social construct than real helped attract and sustain interest from those who could afford attendance, bolstering their sense of supremacy. The sheer level of repetition in the production of these events, as well as the repetition in costumes, suggest that these were a feature of the design rather than a flaw. When a visitor would happen upon these events by invitation or opportunity, some would seek to exploit it through theft and others no doubt would be dumbstruck by the self-serving narrative on display. While it's difficult to ascertain individual motivations in participating in the Regency masquerade, much of this subtext would have been the subconscious play of individuals faced with extraordinary pressures including rising industrialisation and globalisation, imperial expansion and continuing conflict abroad, and a rising middle class challenging the former class structure. Acting out these conflicts with self-soothing rituals, whereby individuals were able to assert their dominance by finding amusement in playacting, marginalised people while also providing a sense that they were actually mingling with this dangerous element and heightened the experience of the masquerade as fun. That masqueraders were rewarded after unmasking by a sumptuous feast of all the delicacies of the season and then continued dancing and drinking, as well as often some sort of celebratory spectacle, served to reposition and comfort masqueraders who, for a time in the early evening, grappled with a variety of identities that ranged from frightening to comedic.

While some critics found, particularly in comparison to European masquerades, that the masquerade itself was incompatible with British national identity, clearly the British masquerade was designed to support and reproduce a specific national identity. One of privilege, power, and exclusivity. It would have been incompatible with both the financial motivations behind introducing this species of entertainment to London but also the things that kept people coming back to these events. The luxurious banquets, feasts for the senses, and entertainment by sharing common values through the mediums of disguise and surprise and the lavish spectacle, functioned to make people feel secure and reinforced in their power and privilege. To even further advance this sense of belonging, caricaturing other cultures helped to create a strong sense of 'us' versus 'them'. Whether this was exacerbated by real anxieties the population doubtless had from being at war is not completely knowable, but the continued emphasis on the military in most aspects of the masquerade suggest that it was both subconscious and top of mind for the power elite of the Regency.

Modern ideas of identity and cultural appropriation, including intersectionality, are challenging to impose on a world and time that was, in many respects, early on in national identity formation. Attitudes towards race, ethnicity, and class were highly dynamic and even volatile during the Regency as debates raged in parliament and beyond over these issues. Costumes are one aspect of the Regency masquerade that clearly demonstrate how bound up identity was, particularly in cultivating a sense of 'us' and 'them'. More importantly, while it may point to key pressures and concerns of the Regency elite, it can also inform the modern interplay of costume and identity.

One identity, gender, has been purposefully left out of this chapter in order to devote a more focused analysis of how gender was played at the Regency masquerade. In part, this is because it's an opportunity to explore how the different genders played differently with masquerading. This information clearly applies to cultural appropriation or transcultural play, as has been discussed with marginalised people and restrictions on their costume and performance. However, the evidence in the record more starkly portrays this when considering gender, and therefore its worthwhile devoting focused attention. The other reason to segregate gender from previous analysis is that there is more evidence of costumes being used as subversive tools when considering gender. We turn to gender next.

## Chapter Twelve

# The Gender Masquerade

At the masquerade, not only could attendees appear in the guise of other religions, ethnicities, or classes but also genders. Donning the garb of the opposite sex or appearing in a non-binary costume was an acceptable form of play. Many of the gendered differences in the Regency era, particularly for upper and middle classes with respect to property, income, and cultural expectations, helped support that play. Yet the play also functioned to reinforce stereotypes and the existing power structure. There are hints of both the subversive and the reproductive throughout the Regency gender masquerade record.

In many ways, this gender play was also an expression of transformations happening within the culture. Upper class women were expected to marry well, joining their fortune or rank with men of similar rank and wealth. Ladies would occupy themselves with 'gentle' pastimes on the whole – painting, music, crafts, and household management were largely seen as the domain of the upper class lady. Upper class men, on the other hand, could engage in more physical pursuits. While there were a limited number of career paths that were deemed acceptable to upper class men, they did have more access to education and significantly more access to money. A specific idea of femininity was taking shape as the country industrialised that would be further cemented throughout the nineteenth century. Masculinity was going through a similar transition, a changing landscape of what the sphere of men would look like.

The masquerade offered people an opportunity to don the costume of a different walk of life. An earl could be a dustman, a fashionable young lady could be a shepherdess, and a serious person could be a harlequin. People played outside their genders, too, with men dressing as old women, often for comedic effect, and women stepping into the power represented by famous or exotic men. This trend is well represented throughout the history of cross-dressing in popular culture; Gubar (1981) identified men in women's clothing falling into two categories of clown or psychopath while women in men's clothing are represented as more erotic or sensual. This binary is evident within the Regency masquerade record and were so commonplace that they were seldom remarked upon other than inclusion in broader coverage of costumes, or with commentary on the performances individuals delivered in keeping with their chosen character. The collective acceptance was that fantasy reigned supreme at a masquerade, at least for those in positions of privilege, and it was an opportunity to present as other that was welcomed as long as it was done in a style and manner that amused others.

The attraction for some was, for others, an aversion. Along with critics who argued masquerades were the sites of degeneracy and vulgarity, there were others who suggested inherent dangers in allowing people to play outside their assigned roles or identities. Fielding's *The Masquerade, A Poem* (1728) warned of the dangers of masquerade, for the masks and clothing allowed the wearer the ability to conceal distinguishing features of their gender and thereby subvert the gender binary.[1] Yet Fielding himself has been acknowledged to be a complex figure hindered or strengthened by his own dualities.[2] And throughout the eighteenth century, masks and masquerades were criticised by female authors as a tool to further patriarchal oppression.[3] Kauer (2007) argued that disguises are an expression of cultural anxiety, an exploration of gendered identity. Costumes represent subversive play whereby the individual can switch identities and be something they are not – funnier, sexier, exotic, foreign, strong, ugly, and so forth. The choices simultaneously reveal something about the individual and the broader culture at large.

The subversive instinct is and is not revolutionary. It is a revolution to the norms, but it's also a fairly simple impulse arguably most humans have to explore a different life through a different form. In fact, there was an element of the mundane about masquerading as a different gender that, while mentioned in the newspaper reporting, resulted in little commentary but the complimentary. Highlighted among the other character and fancy dress at the August 1820 Almack's masquerade was mention of Mrs Mitchell appearing as a haymaker, Lady Caroline Lamb as Don Giovanni, and Miss Crofton as a collegian. Mr Power appeared as a female, and was said to support his character with endless drollery.[4] No shock or awe was expressed as an account of these costumes was explained along with the rest of the party's costumes. Instead, the sentiment was seemingly delight. Yet, in the depths of these presentations was something that doubtlessly subverted the gender binary, tweaking those conventions in most cases for humour, but nonetheless showing that it was possible for a woman to be student, grand lover, or farmer. This was particularly true when women dressed as men. When men dressed as women, the reception as well as the costumes and performance as described leaned more heavily towards reinforcing gender stereotypes tantamount to similar mechanisms of cultural appropriation.

It was not unusual during the Regency masquerade to have at least one gender bending costume in the throng. Mr Dawkins was admired for his support of the character of duenna at Mrs Morton Pitt's June 1801 masquerade.[5] Mr Janes appeared as a farmer's wife at Mrs Walkers June 1801 masquerade. A gentleman of fashion was there in the mask and dress of Queen Elizabeth. The same evening, Lord Courtney appeared as an antiquated woman of fashion and Mrs Champneys embodied Judge Ashurst,[6] a well-known justice who had been immortalised in lines attributed to Erskine.[7] Lady Barrymore's June 1805 masquerade saw Lady Hester Stanhope dressed as a country squire, Lady Gower as an Oxford scholar, Mr Mercer an old maid, and the Duchess of Leeds and several misses dressed as Welsh bards.[8] At the May 1809 Argyll Rooms event, Captain Loftus was pretty as a country girl, while Mr Anstruther dressed as an old lady.[9] Lady Hyde Parker's May 1819 masked ball had an array of character and fancy dress, including the Viscount Lake wearing clothes of a lady from the ancient world and Mr Smith as Matthew's *English Lady in France*.[10] Over and over, memoirs and newspaper accounts would share costume lists that included individuals masquerading as the opposite sex or in non-binary presentations meant to defy gender conventions, titillate, and subvert. Or even reinforce the gender binary.

In some cases, as with the Duchess of Leeds that night in June 1805, the masquerader would appear with others in support of their chosen theme. The extravagance and performance varied on the individual masqueraders. Lord Dungannon's masquerade in January 1816 saw Colonel Phillips and Miss Pigott dressed as a French countess and her daughter, who displayed elegance with a fine waltz.[11] Others would strike out on their own to present as the opposite sex in extravagant fashion. Mr Mellish attended Miss Manner's July 1805 masquerade as a young debutante in a white and pink gown with silver drape. Captain Cotton attended the same event as an antiquated elderly lady in point lace and with a terrifying bonnet and Mr Lawrell also dressed as an elderly woman who amused the group with his act of appearing terrified by the panorama on display.[12] At the Willingham Hall Masquerade in April

1810, Mr Obaldeston appeared as a bespectacled old lady with his brother, Mr Cater, appearing as a young lady of 16 who was being introduced by his brother. The same night Mr Charles Tennyson dressed as a demure lady and Mr Charles Chaplin presented as an oyster wench.[13] These examples showcase the thought and care individuals sought to embody the opposite sex and provide a show for others. In the case of men masquerading as women, particularly elderly with a comedic performance slant, there was a wickedly subtle reinforcement of the gendered stereotypes; the fussy or dotty old woman and the silly young debutante were popular.

Performance, as with other aspects of the British Regency masquerade, was paramount at least in achieving notice by the newspapers or essayists. At the Marchioness of Lansdown's Grand Masquerade in July 1806, several of the gentlemen in attendance appeared as females including Lord Hamilton as a coy young lady, Baron Robec as an old woman, and the Duke of Clarence as a woman of 72 who recounted youthful gambols.[14] The novelty was less in their appearance than in their presentation, the emphasis on how they engaged others by embodying their chosen character. When Colonel Phillips and Miss Pigott appeared as mother and daughter, their waltz in character was what caught the attention of the press. As we have seen over and over in the record, performance was considered necessary to sell the costume and to entertain others, but it was also an opportunity to engage in a dialogue about shared culture and values.

Elderly ladies were a particular favourite gender swap costume for men. From the longer mentions of these costumes, and their emphasis on the performance, we can speculate the goal was primarily of comedic offering. In many cases, they were aping theatrical productions where dressing in drag was done for farcical effect. It would be an easy task to recognise theatrical costumes, a clear signal of the intent to inspire laughter, but also a way to reinforce stereotypes about women. An account of Sir Richard Plasket's 1826 masquerade remarked about several gentlemen in petticoats, saying at first they wanted to find fault with the costumes but some wit observed that many men were naturally old women and that the costumes might be not that much out of character.[15] The implication was clearly a joke on stereotypes of old women as something negative or fussy, and the humour found in comparing men to that stereotype.

In most instances, the emphasis for men was in appearing as a near opposite to their normal identity; a tall athletic man would appear as a frumpy, hunched elderly woman, or a lithe debutante. Conversely, women leaned towards noble and stately men to masquerade as. Whether an exotic leader, avid scholar, hardworking farmer, or famous character it can be understood the main attraction of these character costumes was the difference in power. That women might want, if only for an evening, to try out walking in the shoes of men who benefited from a patriarchal society is unsurprising. What is perhaps more surprising is that there was less Fielding-styled warnings of the danger of gender cosplay. On the whole, the presentation of these gender masquerades was innocuous, taken for granted as part of the normal course of a masked event.

There were the odd disturbances shared by newspaper coverage. On the occasion of the May 1804 Pantheon masquerade, one young man dressed in fanciful female wear caused a disturbance, but the reporter noted that several other males representing as females and females representing as males were present and were not similarly disruptive.[16] Although the account did not detail the disturbance, from context we may glean that it had more to do with the behaviour of the individual rather than the costume itself. The very act of dressing as another gender, in other words, was not what created the offence. Generally, the masquerade accounts were complimentary of individuals appearing in costumes of another gender.

The more standout gender masqueraders had everything to do with spectacle and performance. At the Argyll Rooms in June 1806, the Honourable Mr Neville appeared as Lady Pentweazel, and it was remarked that he was very well dressed. Lady Pentweazel was a character in the Georgian play *Taste* that was famously played by comedian Samuel Foote in drag. The play has been called a high burlesque comedy that lampooned art collectors and dealers, and although it was not wildly successful on stage, the play would be packaged in the next decade with several collections of plays for amateur theatre or books about British drama, and therefore was doubtless a well understood cultural reference. That the author himself appeared in the play's debut in comedic drag doubtless was also an appealing cultural reference that Mr Neville likely traded on to entertain and amuse his fellow masqueraders.

Mr Neville was not alone in his gender bending costume that evening – Captain Cockburn appeared as a female peddler and Mr Barry as an old woman.[17] These less inspired costumes were not uncommon but no doubt played into the idea of comedic contrasts; the characters would be seen as funny because they were opposite in gender and class or age to the people playing them. Sir (Captain) George Cockburn had a lengthy history in the Royal Navy, including acts of heroism during the Napoleonic Wars and the War of 1812 and would later be promoted to an admiral. He died in 1853, one year after inheriting his baronetcy. At the time of the masquerade, the Captain was in his 30s and still single, having returned from the French Revolutionary Wars. A month after the masquerade, he would be given command of the HMS *Captain*. His well distinguished career provided an easy to read contrast with the character of a female peddler, likely the goal to make others laugh.

Lady Pentweazel also made an appearance two years later at the January Argyll Rooms masquerade, and Mr Brooke was praised for his dress and burlesque mimicry of other fashions and manners. On the same night Captain Burke appeared as the Honourable Miss Lucretia McTab.[18] Miss McTab was another character from a comedic play, although it was traditionally played by a woman since its 1801 debut. A few months later at the May Argyll Rooms masquerade, the Marquis of Sligo dressed as Lady Pentweazel.[19] At Mrs Boehm's June 1810 masquerade ball Mr William Ponsonby appeared as Dowager of Quality, described as fubsy.[20] Fubsy was a term used to indicate a short and rotund body shape. Sir William Ponsonby, by the time he appeared as a chubby Dowager, was a well-known politician and British Army officer who would be killed at the Battle of Waterloo, just five years after the masquerade. In contrast with his costume, he had a trim figure that no doubt required padding to pull off the look.

At the same event, Mr Forbes was costumed as an old Irish woman and found to be impossibly funny.[21] At more than one masquerade through the years, reports would mention broom girls with beards, as was the case for six or seven that made an appearance at the May 1828 Argyll Rooms.[22] The Earl Mountedgecumbe was styled as an old maid playing on the guitar at Mrs Walker's masquerade.[23] As a female fortune teller, Mr Crofton wore a doll in place of a child at his back for the July 1804 Duchess of St Alban's masquerade. The masquerade was also visited by Mr Lambe and Mr Kinnaird who wore costumes as a market woman and her daughter, reportedly diverting the party with their witty commentary on everyone's masks.[24] Again, the intent of these costumes can be inferred to be comedic, providing others with the surprise and entertainment of having fashionable or military gentlemen appearing as burlesque, and usually elderly female characters.

Many of the women who masqueraded as men, at least according to the available examples, chose less comedic characters and gravitated toward the exotic, romantic, or rustic. The Duchess of St Alban's masquerade saw the Honourable Miss Butler and Lady Cahier dressed as chimney sweeps, amusing the group with their whimsical appearance.[25] Mrs Arbuthnot, supported by the Duke of Wellington, attracted curiosity when appearing dressed in eastern male attire at the Covent Garden Theatre fancy dress ball in May of 1826. The benefit for Spitalfields' weavers featured much of the royal family and other aristocrats, with an event of over 3000 people, most who appeared in military uniforms or gowns.[26] The Tory party hostess, Harriet Arbuthnot (nee Fane) was a known close friend to Wellington, and her diaries would be published a century later as an important account of life in the Regency era. If her choice of costume was to command attention, she was successful. An Argyll Rooms masquerade in April 1828 was enlivened by the presence of female and male sailors, the females joining in the quadrilles to the amusement of the 1500 people in attendance.[27] At Sir Richard Flasket's December 1826 masquerade ball, a few ladies dressed in male attire, but the newspaper remarked that it was commonplace for ladies to don breeches.[28] The June 1835 Grand Fancy Ball at Hanover Square Rooms featured Lady Burghersh as Louis XIV and Lady Sykes as Sir Joshua.[29] Women favoured the powerful or exotic over the comic, whereas men were more often to go straight for the comedic character.

The examples highlighted in newspaper accounts largely focus on the comedic acting of those appearing in drag, particularly men appearing as women. The nature of drag as we know it today is of an exaggerated performance of the opposite gender for the purpose of entertaining others. Contemporary drag often includes a comedic element in addition to spectacle, meant to enhance the entertainment of the audience. The history with drag, however, had its foundations in a normative approach to misogynistic underpinnings; men historically played all the roles in theatrical productions until trailblazing women like Margaret Hughes in the seventeenth century shook the Restoration conviction that it was immoral for women to appear on stage.[30] By the nineteenth century, women were beginning to impersonate men on stage in a comedic homage, making it clear that the exploitation of gender norms was comedy gold. Or at least, fodder for a cheap laugh.

Beyond laughs, drag has long been a form of self-expression and a way to mine gender roles through exploration of what it means to man or woman.[31]

However, in its infancy drag presented as a source for humour based on surprise and the absurd. The same elements which we expect from modern drag performances are implicit in the account of drag from the Regency masquerades. Performance and the contrast of a masculine personality reduced to age, infirmity, or poverty relied on sparking the humour of those in attendance. Cultural references, like Mrs Pentweazel, provided an instant recognition and surprise sure to inspire laughter. Women chose over the top or exotic costumes to emphasise their masculinity, both as an exercise in humour but also in contrast.

Beyond the comedic and spectacle aspects of gender norm subverting masquerades, there was a broader debate raging in the Regency culture about masculinity, based on effected manners and love of fashion by many of the aristocratic men of the day. Dandies were lauded and loathed for their performance of effortless manners, elegant taste in all things including dress, and indifference to others. The dandy was the quintessential masquerader, their identity tied up in sensual pleasure, leisure, and even a sort of costume departing from the traditional expectations of a gentleman. The emphasis on clothing, dress, and even enhancing their figure and face through cosmetics or supports like garters aligned them with the evolving concept of the feminine.[32]

No one was a bigger target and topic for debate, with respect to masculinity and dandyism, than the Prince Regent himself. A frequent attendee at masquerades, the prince was also known to love fashion and surround himself with notable fashionable people, including Beau Brummel, until their famous fall-out. The Duchess of Devonshire was said to have described the Prince Regent as looking like a woman in man's clothing, which contrasted with a charged political discourse that the prince was a slave to women, in part because of his womanising.[33] While these type of characterisations would largely be employed by his political opponents, there was a resonance to the reputation that hinted at a broader cultural conversation of gender at play. The masquerade could bring this into stark relief, often with the prince as the target or author.

At the Brandenburg House March 1794 event, the prince appeared as a sailor displaying much humour, and making an effective prop of his short pipe and tobacco box.[34] Whether wish fulfilment or another unknowable intent, the contrast between a perceived effeminate royal and his portrayal of working sailor generated amusement. Without the context of the prince's identity, particularly that he was devoted to being fashionable, the costume of sailor would have been mundane; sailors would often mentioned in a droll list of usual suspects for character costumes at masquerades. At another masquerade, he was noted for paying particular attention to a young woman dressed as a nun who was under a sailor's protection. A resulting exchange of heated words called for the constables to be requested, until it was later discovered the sailor was none other than William IV.[35] The Prince Regent's preference for masquerades was aligned with his love of the ostentatious and would provide just these types of opportunity for masking his effeminate characteristics and allow him to seek out liaisons with women.

In contrast, Brummel was a notable fashion icon, but for very different reasons than many of the Prince Regent's set. Known for ushering forth a muted, austere expression of masculinity when compared with the frills, wigs, and spangled heels of the Georgians, Brummel's model demonstrates how gender expression was beginning to cement during the early nineteenth century into a commodifiable binary. A late Georgian or early Regency cant dictionary quickly reveals a litany of derogatory expressions for men devoted to fashion; popinjay, macaroni, court card, fop, coxcomb, flasher, fribble, and milksop were some of the terms applied to an effeminate man or one who dressed in an overly styled fashion. Simultaneously there were as many, if not more, insulting terms for a provincial man implying rough dress and manners, unpolished by Town Bronze. Whereas in more recent Western history there was the rise of the metro-sexual and conversely the lumber-sexual, in the Regency era neither the well-groomed cosmopolitan nor the rugged country man were ideals. Instead, Brummell's definition of fashion and manliness carved out a middle ground of urbane yet understated, stark and refined.

Brummell's influence, scholars have argued, speaks to modernity[36] that aligned with industrialisation. Eschewing the bespoke, individual emphasizing fashions of the earlier Beau, Brummell's preference for black and simple lines were much easier to mass produce. And while that likely had no direct influence on Brummell's style, the reality is the socio-economic machine would embrace this honed, homogeneous style of masculinity. Brummell's name is still conjured to sell products, implying refined taste and an elegant masculinity that has become entwined with Western ideals about what it is to be a man. That it was easy to commodify this version of masculinity, particularly for mass production, is likely why it has had such resonance in Western culture.

Simultaneously, women's fashion was conducted on simpler lines in the early nineteenth century, eschewing wigs, excessive lace, and the bell form, for a more form enhancing and simple empire waist and delicate accessories. Compared with what would evolve in the Victorian era with the bustle and exaggerated woman's form, the Regency woman's silhouette was more attuned with the Romantic, return to nature cultural discourse of the era. Gone were the towering wigs, beauty patches, and overstated maquillage for an understated but also easily commodifiable version of femininity. Beyond the Classical and Romantic influences, there was a more complex socio-economic interchange at play here too. Influence of British Empire expansion, innovations, and the rise of the middle class coupled with ready-made clothing had a marked impact on women's fashions.[37]

The dandy would find its feminine counterpart in the demimonde, who also appreciated the spectacle and earned their reputation and even living at putting themselves on display. This class of women relished in eliciting responses of shock and awe among their audience,[38] often with overt displays of their sexuality that elevated the more natural costume of the upper class Regency lady. Newspaper reports were quick to point to the vulgarity and attention seeking behaviours of the demimonde in attendance at various masquerades. While their genteel counterparts would often gravitate towards more subdued or feminine costumes, these women would embody more risky characters or even opt to go in fancy dress unmasked. They would also occupy the masculine spaces, having no fear to mingle amongst the motley crowds at the large public venues in full view under the blazing lights; a January 1824 description of an Argyll Rooms masquerade stated that the ladies who mingled were almost exclusively Cyprians of higher order, suggesting that masquerades themselves had become a disreputable affair.[39] The same was true for actresses, often paid to be in attendance, and who were regarded by most to be woman of questionable morals. Respectable women, by contrast, would stick to the periphery, hiding in boxes where they could watch the scene without having to participate. Private masquerades were the safest spaces for upper class women, where they could be protected by corruption through an exclusive guest list and curated masquerade experience.

Another layer of women would be completely unseen in these spaces, with the exception of pioneers of pyrotechnics or skilled performance. Middle class and lower class women would be nearly invisible, except as they were summoned in effigy by costume. Many of the masquerade costumes of the era were caricatures of what they aimed to represent. Even when a person was dressing in a manner consistent with societal notions about their assigned gender, the result was often one of the hyper-real. A flower girl was more flower girl than a real flower girl, because the costume stressed the fabric and fashion, as well as performative, symbols of what it was to be a flower girl. In this sense, gender play at a masquerade happened both for those who cross the normative gender lines and those who stayed within their own gender identity, but chose to exacerbate the feminine or masculine.

The notion of seen versus unseen in correlation to gender is something scholars have explored. Barrie (1990) argued that femininity has traditionally been associated with masquerade insomuch as women's identity has historically been associated with the male gaze. Barrie further explores Nietzsche's text on gender, portraying women's non-identity as a sort of mirror meant to reflect the stuff of men's imagination. In this way, western femininity itself is a mask and women the ultimate masqueraders. Regency women dressed as a function of their place in society, demure, simple and modest. As most upper-class women were limited from having their own money, earning funds, or establishing themselves it would have been critical for their livelihood to dress according to the male gaze and in conformance with expectations about their gender. Goldbort (2022) takes the idea of masquerade in everyday life more broadly, focused on the principal argument that gender in itself is drag, and that masquerade was one vehicle used for liberation from social rules on gender. Rich, powerful, white upper class men would benefit less from the cosplay, already being in the position of supremacy and power thereby explaining the broad preference for using gender masquerade as a source of comedy. By comparison, privileged women could take the fantasy of real power further by adopting ordinary and extraordinary masculine identities.

Outside of the masquerade, fashion was strengthening the gender binary in tune to the infancy of capitalism. If fashion is the epitome of an epoch,[40] then the Regency fashion's exploration of gender ideals and homogeneity, contrasted with gender play at masquerades, clearly underscores a nation in the early stages of industrialisation and leaving behind the excess and individuality of the formerly polarised era. If not exactly egalitarian in practice, there was nonetheless a transformation into sameness that was aspirational. And that was an easy sell to a burgeoning class of consumers. The masquerade was a temporary relief from the increasingly stark gender contrast.

Gender masquerading, more generally, was not just something people did in jest or play. *The Lady's Monthly Museum*, in April 1802, published an account of British Amazons. Two sisters, left orphaned and impoverished, sought their fortune by joining the Navy. Eventually, after one was injured and the other fell ill, they were discovered. One sister subsequently was married to her friend on ship, an officer. The account of their masquerade in a popular women's magazine was relatable, tragic, and perhaps also a warning to other women seeking to step outside the bounds of their gender and class to seek their own fortune. But it was not an anomaly. There are other examples throughout history of women masquerading as men to go to war, to get an education, or to simply live their lives as men. Mary Ann Talbot was injured in the French Revolutionary Wars as John Taylor, later publishing her memoirs of the experiences living as a man. The Chevalier d'Eon was known to transition to life as a female while living in England. These examples, often revealed because of death, illness, or discovery were representative of the possibility that many women had to masquerade as men to achieve success limited primarily to men.

Whether transgender or finding the disguise of another gender convenient or necessary, these individual stories represent how fashion and performance of gender were often enough to satisfy others. When the stakes were high, the performance was about passing or authenticity, compared with the masquerade where cross-dressing often was portrayed as performance to entertain or to surprise. Even at play, the choices people made to disguise themselves as another gender demonstrate that women were a marginalised population while men where aspirational; female costumes when donned by men were the butt of jokes, whereas women tended to pick costumes that might earn respect or admiration.

While an emphasis in the literature on the eighteenth-century masquerade has focused on gender subversion, the record for the long Regency masquerades suggests that while subversion may have been an element, gender play also served to reinforce cultural or shared values about the gender binary. This echoes the refrains from many eighteenth-century authors, like Sarah Fielding, who used masks or masquerades as a way to talk about the patriarchy and subjugation of women. Like culturally appropriating costumes, gentlemen's selection of a female representation leaned on either coded comedic characters, like those from farcical productions, or gender stereotypes like the fubsy and fussy elderly lady. While women were increasingly broadening their spheres of influence and economic opportunities, the instinct for those of privilege was to lampoon this to maintain a status quo that would continue to subjugate females. Furthermore, even the comedic displays favoured the male gaze, effectively othering the female audience in much the same way a foreign dignitary might have been excluded or served micro-aggressions in the name of entertainment. The record of Regency masquerades by and large supports that these events did more to support norms, particularly for those in privilege, than they served to subvert them. All the elements deemed necessary for a masquerade's success were about luxury, spectacle, and a shared value of imperialism, Neoclassicism, Romanticism, and maintaining power over marginalised populations. Gender, in the context of a binary, was clearly one nail to hammer in securing the status quo; the cultural conversation on who should attend the masquerade, alone, revealed a strong gender bias.

Yet the masquerade that occurred outside of venues and private ballrooms with respect to gender, in particular, reveals the tension between the industrial capital need for homogeneity and also its need to perpetuate the myth of the individual. Transcultural or gender expressions, both inside and out of the ballroom, represented many things: economic security, differentiation, deviance, and danger. In an era fraught with conflict and rapid change, it makes sense that entertainment and self-expression might try to resolve these conflicts.

## Chapter Thirteen

# Legacy and Influence of the Regency Masquerade

In the preceding chapters, the sights, sounds, and meaning behind the long Regency masquerade have been explored. Themes of national identity, cultural appropriation, gender and class have been examined to understand the meaning behind the relative homogeneous practices of both public and private masquerades. Despite many scholars and contemporaries declaring the masquerade dead after the Georgian era, the reality is the events thrived well into the nineteenth century. And the Regency era was not the end of the masquerade, either.

Many of the Regency venues, including the Lowther Rooms and Vauxhall, would have masquerades into the 1840s. New venues would pop up too, although with less abundance and consistency than counterparts during the Regency era. The décor would still maintain all the brightness and devotion to symbols of the monarchy and Empire. Costumes, too, would show little variability, albeit the industrial machine would begin to support manufacturing of costume and therefore have a heavy hand on costume selection. Guidebooks would pop up in the early Victorian era with specific instruction on how to dress for various characters, requiring little in the way of imagination. Character costumes would follow the trends of theatre and literature, and then cinema, to influence masquerader's choice. Fancy dress without masks would begin to see a rapid increase over the masked events.

During the Regency era, promoted by things like Wellington's Almack's masquerade, fancy dresses would begin to offer an alternative to the masked ball. In some cases, this meant dressing as themes or people, but without a mask to conceal one's own identity. Scholars like Mitchell (2017) have identified a trend among the Victorian fancy dress balls for attendees to prefer representing their own identity, playing off the term fancy to leverage an opportunity to elevate their persona through fantastical garments and masks. This, Mitchell argues, runs contrary to Castle's portrayal of the

Georgian masquerade where costume and disguise helped individuals subvert not only rigid social boundaries, like class, but also self-imposed identity. The Victorian fancy dress ball, in comparison, shifted the emphasis from masquerade to fancy dress, whereby people were more likely to play an extreme version of themselves. In other words, the costume of choice for the Victorian was, for many, an opportunity to elevate and pronounce their identity.

However, this tension was definitely present in the costumes of the long Regency masquerade. Castle (1986) defines three main types of costumes present at the Georgian masquerade that have been consistent with the record of Regency masquerades: dominoes, character costumes, and fancy dress. Just as many masqueraders opted for the simple domino, so did many chose to attend in fancy dress. However, the nuanced definition supplied by Castle of fancy dress was a costume that represented a type of person, a theme, or a similar element, rather than a specific person like the character costume. Mitchell uses the examples of Queen Victoria's fancy dress balls, several with a historical era theme. In this way, it can be understood that Mitchell is suggesting the fancy dress in the Victorian era became more about the individual's true identity than in faithful reproduction of a theme, element, or type of person. In the review of newspaper accounts, there are mentions throughout the long Regency of masqueraders opting to simply dress extravagantly, a more on the nose definition of fancy dress. There is also evidence in critiques, satire, and favourable reviews that many masqueraders deliberately used the opportunity to enhance their own identity or public perception of themselves.

As Pierce Egan's satirical *Life in London* characters plan to attend a Haymarket Masquerade, one suggested the greatest difficulty in the outing was which character to portray would be both easy to manage but also advantageous to one's self. Further on, the narrator argued that the masquerade was an opportunity to exhibit any number of talents including wit, puns, satire, dancing, singing, and severity. Simultaneously, the narrator reflected that masquerades do afford some degree of intimate acquaintance with an array of different classes, sometimes having the impact of displays of impudence. Logic tells Jerry that one of the greatest sources of pleasure and surprise at a masquerade was the unmasking at the supper table. And many of the newspaper stories reflect that the unmasking at supper, particularly for house parties where people were more apt to know each other well, was often a highlight of the event.

There is a duality here, present at many of the Regency masquerades, of the possible types of intent for costumes. In the review of Regency masquerade costumes, simple categories were developed to show potential motivations. And it is likely that an individual had nuanced reasons for their selection of costume ranging from convenience, fit, affordability and accessibility, and then the intended reception. As Logic explains, the surprise and pleasure of the reveal was a highlight likely by and large because of a masquerader's ability to align or not align their chosen costume with their social identity. Egan's portrayal drives home the tension of the masquerade, where individuals could align their everyday persona with a character or fancy dress, or chose to subvert it, depending on their intention.

Egan's portrayal was not the only one that pointed to complex intent behind costumes. *The Tour of Doctor Syntax, in Search of the Picturesque* (1823) devoted a scene of the London tour to attendance at a masquerade, where Syntax delighted his wife by agreeing to take her to a Haymarket masquerade. The lines referenced Fentum's masquerade warehouse and the idea of masking in a monstrous costume and then transitioned into the next canto where a plate revealed Doctor Syntax dressed as some sort of wizard with a wand among other masqueraders dressed as a dragon, harlequin, and other assorted costumes. The Doctor Syntax images describe fantastical motivations, but also speak to aligning a costume with what a person could carry off, according to physical attributes or performance ability.

Sir Richard Plasket's December 1826 grand masquerade ball had the majority of ladies wearing fancy dress. The newspaper coverage subsequently described Swiss peasants, flower girls, and historic costumes. Men at the event, conversely, chose a variety of character costumes including a Gretna Green parson, the Devil, and Hamlet.[1] The author stressed the beauty and good looks of the women in attendance, compared with an emphasis on performance and humour with respect to the gentlemen. While none of the true identities were called out in relation to their costumes, with the exception of the host who wore Spanish inspired fancy dress, the implication is that people both dressed to enhance their physical attributes and performance ability as well as entertain and amuse others. In some respects, the two intents are complementary rather than mutually exclusive. At the well covered Eglinton Castle masquerade, the appearance of the earl's nephew, Master Montgomerie, in attire similar to the Highland garb of his ancestors in portraits hanging in the castle excited much attention and praise. The earl and the countess were dressed but not masked, as they mixed with the crowd that included a broad assortment of character and fancy dress costumes. Members of the Montgomerie clan largely made up the list of notable characters in the newspaper coverage, suggesting that either greater attention was paid to their costume[2] or, like Master Montgomerie, there was amusement in how similar they were to their chosen costume.

Over and over, true and fictional accounts would highlight these competing desires to elevate or oppose a person's common identity during the Regency. In a brief review of Victorian era masquerades, newspaper coverage would frequently reflect nearly identical characters and fancy dress concepts from the previous era. A May 1850 Vauxhall masquerade had the same standard character costumes including harlequins, sultanas, sailors, fruit girls, nuns, devils, and foreign national inspired costumes.[3] Thirty years later, a Mansion House masquerade had an wide variety of costumes, including chimney sweeps, Mephistopheles, Romeo and Juliet, and assorted representations of people from other nations.[4] It is apparent that regardless of individual intent, the same diversity of representation was common several decades into the Victorian era.

Some of the differences highlighted by Mitchell may be in the venue and guest list. The queen would host several noted masquerades that were exclusive and doubtless costly to attire. Several of Queen Victoria's events would emphasise a particular historical period and a devotion to historical accuracy. This would necessitate, at least for the discerning guest, bespoke costumes. Yet even with expensive creations, compared with warehouse costumes, the individual seamstress or tailor and the intended wearer would have influence on the actual representation. As Mitchell points out, it was difficult to truly rid any costume, regardless of the cost, of anachronisms likely due to a devotion to contemporary fashion and the impact on an individual identity. There would also, naturally, be limitations in the style of design and materials used in Victorian England compared with medieval counterparts.

There was also another shift Mitchell highlights to explain a favouring of fancy dress over character costumes. Masquerades had been part of the London experience for nearly two centuries by the late nineteenth century, and commercial masquerade balls were usurped by birthday, anniversary, or other similar celebrations or fundraisers. A reduction in venues offering this entertainment, based on newspaper coverage, bears this out. The shift from public masquerades as commonplace to more emphasis on private or exclusive masquerades, according to Mitchell, legitimised them to the broader masses, at least those that could afford the expense of costume and admittance. It is certainly apparent in the Regency, due to criticisms and commentary, that the stigmas associated with public masquerades were less present for private masquerades. *The London Mercury*, in a review of a King's Theatre masquerade in December 1826, commented that public masquerades were largely a draw for young bucks in London for spring that had more money than sense, and were up for the novelty and promises of risqué goings on that the public masquerades offered. Even the Argyll Rooms frequently had criticisms that only notorious females were ever in attendance at the masquerades, suggesting that most respectable young women were safeguarded away from the events. The appetites for public masquerades, or the ability to capture the same audience over and over, certainly was a natural pressure to lead to the shift. Mitchell also argues that access was easier, particularly due to the new buying power of the middle class. No longer merely the domain of the titled, wealthy, and fashionable, masquerades were accessible to a broader audience.

This broader audience consumed the masquerade both as an event and as a setting or metaphor within the arts. The masquerade's use in literature has supported analysis into the carnivalesque, particularly with respect to gender. Threlkeld-Dent (2017) looked at the carnivalesque used in a variety of Victorian authors' works including Hardy, Forster, Brontë, and Gaskell. Specifically, Threlkeld-Dent examines the use of the masquerade as a transgressive space for women and the working class, concluding that transgressive spaces are important for raising awareness about power dynamics. In this way, the rising fortunes of the middle class would begin to upset the previous order, and providing access to a formerly exclusive activity would feel like an opportunity to further exploit the rapidly decreasing divide between upper orders and the middle. Simultaneously, industrialisation and broader spread wealth was creating a whole new consumer base for entertainment.

Mitchell included in her analysis the 'how to' costume guides that proliferated in the Victorian era. In particular, she highlighted how the authors often suggested that accuracy with respect to historical or cultural details was often not the intent so much as to ensure the costume was appropriate with propriety standards and also matched the wearer's personality and/or body. For women, the guidebooks recommend ways for a woman to enhance her appearance and conformance with normative beauty standards, while the recommendations for men focused on maintaining dignity by not stretching oneself beyond the bounds of their personality or ability to perform. The emphasis was, by the mid-1800s, on enhancement of individual identity rather than trying out a new or subversive persona.

This push for a masquerade as an extension of self was, in part, because the masquerade itself had become a commodity on offer. The middle class now had access to the secrets of a previously exclusive domain through the helpful instruction of publications. The Butterick Publishing Company published a book on masquerades and carnivals in 1892, in an attempt to condense all the information available on masquerades into one book. The book included some narrative musing on masquerades, costume ideas, and even etiquette. It highlighted that a fancy ball required careful pre-planning, more elaborate décor and details than an ordinary ball, and that often a venue would need to be hired to comfortably accommodate the guests and activities. The guidebook then recommended a masquerade or fancy dress ball open with a comedic tableau, an element not common in the Regency masquerade. The full scope instructional would help the burgeoning middle classes decode a former landscape of privilege and power.

On the point of costumes the Butterick guidebook stated that fancy costumes representing historical periods did not have to be strictly authentic and that the other guests would rely on enough similar details to identify the time period. The authors further recommended innovation and creativity when landing on a costume, as to create the most striking, surprise, and pleasure among the other attendees. It is clear this recommendation is geared around the entertainment or amusement of others. In the next paragraph, the guidebook also recommended that individuals should select their costumes based on what might be flattering to their individual characteristics, going so much as to recommend someone with darker colouring chose a nationality that matches. A short list is produced in which brunettes are recommended to dress as Egyptian, Italian, Spanish and Japanese women, while blondes are given a list of Shakespearean fairies and other ethereal characters to emulate.[5]

By the end of the Regency, the fancy dress ball would begin to be distinct from a masquerade through the mere application of a mask. In lieu of the mask, at a fancy dress ball, the Butterick guide stated that a carnival session cap is required. Many of the costume guides for fancy dress balls do, in fact, omit masks as part of the ensembles and instead focus on accessories like jewellery and headwear. The 1881 *Character Suitable for Fancy Costume Balls* has even traditionally masked characters, like a harlequin, unmasked.[6] The cause of this shift towards unmasked costumes is certainly worth exploration and beyond the scope of this book, but its notable in that it hints at a cultural shift; if the Georgians were trying to emulate European counterparts in pursuit of a bacchanalian experience, the Regency masqueraders were experiencing a formalisation, and even sanitation of that experience, likely tied to not only financial but cultural motives. The Victorians then would take that one step further, and in doing so turn their own bodies into spaces of commodification and consumption, anonymity stripped in favour of self-promotion.

Beginning in the Georgian era, public entertainments, rising middle class, and commercialisation helped to capture the public appetite and imagination for masquerades. By the Victorian era, masquerades and fancy dress balls were cemented as cultural institutions. Open to a broader class of people, but with some distinct differences including a sanitisation and prevalence to abandon masks, masquerades and fancy dress balls continued the traditions of cultural appropriation, gender and class cosplay and subversion, and meaning making. National identity, particularly strong during the long Regency in the décor, music, and assorted other elements of the masquerade, would also continue to be tied to the fancy dress ball.

Unlike Castle's vision of the Georgian masquerade, the Victorian masquerade would be less about free love and ritual, and more about enhancing one's self-image. The abandonment of one's own identity was impossible, particularly when unmasked. Yet the Victorian era continued to carry on the nuanced conflict costumes represented of masquerading to enhance one's everyday identity, to explore another identity, and to entertain others with striking contrast to one's everyday identity. This must be a fundamental human dilemma, as it is apparent even today that the intent of the costume wearer can not only be diverse from others but also, in itself, a nuanced form of self-expression and also the destruction of self.

Overall, the legacy of the Regency masquerade would show itself throughout the next century and beyond. While the formula for success would undergo many changes, the desires and intentions of both promoters and attendees cannot be markedly different than contemporary costume balls where people seek to escape the ordinary for a few hours of hedonistic delight and entertainment. What is notable is the further commodification of such experiences through guidebooks, costume manufacturing, and other industrialised mechanisms to make consumption easier and more accessible to a broader audience that could emulate what was once exclusive to the fashionable and wealthy.

## Chapter Fourteen

# Final Thoughts

When I first embarked on research of the long Regency masquerade, I had a different idea of what I would find. I wasn't looking for spectacle or national identity. I wasn't thinking about cultural appropriation. I did not know about the masquerade's origins in Great Britain or expect for these events to be so very similar, decade after decade, in form and function. This process has been one of curiosity and discovery, bringing to life these events in a way I could have never anticipated and I hope translates well onto the page. From the luscious greenery and bright lights to the fantastic spectacle and military connections, to the superstar caterers and creativity of costumes, the Regency masquerade was a ripe space for understanding many aspects of Regency life.

There is more work to be done in this space. So much of the scholarly literature on masquerades in Great Britain focuses on the eighteenth century. While that has been helpful to inform my own research, there are opportunities to continue an examination of masquerades in the long Regency. Future research could expand on nationalism and national identity, Neoclassicism and Romanticism, and some of the complex issues clearly being negotiated at these events. I have examined things mostly from the attendee's perspective, with some highlights on promoters, performers, and other supporting parties, but it would be worthwhile for someone to conduct a detailed look at these public masquerades as an extension of theatre culture in Regency London. There are also opportunities to understand the lower class and middle class participation, service, and perception of the Regency masquerade.

The record is filled with fascinating and unexpected character studies, slices of life, and micro-examples of some of the broader issues and opportunities of the long Regency. But there are also corollaries to many aspects of modern life. Trends, influencers, identity, and group think are at the core alongside the desire that many people have to belong and to entertain their counterparts. Even among the risqué and sometimes lascivious backdrop of the masquerade, there is a sweetness of people coming together to celebrate the absurd, the horrifying, and even the mundane. There are also elements of consumption and scopophilia, including the dominant male, white, Christian gaze, that are still grappled with in Western culture today. We cosplay for very similar motives, a mix of escapism and reinforcement of identity, that brings us very close to our Regency counterparts.

This is nowhere as apparent as in the modern stories we tell of the past. Because it is where my interest was formed, I cannot leave the subject of the Regency masquerade without touching on its prevalence as a plot device in many a Regency romance novel. As a reader, I adore the masquerade theme where in reference to an event or a person masquerading in their life as someone else. This is because not only is it a great vehicle to explore other identities or aspects to our personalities, but it also helps us better understand how others perceive us and the world around them. But in diving deep into the Regency masquerade, I have uncovered some truths that contrast with the picture painted by many historical romance authors. Vauxhall and its secluded walks is a brilliant setting for a clandestine interlude, as is a masked event where a hoydenish heroine secrets inside to get a taste of the wild life. The reader's imagination is filled with crushingly crowded events where the party is masked and a heroine might conceal her identifying features by facial and hair coverings. And while this may have happened a time or two at a Regency masquerade, the reality is there were several constraining factors to real illicit interludes or grand concealment.

First, these events were lit up like daylight. Shadows were banished by the brilliance of thousands of lamps or candles washing out even corners in bright, luxurious light. Near daylight mimicking light was seen as an almost requirement for these events during the long Regency, the brightness frequently highlighted as a key feature. A variety of lamps and candles would be woven throughout the many rooms of venues and private homes, and even in the gardens and outdoor venues lights were a focal point of décor. The anonymity was meant to be largely preserved by the mask and costume one donned, but given the accounts that name the fashionable people in attendance and even share when identities were first elusive, and then rightly figured out, this was more theatre than reality. The well it spaces would leave little opportunity for clandestine affairs.

Second, the masks were pulled off at an early hour, typically before the one o'clock supper or at supper, and given the late starts, inhibition fleeing inspirations like alcohol and dancing were not yet consumed in great enough quantities, unless people had arrived inebriated which the record hints was not the norm. It would be much easier to remember indiscretions of characters in the earlier hours of an event, and therefore unlikely that masked figures were meeting up at the ten or eleven o'clock hour when most guests were arriving to openly engage in vulgar public displays of affections. There were hints that some darkness and privacy was maintained in the private boxes at the large public masquerade venues, and on occasion there were reports of a masquerader who refused to remove their mask. However, by and large, the entertainment of the mask often gave way to other entertainments into the wee hours of the morning. Given the early removal of masks and the brightly lit venues, no person not ordinarily known to be promiscuous would chose a masquerade to engage in such behaviour. On the other hand, someone who enjoyed notoriety or was on the hunt for a risqué encounter might certainly find a willing partner at a public masquerade.

Third, there were limitations on attendance for fashionable women and by and large masquerades were not a popular place for an unmarried debutante to go. Even the Argyll Rooms, one of the most long-standing exclusive venues of the long Regency, would be accused of having a crowd too populated by notorious women. Conversely, the private masquerades that would have been more acceptable for unmarried debutante attendance also had low enough numbers of guests that it's likely everyone in attendance knew each other, or had connections of some kind.

It would be hard for a hoydenish heroine to conceal overmuch in such company. Even in a mask and wig. Georgette Heyer had a good depiction of a young lady's experience at a public masquerade in *Cotillion*, when Kitty must be rescued from vulgar and frightening company by her betrothed, Freddy. Kitty professes that she had no idea it would be so vulgar until she arrived, and then immediately she realised that her appearance at the masquerade was de trop. Given not only much of the criticism but also praise of public masquerades, this experience would have been authentic for any sheltered young lady who happened upon a Pantheon masked ball. What was more likely to occur at the large public masquerades was fraternising between a fashionable man and a member of the demimonde, and there would have been very little scandal as a result, regardless of how vulgar or indecent some would deem such public cavorting.

There is no doubt many of the titled and fashionable circle in the long Regency period enjoyed both public and private masquerades based on the record. And undoubtedly, there was risqué behaviour, bawdy jokes and songs, and some indiscretions that occurred as these events. However, by and large, they were variations on more traditional balls with the opportunity to escape one's typical identity by donning another persona, albeit briefly. This was a dialogical practice, more than anything, relying on the audience's receipt and reaction to that fantastical persona including both costume and dress. At a private ball, in particular, much of the reaction was predicated on either the similarity or the stark difference between the person and that which they chose to represent. Therefore, knowing a person's identity at many of these events was paramount to the desired reaction.

This is not to discourage authors from using the masquerade as a means to bring together characters into a more risqué circumstance. Instead, I am offering a challenge to rethink what we know about the Regency masquerade and that it may have been, more than a means to challenge or subvert norms, a vehicle to strengthen them. Kitty's exposure to the realities of a less curated crowd, for instance, helped drive home how little freedom a young lady, even betrothed, in her position had. With ruination representing such a singular risk for an unmarried lady, attending a masquerade at the Pantheon would have been tantamount to thumbing her nose at respectability. A young buck on the town carousing with friends might venture to the Lowther Rooms to get drunk and fraternise with sex workers as a first exposure to seedier activities available in London. And a peer might attend a masquerade house party to amuse their friends, but also to step temporarily out their duty and be regarded as a labourer for the evening. These were smaller adventures and risks, but poignant nonetheless in a culture heavily constrained by etiquette, rules, and the crushing weight of rapid change and international conflict. The ostentatious display of luxury and wealth amid the rapid change, conflict, and societal shifts is particularly fascinating and worth future exploration.

At the end of my journey of discovery, I am left with more questions than answers about the Regency masquerade. While I have been delighted to tease out patterns and hopefully disprove the assertion that masquerades didn't happen beyond the 1780s, I am also curious about many of the details left unsaid. There is inherent bias in my sources, a slant towards the power elite that infrequently criticised the lavish events all the while there was significant suffering at home and abroad. The ceremonial aspects of praising military, all the while abandoning many returning and wounded veterans or veteran widows to their own devices, is one obvious contradiction in the production of masquerades at odds with the realities of the day. Serving a thirst for the risqué all the while barring entrance through cost or curated guest lists, too, is another contradiction I hope I have teased out but still deserves more contemplation.

A real comparison between masquerades in Europe or elsewhere is also fertile grounds for testing the idea that masquerades are an expression of national identity. For instance, an act was passed in 1829 in New York prohibiting masquerades, meanwhile an 1836 account had some twenty public masquerades happening in one night during Carnival in Madrid.[1] Britian landed somewhere in the middle between excess and prohibition. And that the masquerade was a cultural phenomenon across the oceans also hints at the forces of globalism already at play. There have been hints, too, of influences of technology on these events mostly with respect to décor. Yet unsaid is how technology would begin to change consumption patterns, distances people were able to travel for special events, and even the very idea of anonymity. Were the changes that happened as costumes transitioned from disguise and characters to self-promoting fancy dress prompted by the development of the daguerreotype? Did self-consciousness reflect anxieties about a shrinking gap between the elite and the middle class? Or did the war chests from imperial expansion influence the presentation of self at these special events?

An interest in Regency life is currently popular among many, with the proliferation of Austen adaptations, fan fiction, *Bridgerton* and its spin-offs, and a never-ending stream of young adult and romance fiction set in this era. In its own way, these presentations of the past are their own masquerade, a cosplay of a past both real and imagined, competing themes as complex and nuanced as masquerades were in the era. I have given my recommendations to Regency writers, but would also like to say to the readers to be cautious in your consumption, and allow for these terrible and wonderful contradictions. History is rich and interesting exactly because humans are, and while our modern life loves a binary, especially between good and evil, the reality is we all have the capacity for exciting and mundane, moral and immoral, smart and stupid. So too those masqueraders of the long Regency wanted to escape and escape to, pitching themselves into a fantasy but also maintaining existing systems and hierarchies. What a muddy and murky thing is history.

# Notes

**Introduction**

1. *Derby Mercury* – Friday, 20 June 1777.
2. *Encyclopaedia Britannica; Or, a Dictionary of Arts, Sciences, and Miscellaneous Literature: Constructed on a Plan, by which the Different Sciences and Arts are Digested Into the Form of Distinct Treatises Or Systems, Comprehending the History, Theory, and Practice, of Each, According to the Latest Discoveries and Improvements; and Full Explanations Given of the Various Detached Parts of Knowledge, Whether Relating to Natural and Artificial Objects, Or to Matters Ecclesiastical, Civil, Military, Commercial…, Together with a Description of All the Countries, Cities, Principal Mountains… Throughout the World; a General History …and an Account of the Lives of the Most Eminent Persons in Every Nation, from the Earliest Ages Down to the Present Times.* (1797). United Kingdom: Bell and Macfarquhar.
3. Castle, T. (1983). 'Eros and Liberty at the English Masquerade, 1710–90', *Eighteenth-Century Studies*, 17(2), pp.156–176.
4. Chrissochoidis, I. (2009). 'George I goes to the Masquerade (1721)', *The Scriblerian and the Kit-Cats*, 42(1), pp.47–49.
5. *Fly Leaves: Or, Scraps and Sketches, Literary, Bibliographical and Miscellaneous, Consisting of Notes on Antiquarian and Historical Subjects, Collections Towards Neglected Biography, Memorials of Old London, Choice Specimens of Ancient Poetry, Chiefly from Unpublished Mss., Scraps and Sketches, Curious and Interesting, with Numerous Bibliographical Notices, Etc., Etc.* (1854). United Kingdom: J. Miller.
6. *Derby Mercury* – Thursday, 18 April 1782.
7. *Newcastle Chronicle* – Saturday, 11 May 1782.
8. *Weekly Times* (London) – Sunday, 3 January 1830.

**Chapter One**

1. *Morning Herald* (London) – Wednesday, 4 June 1806.
2. Thornbury, W., Walford, E. (1891). *Old and New London: Westminster and the Western Suburbs.* United Kingdom: Cassell, Petter, and Galpin.
3. Earl of Malmesbury, J. H. (1870). *A Series of Letters: Of the First Earl of Malmesbury, His Family and Friends, from 1745 to 1820.* United Kingdom: R. Bentley.
4. *Sporting Magazine.* (1802). United Kingdom: Rogerson & Tuxford.
5. *Morning Post* – Monday, 21 June 1802.
6. *Saint James's Chronicle* – Saturday, 1 June 1805.
7. *British Press* – Wednesday, 5 June 1805.
8. *Morning Post* – Wednesday, 4 June 1806.
9. *Morning Post* – Tuesday, 1 July 1806.
10. Thomas, D., Carlton, D., Etienne, A. (2007). *Theatre Censorship: from Walpole to Wilson.* Kiribati: OUP Oxford.
11. *Morning Post* – Thursday, 2 July 1807.

12. *Morning Post* – Thursday, 30 June 1808.
13. *Morning Post* – Friday, 26 May 1809.
14. *Sun* (London) – Friday, 16 June 1809.
15. *British Press* – Saturday, 2 June 1810.
16. *Morning Post* – Friday, 8 June 1810.
17. https://www.british-history.ac.uk/survey-london/vols31-2/pt2/pp284-307.
18. *The Fortnightly*. (1927). United Kingdom: Chapman and Hall.
19. *The London Encyclopaedia*, (2011).
20. *Blackwood's Edinburgh Magazine*, (1844).
21. *Star* (London) – Saturday, 24 July 1813.
22. *Morning Herald* (London) – Friday, 29 May 1818.
23. *Saint James's Chronicle* – Tuesday, 2 June 1818.
24. Mercer-Taylor, P. J. (2020). *Gems of Exquisite Beauty: How Hymnody Carried Classical Music to America*. United States: Oxford University Press.
25. *Morning Post* – Thursday, 30 June 1808.
26. *New Times* (London) – Friday, 30 December 1825.
27. *British Press* – Friday, 20 June 1806.
28. *Morning Post* – Thursday, 25 May 1809.
29. *Morning Post* – Friday, 26 May 1809.
30. *Morning Post* – Thursday, 25 May 1809.
31. *Morning Post* – Thursday, 8 June 1809.
32. *National Register* (London) – Sunday, 19 June 1814.
33. *Morning Herald* (London) – Friday, 3 April 1818.
34. *Johnson's Sunday Monitor* – Sunday, 5 February 1826.
35. *Morning Post* – Friday, 29 June 1827.
36. *Coventry Herald* – Friday, 10 June 1825.
37. *Morning Post* – Tuesday, 25 April 1826.
38. *Morning Post* – Tuesday, 13 March 1827.
39. *Age* (London) – Sunday, 29 November 1829.
40. Feltham, J. (1813). *The Picture of London, for 1802*. United Kingdom: (n.p.).

**Chapter Two**

1. *Derby Mercury* – Friday, 8 May 1772.
2. *The Mirror of Literature, Amusement, and Instruction*. (1835). United Kingdom: J. Limbird.
3. *Derby Mercury* – Friday, 8 May 1772.
4. *Kentish Gazette* – Wednesday, 19 May 1773.
5. *Oxford Journal* – Saturday, 1 February 1772.
6. *Chambers's Journal of Popular Literature, Science and Arts*. (1867). United Kingdom: W. & R. Chambers.
7. Thornbury, W. (1873). *Old and New London: A Narrative of Its History, Its People, and Its Places*. United Kingdom: Cassell, Petter & Galpin.
8. Malcolm, J. P. (1808). *Anecdotes of the Manners and Customs of London During the Eighteenth Century; Including the Charities, Depravities, Dresses, and Amusements, of the Citizens of London, During that Period; with a Review of the State of Society in 1807: To which is Added, a Sketch of the Domestic and Ecclesiastical Architecture, and of the Various Improvements in the Metropolis*. United Kingdom: Longman, Hurst, Rees and Orme.

9. *The Gentleman's Pocket Magazine; and Album of Literature and Fine Arts.* (1829). United Kingdom: Joseph Robins, no. 3, Bride Court, Bridge Street.
10. *Railway Bell and London Advertiser* – Saturday, 21 December 1844.
11. *The London Magazine Enlarged and Improved.* (1785). United Kingdom: R. Baldwin.
12. https://www.british-history.ac.uk/survey-london/vols31-2/pt2/pp268-283.
13. Rose, A. (2021). *Empires of the Sky: Zeppelins, Airplanes, and Two Men's Epic Duel to Rule the World.* United States: Random House Publishing Group.
14. *Hereford Journal* – Thursday, 9 March 1786.
15. *The Mirror of Literature, Amusement, and Instruction.* (1835). United Kingdom: J. Limbird.
16. https://www.british-history.ac.uk/survey-london/vols31-2/pt2/pp268-283.
17. *A Narrative of the Minutes of Evidence Respecting the Claim to the Berkeley Peerage: As Taken Before the Committee of Privileges in 1811. Together with the Entire Evidence of the Persons Principally Concerned ..... (1811).* United Kingdom: Sherwood, Neely, and Jones.
18. *Oracle and the Daily Advertiser* – Monday, 20 April 1801.
19. *Taunton Courier and Western Advertiser* – Saturday, 3 September 1938.
20. *Oracle and the Daily Advertiser* – Wednesday, 3 February 1802.
21. *Ipswich Journal* – Saturday, 13 February 1802.
22. *True Briton* – Monday, 19 April 1802.
23. *British Press* – Tuesday, 28 November 1809.
24. *Oracle and the Daily Advertiser* – Monday, 26 January 1801.
25. *True Briton* – Monday, 12 January 1801.
26. *Chambers's Journal of Popular Literature, Science and Arts.* (1867). United Kingdom: W. & R. Chambers.
27. *Oracle and the Daily Advertiser* – Saturday, 2 February 1805.
28. *British Press* – Wednesday, 22 May 1805.
29. *British Press* – Thursday, 17 May 1804.
30. *London Courier and Evening Gazette* – Wednesday, 10 February 1802.
31. *Morning Post* – Friday, 6 May 1803.
32. *Morning Post* – Saturday, 4 February 1804.
33. *Morning Post* – Saturday, 26 February 1803.
34. *Sports and Pastimes in Town and Country: Comprising London Seasons and Sights; Winter, Summer, and Harvest-sports, Fishing and Wateringplace Seasons, Etc.* (1841). United Kingdom: T.H. Coe.
35. *Morning Post* – Wednesday, 7 March 1810.
36. *Morning Post* – Saturday, 26 February 1803.
37. https://www.british-history.ac.uk/survey-london/vols31-2/pt2/pp268-283.
38. London (1843). United Kingdom: Charles Knight & Company.


**Chapter Three**


1. *Morning Post* – Wednesday, 12 February 1806.
2. https://www.british-history.ac.uk/survey-london/vols29-30/pt1/pp223-250.
3. https://www.british-history.ac.uk/survey-london/vols29-30/pt1/pp223-250#h3-0008.
4. Gilliland, T. (1808). *The dramatic mirror: containing the history of the stage from the earliest period to the present time; including a biographical and critical account of all the dramatic writers, from 1660; and also of the most distinguished performers, from the days of Shakespeare to 1807, and a history of the country theatres in England, Ireland, and Scotland. Embellished with seventeen elegant engravings.* London: Printed for C. Chapple, by B. McMillan.

5. *Oracle and the Daily Advertiser* – Thursday, 27 June 1805.
6. *True Briton* – Friday, 13 May 1803.
7. *Morning Herald* (London) – Friday, 20 April 1804.
8. *Imperial Weekly Gazette* – Saturday, 11 April 1818.
9. *World and Fashionable Sunday Chronicle* – Monday, 23 March 1818.
10. *World and Fashionable Sunday Chronicle* – Sunday 5 April 1818.
11. Imperial Weekly Gazette – Saturday, 11 April 1818.
12. Egan, P., Cruikshank, R. (1869). *Tom & Jerry: Life in London, Or, The Day and Night Scenes of Jerry Hawthorn, Esq. and His Elegant Friend Corinthian Tom, in Their Rambles and Sprees Through the Metropolis*. United Kingdom: Hotten.
13. *Morning Post* – Friday, 7 April 1826.
14. *Morning Herald* (London) – Thursday, 28 May 1829.
15. *Morning Post* – Tuesday, 23 February 1830.
16. *Morning Post* – Saturday, 29 March 1834.
17. Lysons, D. (1811). *The Environs of London: Middlesex*. United Kingdom: T. Cadell and W. Davies.
18. Yurchuk, D. (1997). *Ranelagh Gardens and the Recombinatory Utopia of Masquerade*.
19. Knight, C. (1841). *London*. United Kingdom: H. G. Bohn.
20. *Hereford Journal* – Wednesday, 11 May 1791.
21. *Kentish Gazette* – Tuesday, 10 June 1794.
22. Wroth, W. W., Wroth, A. E. (1896). *The London Pleasure Gardens of the Eighteenth Century*. United Kingdom: Macmillan.
23. *Morning Post* – Thursday, 22 January 1801.
24. *Bell's Weekly Messenger* – Sunday, 23 January 1803.
25. *Sun* (London) – Wednesday, 2 June 1802.
26. *True Briton* – Saturday, 5 June 1802.
27. *Morning Post* – Thursday, 3 June 1802.
28. *Morning Post* – Thursday, 2 June 1803.
29. *Statesman* (London) – Saturday, 15 August 1812.
30. Brayley, E. W., Allom, T., Brayley, E. W. (1841). *A Topographical History of Surrey: by E. W. Brayley ... assisted by John Britton ... and E. W. Brayley, jun.... The geological section by Gideon Mantell. (The illustrative department under the superintendence of Thomas Allom.) [With plates.]*. United Kingdom: R. B. Ede.
31. Ibid.
32. Feltham, J. (1802). *The Picture of London, for 1803: Being a Correct Guide to All the Curiosities, Amusements, Exhibitions, Public Establishments, and Remarkable Objects, in and Near London; with a Collection of Appropriate Tables. For the Use of Strangers, Foreigners, and All Persons who are Not Intimately Acquainted with British Metropolis*. United Kingdom: Lewis & Company.
33. William O. Aydelotte. 'Vauxhall Gardens: A Chapter in the Social History of England. By James Granville Southworth (New York: Columbia University Press. 1941. pp.viii, 199. $2.75.)', *The American Historical Review*, Volume 48, Issue 2, January 1943, pp.326–327.
34. *The Picture of London for 1820 ... The Twenty-first Edition*. (1820). United Kingdom: Longman, Hurst, Rees, Orme & Brown.
35. *Particulars of Vauxhall-Gardens ... which will be sold by auction ... April 14, 1818*, etc. (1818). United Kingdom: W. Smith.
36. Platt, J. C., Craik, G. L. (1841). *London*. United Kingdom: Charles Knight & Company.

37. Wroth, W. W., Wroth, A. E. (1896). *The London Pleasure Gardens of the Eighteenth Century*. United Kingdom: Macmillan.
38. *Kentish Gazette* – Friday, 23 May 1794.
39. Wroth, W. W., Wroth, A. E. (1896). *The London Pleasure Gardens of the Eighteenth Century*. United Kingdom: Macmillan.
40. Weber, W. (2009). 'Vauxhall Revisited: Pleasure Gardens and Their Publics, 1660–1880 Tate Britain, London 14–16 July 2008', *Eighteenth-Century Music*, 6(1), pp.151–153.
41. *The Picture of London for 1820 ... The Twenty-first Edition*. (1820). United Kingdom: Longman, Hurst, Rees, Orme & Brown.
42. *Windsor and Eton Express* – Saturday, 29 August 1812.
43. Masquerades, along with Grand Galas, became a feature around 1792 when the daily admission rate was increased from one to two shillings. Special events were typically three shillings. The first successful masked ball, in 1792, was noted for the bright lights and usual character costumes.
44. *New Times* (London) – Wednesday, 25 July 1821.
45. *Morning Post* – Monday, 6 August 1821.

**Chapter Four**

1. Timbs, J. (1872). *Clubs and Club Life in London: With Anecdotes of Its Famous Coffee Houses, Hostelries, and Taverns, from the Seventeenth Century to the Present Time*. United Kingdom: Chatto and Windus.
2. Leigh, S. (1820). *Leigh's New Picture of London: Or, A View of the Political, Religious, Medical, Literary, Municipal, Commercial, and Moral State of the British Metropolis*, .... United Kingdom: S. Leigh.
3. *Morning Post* – Monday, 23 June 1817.
4. Reynolds, L. (2022). *Who Owned Waterloo? Battle, Memory, and Myth in British History, 1815–1852*. United Kingdom: OUP Oxford.
5. *British Press* – Friday, 12 June 1818.
6. *Morning Post* – Wednesday, 7 July 1819.
7. *Morning Post* – Monday, 5 July 1819.
8. *New Times* (London) – Friday, 25 June 1819.
9. *Morning Post* – Friday, 25 June 1819.
10. *Morning Herald* (London) – Thursday, 13 July 1820.
11. Douglass, P. (2004). *Lady Caroline Lamb: A Biography*. United Kingdom: Palgrave Macmillan US.
12. *Morning Chronicle* – Friday, 4 August 1820.
13. *Morning Herald* (London) – Monday, 4 May 1835.
14. *Satirist; or, the Censor of the Times* – Sunday, 27 March 1836.
15. Hill, R. (2008). *God's Architect: Pugin and the Building of Romantic Britain*. United Kingdom: Yale University Press.
16. *English Chronicle and Whitehall Evening Post* – Thursday, 21 November 1833.
17. *Morning Herald* (London) – Wednesday, 19 February 1834.
18. *Morning Herald* (London) – Thursday, 24 December 1835.
19. *True Sun* – Tuesday, 6 June 1837.
20. *Albion: A Weekly Chronicle of Literature, Science and the Fine Arts*. (1835). Germany: (n.p.).
21. *The Idler, and Breakfast-table Companion*. (1837). United Kingdom: George Denney.
22. *Morning Post* – Monday, 21 June 1869.
23. *Edinburgh Evening News* – Friday, 10 October 1879.

24. Wyatt, B. D. (1813). *Observations on the Design for the Theatre Royal, Drury Lane, as Executed in the Year 1812: Accompanied by Plans, Elevation, & Sections, of the Same. Engraved on Eighteen Plates*. United Kingdom: J. Taylor.
25. *Morning Post* – Tuesday, 26 June 1821.
26. *Morning Advertiser* – Monday, 29 June 1829.
27. *Limerick Reporter* – Tuesday, 9 March 1841.
28. Brayley, E. W. (1826). *Historical and Descriptive Accounts of the Theatres of London*. United Kingdom: J. Taylor.
29. *Saint James's Chronicle* – Thursday, 20 February 1817.
30. *Morning Herald* (London) – Wednesday, 9 May 1821.
31. *Morning Herald* (London) – Thursday, 12 November 1835.
32. *Age* (London) – Sunday, 17 January 1836.
33. *London Courier and Evening Gazette* – Monday, 17 May 1802.
34. *Morning Post* – Monday, 17 May 1802.
35. *Dover Telegraph and Cinque Ports General Advertiser* – Saturday, 27 May 1837.
36. *Public Ledger and Daily Advertiser* – Thursday, 1 June 1820.

**Chapter Five**

1. *Morning Post* – Wednesday, 3 June 1801.
2. *London Courier and Evening Gazette* – Wednesday, 3 June 1801.
3. *Morning Post* – Monday, 10 May 1802.
4. *Morning Post* – Friday, 28 May 1802.
5. *Caledonian Mercury* – Saturday, 5 June 1802.
6. *Kentish Gazette* – Tuesday, 1 June 1802.
7. *London Courier and Evening Gazette* – Friday, 1 June 1804.
8. Polden, P. (2002). *Peter Thellusson's Will of 1797 and Its Consequences on Chancery Law*. United States: E. Mellen Press.
9. *Kentish Gazette* – Tuesday, 2 June 1801.
10. *British Press* – Saturday, 14 May 1808.
11. *Morning Post* – Tuesday, 16 June 1801.
12. *English Chronicle and Whitehall Evening Post* – Tuesday, 11 May 1802.
13. *Morning Post* – Friday, 27 July 1804.
14. *Globe* – Saturday, 22 June 1805.
15. *Oracle and the Daily Advertiser* – Tuesday, 25 June 1805.
16. *Bury and Norwich Post* – Wednesday, 24 July 1805.
17. *British Press* – Monday, 9 June 1806.
18. *Morning Post* – Friday, 10 May 1811.
19. *Morning Post* – Wednesday, 26 May 1819.
20. *Morning Post* – Friday, 8 July 1814.
21. *Champion* (London) – Saturday, 9 July 1814.
22. *Morning Post* – Thursday, 5 July 1804.
23. *English Chronicle and Whitehall Evening Post* – Thursday, 29 April 1802.
24. *Morning Post* – Saturday, 25 May 1805.
25. *Sporting Magazine*. (1805). United Kingdom: Rogerson & Tuxford.
26. *British Press* – Wednesday, 8 July 1807.
27. *Morning Advertiser* – Friday, 31 January 1806.
28. *Star* (London) – Friday, 14 June 1805.
29. *Galignani's Messenger: The Spirit of the English Journals. 1819*,1. (1819). France: Brière.

30. Morning Herald – Saturday, 6 June 1835.
31. *Sporting Magazine.* (1807). United Kingdom: Rogerson & Tuxford.
32. Colman, G. (1830). *Random Records. [An autobiography to circa 1790. With a portrait.*] United Kingdom: Henry Colburn & Richard Bentley.

**Chapter Six**

1. *A Guide to all the Watering and Sea Bathing Places in England and Wales , with a description of the Lakes; a sketch of a tour in Wales, and Itineraries ... Illustrated with maps and views. By the Editor of the Picture of London.* (1824). United Kingdom: (n.p.).
2. *Kentish Weekly Post or Canterbury Journal* – Friday, 24 August 1798.
3. Oulton, W. C. (1820). *Picture of Margate and its Vicinity.* United Kingdom: Baldwin.
4. *Porcupine* – Thursday, 3 September 1801.
5. Feltham, J. (1813). *A Guide to all the Watering and Sea Bathing Places; With A Description Of The Lakes; A Sketch Of A Tour In Wales; And Itineraries, By The Editor Of The Picture Of London.* United Kingdom: (n.p.).
6. *The New Margate, Ramsgate and Broadstairs Guide; Containing an Historical Epitome of the Ancient and Present State of the Isle of Thanet, Etc.* (1801). (n.p.)
7. *Morning Post* – Thursday, 1 September 1803.
8. Osborne, R. C. (1840). *New Margate Guide, or steam packet companion.... With a map & ... plates. Fourth edition.* (n.p.): R. C. Osborne.
9. *Globe* – Saturday, 14 September 1805.
10. *New Ramsgate, Margate and Broadstairs guide, etc.* (1850). (n.p.)
11. *London Courier and Evening Gazette* – Wednesday, 27 August 1806.
12. *Star* (London) – Tuesday, 2 August 1808.
13. *Oracle and the Daily Advertiser* – Saturday, 8 September 1804.
14. *Morning Post* – Tuesday, 16 September 1817.
15. *Kentish Gazette* – Friday, 25 January 1833.
16. *Morning Post* – Tuesday, 13 October 1801.
17. *Monmouthshire Merlin* – Saturday, 17 October 1829.
18. *Morning Post* – Saturday, 23 August 1828.
19. *Brighton Gazette* – Thursday, 25 September 1828.
20. *Brighton Gazette* – Thursday, 18 September 1828.
21. *Dublin Evening Packet and Correspondent* – Tuesday, 4 February 1834.
22. *Morning Post* – Tuesday, 14 February 1826.
23. *Norfolk Chronicle* – Saturday, 5 March 1831.
24. *Lancaster Gazette* – Saturday, 26 February 1803.
25. *Liverpool Albion* – Monday, 7 October 1833.
26. *Manchester Courier* – Saturday, 24 September 1836.
27. *Derby Mercury* – Wednesday, 1 February 1826.
28. *Cumberland Pacquet and Ware's Whitehaven Advertiser* – Tuesday, 28 February 1826.
29. *Leicester Chronicle* – Saturday, 8 September 1827.
30. *Newcastle Courant* – Saturday, 16 February 1828.
31. *Western Times* – Saturday, 26 December 1835.
32. *Saunders's News-Letter* – Tuesday, 12 April 1836.
33. *Dublin Evening Post* – Tuesday, 17 May 1808.
34. *Saunders's News-Letter* – Thursday, 22 May 1817.
35. *Calcutta Gazette* – Thursday, 8 January 1795.
36. *London Courier and Evening Gazette* – Saturday, 16 November 1811.

37. *New Times* (London) – Saturday, 19 April 1828.
38. *Morning Post* – Friday, 11 February 1803.
39. *Sun* (London) – Monday, 9 January 1804.
40. *Bristol Mirror* – Saturday, 22 January 1814.
41. *British Press* – Saturday, 24 November 1804.
42. *Stamford Mercury* – Friday, 20 April 1810.
43. *Chester Courant* – Tuesday, 16 January 1816.
44. *Bath Chronicle and Weekly Gazette* – Thursday, 15 April 1824.
45. *Chester Courant* – Tuesday, 21 January 1823.

**Chapter Seven**

1. Conlin, J. (2014). *Big City, Bright Lights? Night spaces in Paris and London, 1660–1820.*
2. Gifford, R. (1988). 'Light, decor, arousal, comfort and communication', *Journal of Environmental Psychology*, 8(3), pp.177–189.
3. Parker, K. W. (2003). 'Sign Consumption in the nineteenth-Century Department Store: An Examination of Visual Merchandising in the Grand Emporiums (1846–1900)', *Journal of Sociology*, 39(4), pp.353–371. https://doi.org/10.1177/0004869003394003.
4. *Party-giving on every scale; or The cost of entertainments [&c.] by the author of 'Manners and tone of good society'*.. (1880). United Kingdom: (n.p.).
5. *Star* (London) – Friday, 4 August 1820.
6. *Morning Chronicle* – Friday, 5 August 1803.
7. *Morning Chronicle* – Monday, 22 August 1803.
8. Boulton, W. B. (1901). *The Amusements of Old London: Being a Survey of the Sports and Pastimes, Tea Gardens and Parks, Playhouses and Other Diversions of the People of London from the 17th to the Beginning of the nineteenth Century.* United Kingdom: J. C. Nimmo.
9. Thornbury, W. (1893). *Old and New London: a Narrative of Its History, Its People, and Its Places ….* United Kingdom: Cassell, Limited.
10. *Globe* – Saturday, 17 June 1809.
11. *Morning Chronicle* – Tuesday, 28 April 1829.
12. *Metropolitan: a Monthly Journal of Literature, Science and the Fine Arts.* (1834). United Kingdom: J. Cochrane and Company.
13. *London Courier and Evening Gazette* – Wednesday, 27 June 1804.
14. *British Press* – Wednesday, 25 May 1808.
15. *The News* (London) – Sunday, 30 August 1812.
16. *Globe* – Saturday, 22 June 1805.
17. *British Press* – Saturday, 14 May 1808.
18. *Caledonian Mercury* – Saturday, 5 June 1802.
19. *Reading Mercury* – Monday, 5 October 1801.
20. *Morning Post* – Thursday, 25 May 1809.
21. *Saint James's Chronicle* – Saturday, 1 June 1805.
22. *British Press* – Saturday, 14 May 1808.
23. *British Press* – Thursday, 16 July 1807.
24. *Cork Constitution* – Tuesday, 30 January 1827.
25. John Plunkett, 'Light work: Feminine Leisure and the Making of Transparencies', in Kyriaki Hadjiafxendi and Patricia Zakreski (eds.), *Crafting the Woman Professional in the Long Nineteenth Century: Artistry and Industry in Britain.* (New York, 2016), pp.43–44.
26. *Oracle and the Daily Advertiser* – Thursday 28 January 1802
27. *London Courier and Evening Gazette* – Wednesday, 10 February 1802.

28. *Morning Post* – Thursday, 3 June 1802.
29. *British Press* – Wednesday, 4 June 1806.
30. *Sun* (London) – Saturday, 7 June 1806.
31. *Globe* – Wednesday, 4 January 1809.
32. *Morning Post* – Saturday, 29 May 1802.
33. *British Press* – Saturday, 14 July 1810.
34. *British Press* – Wednesday, 14 March 1810.
35. *Anti-Gallican Monitor* – Sunday, 19 November 1820.
36. *Morning Advertiser* – Tuesday, 27 January 1829.
37. *Kentish Weekly Post or Canterbury Journal* – Tuesday, 25 March 1817.
38. *Leamington Spa Courier* – Saturday, 24 April 1830.
39. Callaway, A. (2000). *Visual Ephemera: Theatrical Art in Nineteenth-century Australia.* Cocos (Keeling) Islands: UNSW Press.
40. Ogborn, M. (1998). *Spaces of Modernity: London's Geographies 1680–1780.* United Kingdom: Guilford Publications.
41. Potter, R. A. (2010). 'Icebergs at Vauxhall', *Victorian Review*, 36(2), pp.27–31.
42. *Star* (London) – Tuesday, 25 November 1828.
43. *World and Fashionable Sunday Chronicle* – Monday, 6 April 1818.
44. *Sun* (London) – Friday, 28 August 1812.
45. *Public Ledger and Daily Advertiser* – Monday, 4 December 1826.
46. *Morning Herald* (London) – Wednesday, 4 June 1806.
47. *London Courier and Evening Gazette* – Tuesday, 25 August 1801.
48. *Morning Chronicle* – Monday, 4 July 1814.
49. *London Courier and Evening Gazette* – Wednesday, 3 June 1801.
50. *Kentish Gazette* – Friday, 21 May 1802.
51. *Oxford Journal* – Saturday, 22 May 1802.
52. *British Press* – Wednesday, 14 March 1810.
53. *Star* (London) – Friday, 4 August 1820.
54. *Morning Post* – Thursday, 3 June 1802.
55. *True Briton* – Friday, 3 June 1803.
56. *Morning Post* – Friday, 8 June 1810.
57. *Morning Post* – Tuesday, 20 August 1822.
58. *Star* (London) – Friday, 4 August 1820.
59. *The Literary Panorama.* (1810). United Kingdom: (n.p.).
60. Raffald, E. (1799). *The Experienced English Housekeeper ...A New Edition. In which are Inserted Some Celebrated Receipts by Other Modern Authors. [With Plates, Including a Portrait.].* United Kingdom: A. Millar, W. Law, & R. Cater.
61. *Saunders's News-Letter* – Saturday, 6 April 1793.
62. *The Literary Panorama.* (1810). United Kingdom: (n.p.).
63. Whittock, N., Badcock, J., Bennett, J., Newton, C. (1837). *The Complete Book of Trades ...By ...Mr. N. Whittock, Mr. J. Bennett, Mr. J. Badcock, Mr. C. Newton and Others, Etc. [Illustrated.].* United Kingdom: J. Bennett.
64. https://www.cam.ac.uk/news/dreams-of-albion-how-british-identity-is-rooted-in-the-land.
65. 'The Now Vanished Ephemeral Art: Chalking the Regency Ballroom Floor'. Regency Fiction Writers (thebeaumonde.com).
66. Parkes, W. (1841). *Domestic Duties, Or, Instructions to Young Married Ladies, on the Management of Their Households and the Regulation of Their Conduct in the Various*

*Relations and Duties of Married Life*. United Kingdom: Longman, Orme, Brown, Green, & Longmans.
67. *Reading Mercury* – Monday, 4 October 1790.
68. *Aris's Birmingham Gazette* – Monday, 30 August 1790.
69. *Caledonian Mercury* – Saturday, 24 December 1791.
70. *Derby Mercury* – Thursday, 3 June 1802.
71. Enfield, W. (1820). *Young Artist's Assistant: Or, Elements of the Fine Arts, Containing the Principles of Drawing, Painting in General, Crayon Painting, Oil Painting, Portrait Painting, Miniature Painting, Designing, Colouring, Engraving, &c., &c.* United Kingdom: T. Tegg.
72. *London Courier and Evening Gazette* – Thursday, 12 March 1801.
73. *Morning Post* – Monday, 8 April 1816.
74. *Morning Herald* (London) – Wednesday, 4 June 1806.
75. *Morning Post* – Monday, 11 February 1805.
76. *Sun* (London) – Thursday, 26 April 1827.
77. *Morning Herald* (London) – Tuesday, 17 June 1806.
78. *Morning Post* – Saturday, 19 April 1806.
79. *Morning Herald* (London) – Monday, 8 May 1820.
80. Wellings, B. (2002). 'Empire-nation: National and imperial discourses in England', *Nations and Nationalism*, 8(1), pp.95–109.
81. Díaz-Andreu, M. (2007). *A World History of Nineteenth-Century Archaeology: Nationalism, Colonialism, and The Past*. OUP Oxford.

**Chapter Eight**

1. *Johnson's Sunday Monitor* – Sunday, 16 February 1817.
2. *Morning Post* – Tuesday, 7 February 1826.
3. *Morning Chronicle* – Monday, 4 July 1814.
4. Wilson, T. (1816). *A Companion to the Ball Room, Containing a Choice Collection of Country Dance ...and Waltz Tunes, with ...Appropriate Figures, the Etiquette, and a Dissertation on the State of the Ball Room*. United Kingdom: Button, Whittaker & Company.
5. *Caledonian Mercury* – Monday, 31 August 1801.
6. *Stamford Mercury* – Friday, 20 April 1810.
7. *Morning Post* – Saturday, 20 July 1805.
8. *Bath Chronicle and Weekly Gazette* – Thursday, 8 January 1801.
9. *Madras Courier* – Tuesday, 22 December 1812.
10. *British Luminary* – Sunday, 31 January 1819.
11. *Morning Post* – Monday, 18 February 1822.
12. *Morning Advertiser* – Tuesday, 30 June 1829.
13. *Star* (London) – Tuesday, 28 April 1829.
14. *New Times* (London) – Tuesday, 30 December 1823.
15. *New Times* (London) – Tuesday, 11 January 1825.
16. *Morning Chronicle* – Monday, 4 July 1814.
17. *World and Fashionable Sunday Chronicle* – Monday, 6 April 1818.
18. *Saunders's News-Letter* – Wednesday, 20 May 1818.
19. *London Courier and Evening Gazette* – Wednesday, 4 February 1801.
20. *Morning Post* – Saturday, 4 February 1804.
21. *Oracle and the Daily Advertiser* – Thursday, 27 June 1805.

22. Herbert, T., & Barlow, H. (2013). *Music & The British Military in the Long Nineteenth Century*. Oxford University Press, USA.
23. Rogan, J. M. (1903). 'Military Bands and Military Music: A Series of Three Lectures', *Journal of the Royal United Services Institution*, 47(308), pp.1099–1115.
24. *Imperial Weekly Gazette* – Saturday, 11 April 1818.
25. *Kentish Gazette* – Friday, 21 May 1802.
26. *Morning Herald* (London) – Wednesday, 26 June 1805.
27. Herbert, T. (2020). '"The band is the instrument": military bands, the martial paradigm, the crowd and the legacy of the long nineteenth century', in Pestana, Maria do Rosário; Granjo, André; Sagrillo, Damien François; Lorenzo, Gloria Rodriguez (orgs.), *Our Music, Our World: Wind Bands and Local Social Life*, pp.17–26.
28. *British Press* – Thursday, 20 June 1811.
29. https://artandmusic.yale.edu/handels-london/vauxhall-gardens/vauxhall-gallery2-instruments-music-pandean-minstrels-performance.
30. Lidington, T. (n.d.). *'Don't Forget The Pierrots!' The Complete History of British Pierrot Troupes & Concert Parties*. United Kingdom: Taylor & Francis.
31. https://www.regencydances.org/paper022.php.
32. *Saint James's Chronicle* – Saturday, 6 July 1805.
33. *London Courier and Evening Gazette* – Wednesday, 27 June 1804.
34. *Morning Post* – Saturday, 25 April 1801.
35. *Oracle and the Daily Advertiser* – Thursday, 28 January 1802.
36. *True Briton* – Thursday, 25 February 1802.
37. *True Briton* – Friday, 12 February 1802.
38. *Morning Post* – Saturday, 17 May 1828.
39. *Morning Advertiser* – Tuesday, 29 December 1829.
40. *True Sun* – Tuesday, 6 June 1837.
41. *Sun* (London) – Saturday, 19 April 1823.
42. *Brunswick or True Blue* – Sunday, 6 May 1821.
43. *New Times* (London) – Wednesday, 25 July 1821.
44. *Morning Advertiser* – Saturday, 21 June 1828.
45. *Imperial Weekly Gazette* – Saturday, 11 April 1818.
46. *British Press* – Thursday, 17 May 1804.
47. *Morning Herald* (London) – Wednesday, 4 June 1806.
48. *Morning Advertiser* – Tuesday, 29 December 1829.
49. *Morning Post* – Saturday, 21 June 1828.
50. *Morning Post* – Thursday, 3 June 1813.
51. Brock, A. S. H. (1922). Pyrotechnics: the History and Art of Firework Making. D. O'Connor.
52. Ibid.
53. Partington, C. F. (1822). *A Brief historical and descriptive Account of the Royal Gardens, Vauxhall. [By C. F. Partington.]*. United Kingdom: (n.p.).
54. https://vauxhallhistory.org/fireworks-at-vauxhall/.
55. https://www.british-history.ac.uk/old-new-london/vol6/pp447-467.
56. *Saint James's Chronicle* – Saturday, 1 July 1837.
57. Colles, H. C. (1927). *Grove's Dictionary of Music and Musicians*. United Kingdom: Macmillan.
58. *Morning Chronicle* – Wednesday, 29 June 1808.

59. *The Kaleidoscope; Or, Literary and Scientific Mirror: Containing a Variety of Original and Select Articles, Literature, Men and Manners, Amusement, Criticism, Elegant Extracts, Poetry, Anecdotes, Biography, Meteorology, the Drama, Arts and Sciences, Voyages and Travels, Natural History, Diary of the Months, Fashions, &c..... (1823).* United Kingdom: E. Smith and Company.
60. *The Art of Making All Kinds of Fireworks ... To which is Added the History of Guy Fawks, and Gunpowder Plot ... Third Edition.* (1813). United Kingdom: W. Mason.
61. Grotz, C. (1820). *The Art of Making Fireworks.* Ireland: (n.p.).
62. Hill, C. (1904). *Jane Austen: Her Homes and Her Friends.* United Kingdom: John Lane.
63. *Complete Works of Frances Burney* (Delphi Classics). (2015). Hungary: Delphi Classics.
64. *Annual Register of World Events.* (1764). United Kingdom: (n.p.).
65. *Leicester Chronicle* – Saturday, 1 September 1827.
66. *Morning Chronicle* – Wednesday, 21 June 1815.
67. *Johnson's Sunday Monitor* – Sunday, 16 February 1817.
68. *New Times (London)* – Tuesday, 22 June 1819.
69. *Literary Gazette and Journal of Belles Lettres, Arts, Sciences, Etc.* (1817). United Kingdom: H. Colburn.
70. *Morning Herald* (London) – Tuesday, 27 June 1826.
71. *Leamington Spa Courier* – Saturday, 24 April 1830.
72. Gaard, G. (2017). *Critical Ecofeminism.* United States: Lexington Books.
73. *Sun* (London) – Friday, 28 August 1812.
74. *Bell's Life in London and Sporting Chronicle* – Sunday, 31 December 1826.
75. *Sun* (London) – Saturday, 19 April 1823.
76. *Imperial Weekly Gazette* – Saturday, 11 April 1818.
77. *Sun* (London) – Friday, 28 August 1812.
78. *Morning Post* – Tuesday, 26 June 1821.
79. Bishop, J. G. (1892). *'A Peep Into the Past': Brighton in the Olden Time, with Glances at the Present.* United Kingdom: J. G. Bishop.
80. *Eliza Cook's Journal.* (1852). United Kingdom: John Owen Clarke.
81. Banerjee, S. (2011). 'The Mysterious Alien: Indian Street Jugglers in Victorian London', *Economic and Political Weekly*, pp.59–65.
82. *National Register* (London) – Sunday, 3 July 1814.
83. *Brighton Gazette* – Thursday, 18 September 1828.
84. *Bell's Life in London and Sporting Chronicle* – Sunday, 31 December 1826.
85. *Morning Herald* (London) – Wednesday, 23 June 1824.
86. *Morning Post* – Monday, 18 February 1822.
87. *Brunswick or True Blue* – Sunday, 6 May 1821.
88. *British Press* – Monday, 5 February 1821.
89. *Sun* (London) – Friday, 20 June 1828.
90. *Morning Advertiser* – Monday, 29 June 1829.
91. *New Times* (London) – Tuesday, 30 June 1829.
92. *True Briton* – Monday, 10 January 1803.
93. *Morning Chronicle* – Monday, 4 July 1814.

**Chapter Nine**

1. Willich, A. F. M. (1802). *The Domestic Encyclopaedia: Or, A Dictionary of Facts, and Useful Knowledge, Comprehending a Concise View of the Latest Discoveries, Inventions,*

*and Improvements, Chiefly Applicable to Rural and Domestic Economy ....* United Kingdom: Murray and Highle.
2. *The Gentleman's Magazine*. (1898). United Kingdom: Bradbury, Evans.
3. Rover, W. (1882). *The Neptune at the Golden Horn*. United States: P. O'Shea, agent.
4. Henderson, W. A. (1809). *The Housekeeper's Instructor ....* United Kingdom: J. Stratfored.
5. Cox, J. (1822). *The Practical Confectioner, Embracing the Whole System of Pastry, and Confectionery, in All Their Various Branches; Containing Upwards of 260 Genuine and Valuable Receipts, Etc. [With Plates.]*. United Kingdom: Longman, Hurst, Rees, Orme & Browne.
6. *True Briton* – Monday, 19 April 1802.
7. *Morning Advertiser* – Tuesday, 29 December 1829.
8. Whitehead, J. (1889). *The Steward's Handbook and Guide to Party Catering*. United States: J. Anderson & Company, printers.
9. *New Times* (London) – Wednesday, 25 July 1821.
10. *Oracle and the Daily Advertiser* – Monday, 16 May 1808.
11. *Oracle and the Daily Advertiser* – Wednesday, 4 May 1803.
12. *Oracle and the Daily Advertiser* – Monday, 16 May 1808.
13. *Oracle and the Daily Advertiser* – Thursday, 15 January 1801.
14. Pascoe, C. E. (1888). *London of To-day: An Illustrated Handbook for the Season*. United Kingdom: Sampson Low, Marston, Searle, and Rivington Limited, St. Dunstan's House, Fetter Lane, Fleet Street.
15. *Figaro in London*. (1836). United Kingdom: W. Strange.
16. *New Monthly Magazine, and Universal Register*. (1840). United Kingdom: Henry Colburn.
17. *Cobbett's Political Register*. (1833). United Kingdom: William Cobbett.
18. *Sporting Magazine*. (1812). United Kingdom: Rogerson & Tuxford.
19. *Oracle and the Daily Advertiser* – Wednesday, 20 April 1803.
20. *Oracle and the Daily Advertiser* – Thursday, 30 April 1807.
21. *Morning Post* – Saturday, 26 February 1803.
22. *Sun* (London) – Saturday, 19 April 1823.
23. *Sun* (London) – Saturday, 19 July 1823.
24. *Morning Herald* (London) – Saturday, 29 December 1821.
25. Palmerston, H. J. T., Croker, J. W., Peel, R. (1819). *The New Whig Guide*. United Kingdom: W. Wright.
26. *Morning Herald* (London) – Friday, 20 April 1804.
27. *Oracle and the Daily Advertiser* – Saturday, 29 June 1805.
28. *Morning Herald* (London) – Thursday, 13 February 1806.
29. *Oracle and the Daily Advertiser* – Tuesday, 5 February 1805.
30. *The Epicure's Almanack; Or Calendar of Good Living: Containing a Directory to the Taverns, Coffee-houses, Inns, Eating-houses, and Other Places of Alimentary Resort in the British Metropolis and Its Environs ... To be Continued Annually*. (1815). United Kingdom: Longman's & Company.
31. *Sun* (London) – Friday, 27 May 1803.
32. *The year 1800, or The sayings and doings of our fathers and mothers 60 years ago, as recorded in the newspapers and other periodicals, prepared by F. Perigal*. (1860). United Kingdom: Thomas Sanderson.
33. *The Epicure's Almanack; Or Calendar of Good Living: Containing a Directory to the Taverns, Coffee-houses, Inns, Eating-houses, and Other Places of Alimentary Resort in*

*the British Metropolis and Its Environs ... To be Continued Annually*. (1815). United Kingdom: Longman's & Company.
34. *Morning Herald* (London) – Wednesday, 1 January 1834.
35. *Satirist; or, the Censor of the Times* – Sunday, 16 December 1832.
36. *British Press* – Tuesday, 4 May 1824.
37. *Morning Post* – Wednesday, 18 February 1824.
38. *Morning Post* – Saturday, 12 February 1803.
39. *Morning Post* – Saturday, 13 November 1824.
40. *One Thousand Hints for the Table: With a Few Words on Wines*. (1862). United Kingdom: Routledge, Warne, & Routledge.
41. *Morning Post* – Friday, 8 June 1810.
42. *Morning Post* – Monday, 22 June 1812.
43. *Morning Post* – Friday, 11 February 1803.
44. *Caledonian Mercury* – Thursday, 5 January 1809.
45. *London Courier and Evening Gazette* – Friday, 17 May 1805.
46. *Bath Chronicle and Weekly Gazette* – Thursday, 15 April 1824.
47. *Etiquette for Ladies: With Hints on the Preservation, Improvement, and Display of Female Beauty*. (1838). United States: Carey, Lea & Blanchard.
48. *Oracle and the Daily Advertiser* – Friday, 11 February 1803.
49. *Oracle and the Daily Advertiser* – Monday, 16 May 1808.
50. *Oracle and the Daily Advertiser* – Friday, 30 April 1802.
51. *British Press* – Saturday, 2 June 1810.
52. *Morning Herald* (London) – Monday, 20 April 1818.
53. *Morning Herald* (London) – Saturday, 12 April 1817.
54. *Globe* – Saturday, 4 April 1818.
55. *Globe* – Thursday, 14 February 1811.
56. *Sun* (London) – Friday, 11 May 1810.
57. *True Briton* – Tuesday, 31 May 1803.
58. *London Courier and Evening Gazette* – Tuesday, 14 April 1801.
59. *Public Ledger and Daily Advertiser* – Saturday, 22 August 1812.
60. *English Chronicle and Whitehall Evening Post* – Thursday, 1 January 1824.
61. *Tavern Anecdotes and Reminiscences of the origin of signs, clubs, coffee-houses, ... &c. intended as a lounge-book for Londoners and their country cousins. By one of the old School [W. West]*.. (1825). United Kingdom: (n.p.).
62. *Oracle and the Daily Advertiser* – Saturday, 29 June 1805.
63. *Morning Post* – Wednesday, 5 May 1824.
64. *True Sun* – Friday, 4 April 1834.
65. *Town Talk 1822* – Sunday, 21 April 1822.
66. *Morning Post* – Tuesday, 11 January 1825.
67. *Evening Mail* – Friday, 29 December 1826.
68. *Morning Post* – Wednesday, 4 June 1806.
69. *Morning Chronicle* – Friday, 30 December 1825.
70. *Fleming's Weekly Express* – Sunday, 1 January 1826.
71. *Morning Post* – Tuesday, 2 February 1830.
72. *Public Ledger and Daily Advertiser* – Saturday, 17 February 1816.
73. *Kentish Gazette* – Friday, 21 May 1802.
74. *Morning Herald* (London) – Saturday, 5 May 1810.
75. *Oracle and the Daily Advertiser* – Saturday, 7 February 1807.

76. *Morning Herald* (London) – Thursday, 30 April 1807.
77. *Derby Mercury* – Thursday, 3 June 1802.
78. *Saint James's Chronicle* – Saturday, 6 July 1805.
79. *Chester Chronicle* – Friday, 18 July 1806.
80. *Morning Herald* (London) – Thursday, 18 April 1822.
81. *Morning Herald* (London) – Friday, 25 December 1829.
82. *Morning Herald* (London) – Monday, 2 February 1801.
83. *Morning Herald* (London) – Thursday, 30 April 1807.
84. *Morning Herald* (London) – Monday, 2 February 1801.
85. *Johnson's Sunday Monitor* – Sunday, 16 February 1817.
86. *Morning Post* – Friday, 7 April 1826.

**Chapter Ten**

1. *Johnson's Sunday Monitor* – Sunday, 18 June 1820.
2. *Morning Post* – Saturday, 12 February 1803.
3. *Walker's Hibernian Magazine, Or, Compendium of Entertaining Knowledge*. (1800). Ireland: R. Gibson.
4. *The Scotsman* – Wednesday, 9 July 1823.
5. *Morning Herald* (London) – Friday, 20 April 1804.
6. *New Times* (London) – Wednesday, 1 April 1818.
7. *True Briton* – Friday, 18 February 1803.
8. *Morning Herald* (London) – Monday, 27 April 1818.
9. *New Times* (London) – Thursday, 6 February 1823.
10. *Oxford University and City Herald* – Saturday, 17 August 1811.
11. https://thechaptercatcher.com/dr-syntax-worlds-first-cartoon/.
12. *Star* (London) – Friday, 17 April 1801.
13. *Oracle and the Daily Advertiser* – Friday, 11 February 1803.
14. *Morning Herald* (London) – Wednesday, 26 June 1805.
15. *Morning Herald* (London) – Saturday, 26 April 1834.
16. *Staffordshire Advertiser* – Saturday, 11 May 1799.
17. *New Times* (London) – Thursday, 28 December 1826.
18. *Morning Post* – Thursday, 22 January 1801.
19. *Caledonian Mercury* – Thursday, 5 January 1809.
20. *Bath Chronicle and Weekly Gazette* – Thursday, 8 January 1801.
21. *Kentish Gazette* – Tuesday, 2 June 1801.
22. *Sussex Advertiser* – Monday, 20 June 1825.
23. Nigro, J. A. (2010). 'Mystery Meets Muslin: Regency Gothic Dress in Art, Fashion, and the Theater', *Persuasions: The Jane Austen Journal On-Line*, 31(1).
24. Winter, C. (2020). *Gothic economics: gothic literature and commercial society in Britain, 1750–1850* (Doctoral dissertation).
25. *Morning Post* – Wednesday, 4 June 1806.
26. Sloan, C. L. (2017). The Gothic Sartorial: Fashion and Costume in Novels from the Long Nineteenth Century (Doctoral dissertation).
27. *Morning Post* – Saturday, 28 April 1804.
28. *Star* (London) – Friday, 4 August 1820.
29. Jarvis, A. (1982). '"There was a Young Man of Bengal..." The Vogue for Fancy Dress, 1830–1950', *Costume*, 16(1), pp.33–46.
30. Myerly, S. H. (1992). '"The Eye Must Entrap the Mind": Army Spectacle and Paradigm in Nineteenth-Century Britain', *Journal of Social History*, pp.105–131.

31. *British Press* – Friday, 12 June 1818.
32. *Morning Herald* (London) – Wednesday, 24 December 1828.
33. *London Courier and Evening Gazette* – Tuesday, 21 April 1801.
34. *Sun* (London) – Saturday, 29 May 1802.
35. *True Sun* – Tuesday, 6 June 1837.
36. *Bury and Norwich Post* – Wednesday, 3 December 1806.
37. *Englishman* – Sunday, 21 May 1826.
38. *Leamington Spa Courier* – Saturday, 2 May 1835.
39. *Fleming's Weekly Express* – Sunday, 13 June 1824.
40. *Star* (London) – Tuesday, 28 April 1829.
41. *London Courier and Evening Gazette* – Wednesday, 3 June 1801.
42. *Staffordshire Advertiser* – Saturday, 11 May 1799.
43. *Oracle and the Daily Advertiser* – Saturday, 7 February 1807.
44. *London Courier and Evening Gazette* – Tuesday, 2 June 1801.
45. *Morning Post* – Friday, 27 May 1808.
46. *Johnson's Sunday Monitor* – Sunday, 12 April 1818.
47. *Star* (London) – Friday, 4 August 1820.
48. *Morning Post* – Monday, 18 February 1822.
49. *British Press* – Tuesday, 11 January 1825.
50. *Star* (London) – Friday, 4 August 1820.
51. *Caledonian Mercury* – Monday, 31 August 1801.
52. *Morning Post* – Friday, 8 June 1810.
53. *Newcastle Courant* – Saturday, 18 June 1825.
54. *Morning Post* – Thursday, 25 May 1809.
55. *Morning Herald* (London) – Wednesday, 31 December 1823.
56. *Derby Mercury* – Thursday, 3 June 1802.
57. *Newcastle Courant* – Saturday, 18 June 1825.
58. *Morning Post* – Friday, 8 June 1810.
59. *Reading Mercury* – Monday, 4 October 1790.
60. *Morning Chronicle* – Friday, 28 December 1832.
61. *Englishman* – Sunday, 21 May 1826.
62. *Morning Post* – Saturday, 22 May 1802.
63. *Star* (London) – Friday, 4 August 1820.
64. *Morning Post* – Friday, 27 July 1804.
65. *Morning Post* – Friday, 8 June 1810.
66. *Morning Post* – Thursday, 25 May 1809.
67. *Morning Post* – Friday, 28 April 1809.
68. *Morning Post* – Wednesday, 3 June 1801.
69. *Morning Herald* (London) – Wednesday, 8 June 1825.
70. *Morning Advertiser* – Tuesday, 27 January 1829.
71. *Morning Post* – Monday, 29 June 1835.
72. *Morning Chronicle* – Wednesday, 2 June 1802.
73. *Morning Post* – Thursday, 25 May 1809.
74. *Morning Post* – Wednesday, 5 May 1824.
75. *Star* (London) – Friday, 4 August 1820.
76. *Morning Advertiser* – Saturday, 21 June 1828.
77. *Morning Post* – Monday, 10 February 1812.
78. *London Courier and Evening Gazette* – Tuesday, 25 August 1801.

79. *Morning Chronicle* – Monday, 7 June 1802.
80. *Star* (London) – Friday, 4 August 1820.
81. *Saint James's Chronicle* – Thursday, 20 February 1817.
82. Brownie, B. (2013). 'Dressing Down: Costume, Disguise and the Performance of Ordinariness', *Clothing Cultures*, 1(1), pp.45–57.
83. *Star* (London) – Tuesday, 25 November 1828.
84. *Morning Post* – Friday, 20 January 1826.
85. *Coventry Herald* – Friday, 6 January 1826.
86. *Age* (London) – Sunday, 8 March 1840.
87. *Bath Chronicle and Weekly Gazette* – Thursday, 8 January 1801.
88. *Morning Chronicle* – Friday, 28 December 1832.
89. Klapp, O. E. (1954). 'Heroes, villains and fools, as agents of social control', *American Sociological Review*, 19(1), pp.56–62.
90. DuBois, A. E. (1934). 'Shakespeare and Nineteenth-Century Drama', *Journal of English Literary History*, 1(2), pp.163–196.
91. Lublin, R. I. (2016). *Costuming the Shakespearean Stage: Visual Codes of Representation in Early Modern Theatre and Culture*. Routledge.
92. *London Courier and Evening Gazette* – Wednesday, 3 June 1801.
93. *Morning Post* – Thursday, 25 May 1809.
94. *New Times* (London) – Friday, 30 December 1825.
95. *Star* (London) – Tuesday, 28 April 1829.
96. *Oxford Journal* – Saturday, 28 January 1797.
97. *Weekly True Sun* – Sunday, 17 May 1835.
98. *London Courier and Evening Gazette* – Wednesday, 3 June 1801.
99. *Belle Assemblée: Or, Court and Fashionable Magazine; Containing Interesting and Original Literature, and Records of the Beau-monde*. (1819). United Kingdom: J. Bell.
100. Castle, T. (1986). *Masquerade and Civilization: The Carnivalesque in Eighteenth-Century English Culture and Fiction*. Stanford University Press.
101. *London Courier and Evening Gazette* – Tuesday, 21 April 1801.
102. *Caledonian Mercury* – Monday, 31 August 1801.
103. *Star* (London) – Friday, 4 August 1820.
104. *New Times* (London) – Thursday, 24 April 1823.
105. *New Times* (London) – Tuesday, 11 January 1825.
106. *Morning Post* – Saturday, 12 February 1803.
107. *Morning Post* – Saturday, 26 February 1803.
108. *Bath Chronicle and Weekly Gazette* – Thursday, 8 January 1801.

**Chapter Eleven**

1. Smith, A. D. (2013). *Nationalism: Theory, Ideology, History*. John Wiley & Sons.
2. Colley, L. (2005). *Britons: Forging the Nation, 1707–1837*. Yale University Press.
3. *Bath; a glance at its public worship, style of dress, cotillons, masquerades, &c. &c. Second edition*. (1814). United Kingdom: Meyler & Son.
4. *Evening Mail* – Monday, 14 February 1803.
5. *Brighton Gazette* – Thursday, 25 September 1828.
6. *The Comic Offering; Or Ladies' Melange of Literary Mirth, for MDCCCXXXI [-MDCCCXXXV.]*. (1835). United Kingdom: Smith, Elder, and Company.
7. *Reading Mercury* – Monday, 16 November 1835.
8. *Nation* – Friday, 11 June 1824.

9. *Evening Mail* – Monday, 25 April 1803.
10. *British Press* – Thursday, 17 May 1804.
11. *New Times* (London) – Friday, 30 December 1825.
12. *Bombay Gazette* – Wednesday, 17 November 1824.
13. *Morning Herald* (London) – Wednesday, 31 December 1823.
14. *London Life as it is; or, a hand-book to all the attractions, wonders, and enjoyments of the great city, etc.* (1851). United Kingdom: (n.p.).
15. *British Press* – Tuesday, 25 April 1826.
16. Matthews, H. (1836). *The Diary of an Invalid; the Journal of a Tour in Portugal, Italy, Switzerland and France.* France: (n.p.).
17. Lemaistre, J. G. (1806). *Travels After the Peace of Amiens, Through Parts of France, Switzerland, Italy, and Germany, Etc.* United Kingdom: (n.p.).
18. *Bell's Weekly Messenger* – Sunday, 14 March 1802.
19. Beckford, P. (1805). *Familiar Letters from Italy, to a Friend in England.* United Kingdom: J. Easton.
20. MacGill, T. (1808). *Travels in Turkey, Italy and Russia During the Years 1803, 1804, 1805, and 1806: With an Account of Some of the Greek Islands.* United Kingdom: J. Murray.
21. Sloan, J., Lyman, T. (1818). *Rambles in Italy: In the Years 1816....17.* United States: N. G. Maxwell, J. Robinson, Printer.
22. *Morning Herald* (London) - Wednesday, 8 June 1825.
23. *London Packet and New Lloyd's Evening Post* – Wednesday, 28 June 1826.
24. *English Chronicle and Whitehall Evening Post* – Thursday, 1 January 1824.
25. Weber, W. (2009). 'Vauxhall Revisited: Pleasure Gardens And Their Publics, 1660–1880 Tate Britain, London 14–16 July 2008', *Eighteenth-Century Music,* 6(1), pp.151–153.
26. Wolffe, J. (2008). 'Anti-Catholicism and the British Empire, 1815–1914', in *Empires of Religion* (pp.43–63). London: Palgrave Macmillan UK.
27. Cauthen, B. (2004). 'Covenant and continuity: ethno-symbolism and the myth of divine election', *Nations and Nationalism,* 10(1-2), pp.19–33.
28. *British Press* – Tuesday, 4 May 1824.
29. *Morning Post* – Monday, 29 June 1835.
30. *Hereford Journal* – Wednesday, 11 May 1791.
31. *Morning Post* – Saturday, 12 February 1803.
32. Eskandari-Qajar, M. (2011). 'Persian Ambassadors, their Circassians, and the Politics of Elizabethan and Regency England', *Iranian Studies,* 44(2), pp.251–271.

**Chapter Twelve**

1. Craft-Fairchild, C. A. (1993). *Masquerade and Gender: Disguise and Female Identity in Eighteenth-Century Fictions By Women.* Penn State Press.
2. Campbell, J. (1995). *Natural Masques: Gender and Identity in Fielding's Plays and Novels.* Stanford University Press.
3. Craft-Fairchild, C. (2010). *Masquerade and Gender: Disguise and Female Identity in Eighteenth-Century Fictions By Women.* Penn State Press.
4. *Morning Chronicle* – Friday, 4 August 1820.
5. *Morning Post* – Tuesday, 16 June 1801.
6. *London Courier and Evening Gazette* – Wednesday, 3 June 1801.
7. *Dictionary of National Biography.* (1885). United Kingdom: Smith, Elder, & Company.
8. *Morning Herald* (London) – Monday, 24 June 1805.
9. *Morning Post* – Thursday, 25 May 1809.

10. *Morning Post* – Wednesday, 26 May 1819.
11. *Chester Chronicle* – Friday, 19 January 1816.
12. *Morning Post* – Saturday, 20 July 1805.
13. *Stamford Mercury* – Friday, 20 April 1810.
14. *Chester Chronicle* – Friday, 18 July 1806.
15. *Public Ledger and Daily Advertiser* – Monday, 4 December 1826.
16. *London Courier and Evening Gazette* – Thursday, 17 May 1804.
17. *Morning Post* – Wednesday, 4 June 1806.
18. *Morning Post* – Tuesday, 5 January 1808.
19. *Morning Post* – Thursday, 25 May 1809.
20. *Morning Post* – Friday, 8 June 1810.
21. Ibid.
22. *Johnson's Sunday Monitor* – Sunday, 18 May 1828.
23. *London Courier and Evening Gazette* – Wednesday, 3 June 1801.
24. *Morning Post* – Friday, 27 July 1804.
25. Ibid.
26. *Drakard's Stamford News* – Friday, 19 May 1826.
27. *Sussex Advertiser* – Monday, 21 April 1828.
28. *Public Ledger and Daily Advertiser* – Monday, 4 December 1826.
29. *Morning Post* – Monday, 29 June 1835.
30. https://villagetheatre.wordpress.com/2021/03/03/women-in-theatre-history/.
31. https://www.cbc.ca/comedy/the-history-of-drag-on-screen-strutting-from-ancient-times-to-cbc-s-queens-1.5699542.
32. Alharbi, F. A. M. (2021). *The Demimonde as a Female Dandy: Masks, Masquerade, and the Making of the Dandy's Personae in Nineteenth-Century British Culture* (Doctoral dissertation, University of Colorado at Boulder).
33. Handley, M. (2018). 'Flying the Feather-George, Prince of Wales and the Performance of Masculinity on the Late-Eighteenth-Century Stage', *European Drama and Performance Studies*, 2018(10), pp.29–49.
34. *Caledonian Mercury* – Saturday, 1 March 1794.
35. Huish, R. (1830). *George, I. V. Memoirs of George the Fourth: descriptive of the most interesting scenes of his private and public life, and the important events of his memorable reign: with characteristic sketches of all the celebrated men who were his friends and companions as a prince, and his ministers and counsellors as a monarch.*
36. George, L. (2004). 'The emergence of the Dandy', *Literature Compass*, 1(1).
37. Cantoni, J. (2008). 'Victorian Fashion: A Middle-Class Makeover' (Doctoral dissertation).
38. Alharbi, F. A. M. (2021). 'The Demimonde as a Female Dandy: Masks, Masquerade, and the Making of the Dandy's Personae in Nineteenth-Century British Culture' (Doctoral dissertation, University of Colorado at Boulder).
39. *English Chronicle and Whitehall Evening Post* – Thursday, 1 January 1824.
40. Laver, J. (1944). 'Fashion and War', *Journal of the Royal Society of Arts*, 92(4666), pp.303–311.

**Chapter Thirteen**

1. *Public Ledger and Daily Advertiser* – Monday, 4 December 1826.
2. *Caledonian Mercury* – Thursday, 5 January 1809.
3. *Morning Advertiser* – Thursday, 30 May 1850.

4. *Christian World* – Thursday, 5 February 1880.
5. Wandle, J. T. (1892). *Masquerade and Carnival: Their Customs and Costumes.* United States: Butterick Publishing Company (limited).
6. Schild, M. (1881). *Character Suitable For Fancy Costume Balls.* United Kingdom: S. Miller.

**Chapter Fourteen**

1. Mackenzie, A. S. (1836). *Spain Revisited.* United Kingdom: Harper & Brothers.

# Bibliography


Aycock, C., & Scott, M. (eds.) (2014). *The First Black Boxing Champions: Essays on Fighters of the 1800s to the 1920s*. McFarland.

Barczewski, S. (2000). *Myth and National Identity in Nineteenth-Century Britain: The Legends of King Arthur and Robin Hood*. United Kingdom: OUP Oxford.

Barrie, L. (1990). 'On Masquerade', *Interstices: Journal of Architecture and Related Arts*, pp.148–161.

BaVaro, V. (2018). '"Taking Back One's Narrative": Dear White People, Cultural Appropriation, and the Challenge of Anti-essentialism', *RSA JOURNAL*, 29, pp.19–37.

Berry, M. (1802). *The Fashionable Friends* ... [By Mary Berry] The Second Edition. United Kingdom: J. Ridgway.

Blažeković, Z. (2017). 'On the Margins of Performance: Theaters, Their Decorations, and Audience Habits', *Music in Art*, 42(1–2), pp.1–16.

Brownie, B. (2013). 'Dressing down: Costume, disguise and the performance of ordinariness', *Clothing Cultures*, 1(1), pp.45–57.

Castle, T. (1986). *Masquerade and Civilization: The Carnivalesque in Eighteenth-Century English Culture and Fiction*. United Kingdom: Stanford University Press.

Cauthen, B. (2004). 'Covenant and continuity: ethno-symbolism and the myth of divine election', *Nations and Nationalism*, 10(1–2), pp.19–33.

Champion, T. (2016). 'Beyond Egyptology: Egypt in 19th and 20th century archaeology and anthropology', in *The Wisdom of Egypt* (pp.161–185). Routledge.

Chatterjee, D. (2020). 'Cultural appropriation: Yours, mine, theirs or a new intercultural?', *Studies in Costume & Performance*, 5(1), pp.53–71.

Díaz-Andreu, M. (2007). *A World History of Nineteenth-Century Archaeology: Nationalism, Colonialism, and the Past*. OUP Oxford.

Ermilova, D. Y. (2020). 'Costume as a form of visualization of ethnicity: From tradition to modernity', *Rupkatha Journal on Interdisciplinary Studies in Humanities*, 12, v12n620.

Feltham, J. (1809). *The Picture of London, for 1802*. United Kingdom: (n.p.).

Goldbort, S. (2022). 'Masquerade and Authenticity: Women's Ambiguous Subjectivity in British Literature, 1720–1860'. (Doctoral dissertation, State University of New York at Buffalo.)

Gubar, S. (1981). 'Blessings in disguise: Cross-dressing as re-dressing for female modernists', *The Massachusetts Review*, 22(3), pp.477–508.

Ickow, Sara. 'Egyptian Revival', in *Heilbrunn Timeline of Art History*. New York: The Metropolitan Museum of Art, 2000. http://www.metmuseum.org/toah/hd/erev/hd_erev.htm (July 2012).

Jarvis, A. (1982). '"There was a Young Man of Bengal..." The Vogue for Fancy Dress, 1830–1950', *Costume*, 16(1), pp.33–46.

Kauer, U. (2007). *Masks and Masquerades in the 18th Century Novel: Sarah Fielding and Samuel Richardson*.

Klein, M. (2020). 'Louis XIII, Richard I, and the Duchess of Devonshire: Nineteenth-Century Jews in Fancy Dress Costume', *Images*, 14(1), pp.54–81.

Leerssen, J. (2013). 'Notes toward a definition of romantic nationalism', *Romantik: Journal for the Study of Romanticisms*, 2(1), pp.9–35.

Li, P. (2019). *The Spectacle of the Masquerade and the Pleasure Gardens: English Society in the Eighteenth Century*. Research in Disciplines/Fashion. Rutgers Undergraduate Research Writing Conference.

Livesay, D (2018). *Children of Uncertain Fortune: Mixed Race Jamaicans in Britain and the Atlantic Family, 1733–1833.* Chapel Hill, University of North Carolina Press.

Lublin, R. I. (2016). *Costuming the Shakespearean Stage: Visual Codes of Representation in Early Modern Theatre and Culture*. Routledge.

McLeod, H. (1999). 'Protestantism and British National Identity, 1815–1945', *Nation and Religion: Perspectives on Europe and Asia*, *44*, p.70.

Mitchell, R. N. (2017). 'The Victorian fancy dress ball, 1870–1900', *Fashion Theory*, 21(3), pp.291–315.

Mosley, A. J., & Biernat, M. (2021). 'The new identity theft: Perceptions of cultural appropriation in intergroup contexts', *Journal of Personality and Social Psychology*, 121(2), p.308.

Smith, A. and Hutchinson, J. (eds.). *Nationalism*. (1994). United Kingdom: Oxford University Press.

Příhodová, B. (2012). 'Costume and the performing body' in *The Disappearing Stage: Reflections on the 2011 Prague Quadrennial*, pp.74–83.

Rogers, R. A. (2006). 'From cultural exchange to transculturation: A review and reconceptualization of cultural appropriation', *Communication Theory*, 16(4), pp.474–503.

Rust, F. M. (1968). *The Dance and Society. A Sociological Analysis of the Inter-Relationship of the Social Dance and Society in England from the Age of Chaucer to the Present Day*. University of London, Bedford College (United Kingdom).

Segal, B. *Henrys and Harlequins: masquerade balls in 18th-century England.*

Smith, A. D. (1991). *National Identity*. United Kingdom: University of Nevada Press.

Threlkeld-Dent, D. (2017). *Victorian Women and the Carnivalesque in Six Novels.*

Toulmin, V. (1997). 'Fun Without Vulgarity: Community, Women and Language in Showland Society'. (Doctoral dissertation, University of Sheffield).

Wolffe, J. (2008). 'Anti-Catholicism and the British empire, 1815–1914', in *Empires of Religion* (pp. 43–63). London: Palgrave Macmillan UK.

Wild, B. L. (2020). 'Critical reflections on cultural appropriation, race and the role of fancy dress costume', *Critical Studies in Fashion & Beauty*, 11(2), pp.153–173.

# Index